Da Capo
BEST
MUSIC
WRITING
2001

The Year's Finest Writing on
Rock, Pop, Jazz, Country & More

Nick Hornby
GUEST EDITOR

Ben Schafer
SERIES EDITOR

DA CAPO PRESS

List of credits/permissions for all pieces can be found on page 335.

Copyright © 2001 by Da Capo Press

Designed by Jeffrey P. Williams
Set in 10-point Janson Text by Perseus Publishing Services

Cataloging-in-Publication data for this book is available from the Library of Congress.

First Da Capo Press edition 2001
ISBN 0–306–81066–2

Published by Da Capo Press
A Member of the Perseus Books Group
http://www.dacapopress.com

Da Capo Press books are available at special discounts for bulk purchases in the U.S. by corporations, institutions, and other organizations. For more information, please contact the Special Markets Department at the Perseus Books Group, 11 Cambridge Center, Cambridge, MA 02142, or call (617) 252–5298.

1 2 3 4 5 6 7 8 9—05 04 03 02 01

CONTENTS

Introduction   I
by Nick Hornby

STEVEN DALY, DAVID KAMP, AND BOB MACK   7
The Rock Snob's Dictionary
Vanity Fair

RICHARD MELTZER   22
Third Spud from the Sun:
   Cameron Crowe Then and Now
San Diego Reader

MIKE DOUGHTY   35
I Like It Warm and Fuzzy
New York Press

N.R. KLEINFIELD   39
Guarding the Borders of the Hip-Hop Nation
New York Times

RIAN MALAN   59
In the Jungle
Rolling Stone

MONICA KENDRICK   88
This Wreckage Was No Accident:
   The Complete Fun House Sessions
Chicago Reader

STEVE ERICKSON   93
Neil Young on a Good Day
New York Times Sunday Magazine

LORRAINE ALI   102
West Bank Hard Core
Raygun

ROBERT GORDON   113
Northern Light
Oxford American

ERIC BOEHLERT   119
Invisible Man: Eminem
Salon.com

GILBERT GARCIA   128
The Tao of Esteban
Phoenix New Times

CHARLES C. MANN   144
The Heavenly Jukebox, Part 3:
   They're Paying Our Song
Atlantic Monthly

CARLY CARIOLI   152
Napster Nation
Boston Phoenix

LORI ROBERTSON   160
Golden Oldies
American Journalism Review

Contents

JIM DeROGATIS   173
Singer Gets an Eye for Eye
Chicago Sun-Times

BILL BUFORD   179
Delta Nights: A Singer's Love Affair with Loss
New Yorker

NICK TOSCHES   210
Hipsters and Hoodlums
Vanity Fair

JONATHAN LETHEM   240
Not a Go-Betweens Piece: A Letter from
    Jonathan Lethem, on His Favorite Band
Open Letters

SARAH VOWELL   245
Singing Lead
Salon.com

DAVID RAKOFF   248
Barbra's Farewell: A City *Verklempt*
New York Observer

ROBBIE FULKS   255
If I Said You Had a Beautiful Gross Adjusted Income
    Would You Hold It Against Me?
Open Letters

METAL MIKE SAUNDERS   266
Disney Dreams Up the Best Radio Station in 30 Years
Village Voice

ANTHONY DeCURTIS   275
Johnny Cash Won't Back Down
Rolling Stone

WILLIAM GAY   289
Sitting On Top of the World
Oxford American

WHITNEY BALLIETT   299
Seeing Music: Django Reinhardt
New Yorker

FRANCIS DAVIS   306
Our Lady of Sorrows: Billie Holiday
Atlantic Monthly

GREIL MARCUS   316
Raising the Stakes in Punk Rock: Sleater-Kinney
New York Times

Other Notable Essays of 2000   325
List of Contributors   329
Credits   335

Introduction

Sure, I had a methodology for choosing the selection that makes up this book, and it was a good one, too. It's just that . . . well, I sort of had to abandon it. It didn't work, for reasons which I will try to explain. First of all, there's the whole question of my age, which I'd hoped wouldn't rear its wizened head, but which became unavoidable after a while (in truth, about halfway through the first piece I read). Oh, I know I'm old. I knew I was old even before I accepted the honor of this job; in fact, I'd built my age right into my methodology. One of the pieces in this book, "Golden Oldies," by Lori Robertson, raises the question of whether older people—and sixteen-year-old Limp Bizkit fans might argue that the comparative form of the adjective is redundant here, although they would articulate the argument in a different way—can and should write about what's currently going on in rock'n'roll (except of course it's probably not called rock 'n' roll any more, and nobody told me). It's something I find myself thinking about a lot: I'm halfway through my fifth decade, and I have recently embarked on my first-ever regular music-writing gig, for the *New Yorker*. Has it come twenty years too late?

Let's leave aside for now the fact that the *New Yorker* probably wouldn't have given me the job twenty years ago, when I was unpublished, teaching recalcitrant fourteen-year-olds, and attempting to write awful screenplays in my spare time; would I have been better equipped for, or better suited to, a job as a music critic than I am now? Well, of course, in most ways I am certainly better equipped now, just as I am better equipped to review books: I know

1

more than I did. This knowledge, however, is as much a curse as a blessing, because the more you know, the harder it becomes to feel wildly enthusiastic about anything. Much pop music is derivative, but when you're young, of course, you don't know that. Robert Christgau or Richard Meltzer or I may well have spotted that Pink Lunchbox or whoever is a laughable Velvets knockoff, with a little Neil Young thrown in, but if you've never listened to the Velvets, you're not going to be able to say that. In other areas of art criticism, this would simply make you a bad critic, but there is a special case to be made for music writing, I think. Pop music has never been about expertise or a veneration for the past; "No Elvis, Beatles, or the Rolling Stones in 1977," Joe Strummer sang in . . . a long time ago now (and of course my ability to quote the line verbatim is kind of ironic in this context). Pop music needs energy and cheek, and a lot of old codgers stroking their beards and pointing out that Pink Lunchbox isn't as good as ? and the Mysterians is as effective a way as any of killing that energy. There's no real excuse for ignorance in any field of journalism (or in any field of anything, come to think of it), but I'd rather read someone who loves Pink Lunchbox with a passion that brooks no reason, and can communicate with wit and style how the Lunchbox (the Lunchies?) has changed his or her life, than someone who can no longer be bothered to listen to track 2 of any CD because nothing is as good as *Exile on Main Street*. This may well be true—in which case, pal, it's about time you got yourself a different job. What's the point of sticking with this one? So. In my book—in this book—old was going to be out, and young was going to be in . . . except so many of the best pieces turned out to be written by older people, and to exclude these pieces would have done a lot of damage to the quality of this volume.

OK, so, no upper age limit. But pop music writing should still reflect what's going on out there, even if these reflections are made by people in their forties and fifties and sixties, right? Unfortunately the world is no longer that simple. I was as excited as any eighteen-year-old webzine editor when free CDs started pouring through my letterbox last year, but I don't think that my age has anything to do with the nausea I felt within a month of being on record company mailing lists. The first communication I had from a major label wasn't a pre-release by a favorite artist; it was a press release telling me that a leading female artist had signed an exclusive deal with Redken Hair Products. (And I knew about it before just about anyone else! How cool was that?) But the information contained in this press release serves as a useful counterpoint to the Pink Lunchbox dilemma: If I'm arguing that music writing, and therefore this book, should reflect what's happening, then maybe I should have included the hair products letter. What, after all, is more representative of the zeitgeist than this sort of crap? Isn't this what they mean by synergy? And isn't synergy the main purpose of a lot of contemporary music? Wrestling sells rap metal sells wrestling? Will Smith (or Mariah Carey or Geri Halliwell) sells a movie sells Will Smith? And does this mean that pretty blonde singer sells Redken hair products sells *Da Capo Best Music Writing 2001*? Probably not. And, yes, postmodernism has given us the tools to write about hair products in a different way (in other words, anyone with a high school education is capable of decoding it), but I wouldn't want to read a book full of deconstructions of pretty blonde singers or shampoo, and I wouldn't want to try to sell you one, either.

Of course there is a lot of writing in this book that could not have been produced at any other time. Eminem, *Almost Famous*, Radio Disney, Third Eye Blind, Napster, the weird incursions that hip-hop is making into other cultures: None of this could have been written at any time other than the turn of the millennium. But the whole question of what's going on out there is very complicated. A story about Johnny Cash could have appeared in *Best Music Writing 1961* or any year thereafter; but a piece about Johnny Cash as he approaches the end of his life and spectacular career (and in the year that he made one of his very best records)—that could only have been written now, which means that Johnny Cash, or this version thereof, is going on now too. If I had to pick a particular favorite from this collection, it would be Rian Malan's piece about "The Lion Sleeps Tonight," a song which (it turns out) was first recorded in 1939. Malan's story is about the long, sad, strange life of the song; had it appeared any earlier, it would have been missing a few chapters, like a Haley Joel Osment biography.

Pop music's past, it turns out, is happening just as much as Eminem is happening. Look at the recent critical reaction to the work of Harry Smith, a now-dead musicologist who "happened" fifty years ago, and whose startling collection of folk and blues recordings "happened" before that, even, but which have been re-released in the last couple of years and sound utterly extraordinary—maybe more extraordinary than they have ever sounded. And then David Johansen makes a great blues album—in the year 2000—called *David Johansen and the Harry Smiths*, and it turns out that Harry Smith is happening all over the place. And Woody Guthrie's got more life in him than we thought, too, thanks to Billy Bragg and Wilco, and anyway the past is always with us, thanks to sampling and oldies stations and boxed sets. . . .

It was inevitable that pop music would eventually develop a sense of its own history, although it took its time. When I was fourteen the world was divided into oldies and good stuff (i.e., Led Zeppelin and Black Sabbath), but a recent browse through a teenage CD collection turned up albums by Hendrix and Pink Floyd and Al Green. Like it or not, there is a canon now, exactly equivalent to a literary canon, with Elvis as Shakespeare, Howlin' Wolf as Chaucer, Aretha as George Eliot (although listening to these guys is a lot more fun than this makes it sound). Some people would have you believe that a canon has emerged because the music is dying, but it seems to me to be a sign of cultural maturity, a recognition that this music takes itself seriously as an art form (and that's not the same thing as taking itself seriously) to acknowledge that it has a past, and that past impacts on the present in all sorts of ways. It doesn't seem to me either paradoxical or undesirable that a book entitled *Da Capo Best Music Writing 2001* contains pieces about the Stooges and Django Reinhardt.

So my carefully-wrought preconceptions now lie in shreds at my feet, and this book, luckily for you, has turned into a dip full of good stuff. Of course, a few of my prejudices have remained intact:

Good rock writing is the same as good writing in any other medium, and only Lester Bangs could be Lester Bangs with any degree of success (sometimes one wishes to remind the Bangs wannabes that other people wrote some pretty decent prose too—Pauline Kael, say, or Mark Twain); real, loud, sustained hatred for an artist or an album suggests that it's maybe about time that the writer had kids, or got a job as an aid worker, or did anything which might help him (or . . . no, let's not even pretend there's no gender discrimination on that one) gain a sense of perspective; and, last but not least, most pop music is pretty funny, most of it unwittingly so, and therefore jokes about it are not only advisable but vital. Who else is going to laugh at the pomposity of pop music, its self-importance and narcissism and its eye-popping idiocies?

Oh, and one last thing: Like the musician Mike Doughty, whose piece made me want to pick him up and carry him in triumph around the nearest Tower Records, I don't understand how art can ever be dangerous, and I am deeply suspicious of anyone who thinks otherwise. I am especially suspicious of those writers who think that all art, especially rock music, should be dangerous all of the time—that there is no room for sweetness, regret, joy, or any of the other things that permeate so many of my favorite songs—and who by some weird process of imaginary osmosis have clearly ended up regarding themselves as dangerous. They're not. Granted, they're tedious, and like, say, jogging, tedium can have some unpleasant and possibly even fatal side effects, but that doesn't make tedium and danger synonymous.

In the end, it's a tricky business, writing about this stuff. Music matters to me as much as just about anything that doesn't have two legs (and infinitely more than anything with four): It's a fuel, a companion, a constant source of literary inspiration, a consolation, an energizer, a means of self-expression when, as so often happens, the means I have at my disposal fail me. So it stands to reason that anything attempting to describe or appraise or contextualize it is going to be important to me too. Hanif Kureishi once said that "pop is a form crying out not to be written about. It is physical, sensual, of the body rather than the mind." But it seems to me that if we accept this as an idea, we also accept that words are of limited use—that the pleasures of food, and sex, and dance, and sport are beyond them, that they cannot explain rage, or grief, or tiredness, or despair, or physical pain—and as a writer, I'm not prepared to do that. If I thought that words were really so limited in their application, then I'd quit my day job and learn the guitar. . . .

. . . Which is, of course, what all of us who have contributed in some way to this book really wanted to do, and probably have done at some time or another, to usually unsatisfying effect. Every critic is a fan, and fandom can often be shot through with envy; it takes a steady nerve and a great generosity of spirit to keep that envy out of the writing. You won't find much that is mean in this book (maybe one or two pieces, just for seasoning); but you will find lots of stuff trying to explain why music matters, what it means, where it, and the impulse to make it, comes from. In other words, this book is hopefully not about music at all, but about what makes us human.

NICK HORNBY

COMPILED BY STEVEN DALY,
DAVID KAMP, AND BOB MACK

The Rock Snob's Dictionary

The Rock Snob is a confounding person in your life. On one hand, he (and he almost always is a he) brooks no ignorance of pop-music history, and will take violent umbrage at the fact that you've never heard of Jack Nitzsche, much less heard Nitzsche's ambitious pop-classical album *St. Giles Cripplegate*. On the other hand, he will not countenance the notion that you may actually know more than he about a certain area of music. If, for example, you mention that *Fun House* is your favorite Stooges album, he will respond that it "lacks the visceral punch of 'I Wanna Be Your Dog' from a year earlier, but it's got some superb howling from Iggy and coruscating riffing from Ron Asheton, though not on the level of James Williamson's on *Raw Power*"—this indigestible clump of words acting as a cudgel with which the Rock Snob is trumping you and marking the turf as his. *The Rock Snob's Dictionary* enables you to hold your own in such situations, with the added benefit of saving you the trouble of actually listening to the music.

The Rock Snob's Dictionary makes no claim to be a comprehensive reference in the vein of *The* Rolling Stone *Encyclopedia of Rock & Roll*. Indeed, just because a musician has enjoyed lasting success and critical acclaim doesn't mean he warrants inclusion here. *Only persons and entities that are the psychic property of Rock Snobs make the cut.* For example, there is no entry for David Crosby, because practically every person over 30 knows who he is and can hum a few bars of "Teach Your Children." However, the late Gene Clark, Crosby's colleague in the original lineup of the Byrds, warrants an entry because, while the average Joe hasn't the faintest idea who he is, the Rock Snob has fetishized him for his poor-selling post-Byrds output of country rock.

It bears mentioning that the Rock Snob is hardly some hidebound, patchouli-drenched anachronism. He is, by definition, *in touch*—in touch with anything that will allow him to lord it over mere rock aficionados (the lightweights!). The Rock Snob's fear of calcification ensures that artists in such exotic genres as world music and hip-hop will one day enter the pantheon alongside such unimpeachables as Syd Barrett and Big Star. The editors of *The Rock Snob's Dictionary* will be vigilant in keeping track of such developments for future editions.

Alt.country. Self-righteous rock-country hybrid genre whose practitioners favor warbly, studiedly imperfect vocals, nubby flannel shirts, and a conviction that their take on country is more "real" than the stuff coming out of Nashville. Heavily influenced by GRAM PARSONS. Also known as the No Depression movement, after the title of an album by the SEMINAL alt.country band Uncle Tupelo (which itself purloined the title from The Carter Family song "No Depression in Heaven"). Current alt.country standard-bearers include the Jayhawks, Freakwater, and Whiskeytown, plus the Uncle Tupelo splinter groups, Wilco and Son Volt.

Anthology of American Folk Music, The. Multivolume collection, first issued by the Folkways label in 1952, of obscure and semi-obscure folk recordings as compiled by eccentric musicologist Harry Smith (1923–1991). Significant for having allegedly triggered the late-50s-early-60s "folkie" movement that gave us Bob Dylan (*see also* ZIMMY)—and therefore, by extension, for making pop music subversive, turning the Beatles into druggies, and irreparably rending the fabric of our society.

Bacharach, Burt. Rehabilitated songwriter whose metrically and melodically unorthodox 60s popluxe hits, such as "Anyone Who Had a Heart" and "I Say a Little Prayer" (written with lyricist Hal David), were dismissed for two decades as square and Muzak-y until Rock Snobs decided in the 1990s that it was O.K. to like them again. Particularly active latter-day boosters have been Noel Gallagher of Oasis and Elvis Costello, with whom Bacharach recorded a 1998 "comeback" album. *That song has a very* Bacharach-*esque flügelhorn part.*

Bad Brains. Hard-luck jazz-fusion weirdos from Washington, D.C., who cashed in on the New York hard-core punk scene in 1980 with their minute-and-a-half-long single "Pay to Cum." The subsequent introduction of reggae and heavy-metal elements into Bad Brains' sound did little for their sales but everything for their legend, as evidenced by the band's feverish championing by the Rock Snob collective the Beastie Boys.

Bangs, Lester. Dead rock critic canonized for his willfully obnoxious, amphetamine-streaked prose. Writing chiefly for *Creem* magazine, Bangs stuck two fingers down the throat of the counterculture elite and kept alive the scuzzy legacy of bands such as the Velvet Underground, the STOOGES, and the MC5. Though every Rock Snob worth his salt reveres Bangs (a heavy biography by Rock Snob author Jim DeRogatis was published earlier this year), his writing has aged rather less well than that of his less strident contemporaries Richard Meltzer and Nick Tosches. *They're all pussies at* Rolling Stone *now, man; not a* Lester Bangs *among them.*

Barrett, Syd. Founding member of Pink Floyd who defined the group's early sound with his juvenile, peculiarly English take on psychedelia. Already in the process of becoming rock's most celebrated acid casualty at the time of Pink Floyd's 1967 debut. Barrett left the band in 1968, managing to record two solo albums of skeletal meanderings (one of them entitled *The Madcap Laughs*) before drifting into the permanent twilight in which he lives today. The post-Barrett Floyd song "Shine On You Crazy Diamond" is about him.

Beefheart, Captain. Performing name of Don Van Vliet, a California-desert kid and childhood friend of Frank Zappa's whose 1969 album, *Trout Mask Replica*, is, Rock Snobs swear, a classic whose brilliance will reveal itself after you've listened to it 6,000 times or so. A typical Beefheart song showcased Van Vliet yawping dementedly over the intricately arranged yet chaotic-sounding playing of his backing group, the Magic Band, whose members used "wacky" stage names such as Zoot Horn Rollo and Antennae Jimmy Semens. Van Vliet retired from music in the early 80s and is now a painter. *I'm feeling nostalgic, honey—let's drop some acid and put on some* Beefheart.

Big Star. Anglophilic early-70s American combo whose first two albums, *# 1 Record* and *Radio City*, have Koran-like status in POWER-POP circles. Led by Memphis native Alex Chilton, who began his career as a teenager with the blue-eyed-soul boys the Box Tops ("The Letter"). Big Star recorded tunes that, while catchy, were too fraught with druggy tension to be commercial—thereby guaranteeing the group posthumous "great overlooked band" mythology. Chilton, who later had a REPLACEMENTS song named after him, is now a rheumy-eyed eccentric with a reputation for self-immolating live shows.

Buckley, Tim and Jeff. Symmetrically ill-fated father-and-son artists whose early deaths, swooping voices, and Pre-Raphaelite beauty are irresistible to the romantic wing of Rock Snobbism. Jeff Buckley was eight years old when his father, a honey-voiced folkie turned jazz dabbler, died of a drug overdose, aged 28, in 1975; Buckley *fils* went on to become a singer-songwriter of equal repute, winning raves for his 1994 debut album, *Grace*, but drowned in Memphis, aged 30, before he could complete a studio follow-up.

Clark, Gene. Brooding, handsome founding member of the Byrds who quit the band in 1966 after having written songs that included "Feel a Whole Lot Better" and "Eight Miles High." (Ironically, Clark's fear of flying contributed to his exit.) Subsequent albums such as *Echoes* (1967) and *No Other* (1974) achieved cult status for their audacious blend of pop, country, and gospel, and a 1968 collaboration with banjoist Doug Dillard, *The Fantastic Expedition of Dillard & Clark*, is also considered a Rock Snob classic. But none of these albums sold beans, their poor commercial performance hastening Clark's alcohol-related decline and premature death in 1991.

Crawdaddy! The first mainstream rock magazine, founded in 1966, a year before *Rolling Stone*, by Paul Williams. Though it ceased publication in 1979, Williams revived it as a newsletter in 1993. Just about every major rock biography seems to rely heavily on ancient *Crawdaddy!* interviews.

Drake, Nick. Sad-sack, compulsively muted English singer-songwriter from posh background, posthumously canonized by Rock Snobs for the three plaintive, delicately wrought albums he recorded before dying, an apparent suicide, in 1974 at the age of 26. Was frequently photographed standing dolefully among trees. Achieved a measure of posthumous fame when his song "Pink Moon" was used in a Volkswagen TV commercial.

Earle, Steve. World-weary singer-songwriter, hailed in Rock Snob circles as the only contemporary country artist (as opposed to ALT.COUNTRY artist) fit to polish Hank Williams's cowboy boots. Earle made a triumphant debut with his 1986 album, *Guitar Town*, only to fritter away his early promise on a five-year drugs-and-drink bender. Now clean and 45 years old, he inspires a Springsteen-like reverence among fans and critics, both for his storytellin' songs and his impassioned political positions, such as his anti-death-penalty stance.

Eno, Brian. Egghead producer and electronics whiz with appropriately futuristic name and aerodynamic pate. Eno started out as the keyboard player for Roxy Music and went on to make his name as a producer (Talking Heads, Devo, U2) and pioneer of ambient music, the soundtrack for everything from aromatherapy to recreational drug use to booting up Windows 95. Eno enjoys his greatest Rock Snob status, however, for his 70s solo albums, *Another Green World*, *Here Come the Warm Jets*, and *Before and After Science*.

Erickson, Roky. Texas psychedelia kingpin often championed, like SKIP SPENCE, as North America's answer to SYD BARRETT. The oddball lead singer of the 13th Floor Elevators, Erickson was arrested for possession of drugs in 1968. Attempting to avoid jail time, he pleaded insanity and was committed to Texas's Rusk State Hospital for the Criminally Insane, where electroshock therapy exacerbated his eccentric tendencies more than drugs ever did. Now lives like a hobo in Austin, occasionally recording gonzo albums that actually get decent reviews.

Fender Rhodes. Electric piano with resonant, fuzzy timbre that bestows instant sensitivity upon its user. Originally a jazz-club staple, the Rhodes became ubiquitous in the squishy mid-70s, appearing on everything from jazz-rock fuzak albums to the Rolling Stones' "Fool to Cry," and has recently been revived by mood-music trendsetters such as Air and Portishead.

Gainsbourg, Serge. Raffish, *joli laid* French balladeer revered by kitsch-loving Rock Snobs for his sleazy-listening pop of the 1960s and 70s. Despite hangdog looks and an inability to actually sing, Gainsbourg embodied the pungent flower of French manhood in all its Gallic glory, duetting and getting busy with such hotties of the period as Brigitte Bardot and English dolly bird Jane Birkin. A less edifying collaboration was 1984's "Lemon Incest," a duet with his 12-year-old daughter, Charlotte. Gainsbourg died in 1991, five years after saying "I want to *fouck* you" to Whitney Houston on live television.

Hazlewood, Lee. Hard-drinkin', ultra-manly producer of Native American extraction who first made his name working with twangy guitar slinger Duane Eddy and went on to become the premier *auteur* of Rat Pack–offspring kitsch, writing and producing material for Dino, Dest & Billy, and, most notoriously, for Nancy Sinatra ("These Boots Are Made for Walkin'"). Following a 1973 solo debut candidly titled *Poet, Fool or Bum*, Hazlewood moved to Sweden and made lousy movies. Currently living in America again, where his oeuvre is being reissued by a small label owned by Sonic Youth drummer and confirmed Rock Snob Steve Shelley.

Krautrock. Blanket term for offbeat hippie-era music recorded by Germans, meaning everything from the proto-"Sprockets" stylings of Kraftwerk to the meandering soundscapes of Tangerine Dream to the starkly aggressive output of the dauntingly named bands Can, Neu, and Faust (the last of which actually recorded a song called "Krautrock"). *Some of that last R.E.M. album was, like, total* Krautrock!

Lo-fi. Luddite recording aesthetic championed by contemporary artists who tend toward sparse, raw production and believe that older, analog equipment produces a more "honest" or "organic" sound; or, more realistically, by artists too musically incompetent and undisciplined to record crafted, finished music. *Pavement combines Phi Beta Kappa smarts with an endearing* lo-fi *slipshodness.*

Love. Baroque mid-60s L.A. popsters led by Arthur Lee, a black hippie of prodigious talent and erratic discipline. Love's ability to combine such seemingly irreconcilable genres as psychedelia, West Coast sophisto-pop, mariachi, and garage-punk reached its apex with the band's 1967 album *Forever Changes.* Lee is currently serving time in a California prison on an illegal-firearms possession charge.

MC5, the. Wild-eyed, butt-ugly rhetoricians who emerged from Detroit's White Panther enclave in 1969 to debut with the insurrectionary live album *Kick Out the Jams* (whose title song amended this command with the word "motherfuckers!"). *Kick Out the Jams* and its follow-up, *Back in the USA,* stood in bracing contrast to the hippie noodlings offered up by other bands of the era; dropping the MC5's name—and that of its decadent Detroit neighbors the STOOGES—was positively de rigueur for British punk's class of 1977.

Mellotron. Primitive 60s synthesizer whose keys, when pressed, activate prerecorded tape loops; used to famous effect in the opening bars of "Strawberry Fields Forever." Vintage mellotrons are now purchased at great cost (approximately $10,000) by retro rockers angling to sound Beatles-esque. *Oasis went too far with that mellotron on "Go Let It Out"*

Mojo. Seven-year-old English magazine offering an exuberant, high-production-values take on Rock Snobbism. A typical issue offers a reverent interview with a crinkly rocker of 60s vintage, a couple of multipage, photoladen articles on suitably obscurist topics (such as the Doug Yule–era Velvet Underground, or the triumphal years of English blues plodders Free), and some sort of article on NICK DRAKE.

Moog. Squelching old-school synthesizer invented in 1965 and first popularized by Walter Carlos's bachelor-pad suite *Switched-On Bach*. The prodigiously corded instrument (and its *Austin Powers* sounding offspring, the MiniMoog) went on to become a staple of prog rock and KRAUTROCK. Today, the Moog is fetishized by instrument snobs such as Beck, as well as dance-music acts such as the Prodigy and Fatboy Slim, who remixed a track on this year's kitschy *Best of Moog* compilation.

Neil, Fred. Ringleted, mild-mannered folkie and early Dylan acolyte best known for his anti-urban plaint "Everybody's Talkin'," which was sung by HARRY NILSSON on the *Midnight Cowboy* soundtrack. Painfully shy and empathetic, Neil identified more with dolphins than with humans (his elegiac song "Dolphins" was covered by TIM BUCKLEY), and now lives in blissful anonymity in the Florida Keys, paining Rock Snobs by refusing to record new music.

Nilsson, Harry. Powerfully piped singer-songwriter equally famous for well-realized retro-pop albums such as *Nilsson Schmilsson* (1971) and for being John Lennon's drinking buddy/partner in crime during the latter's "Lost Weekend" period in Los Angeles. (Nilsson was once rumored to be joining the Beatles.) After he died of a heart attack in 1994, Nilsson's oeuvre acquired significant hipster cachet.

Nitzsche, Jack. Runty, cantankerous, recently deceased Phil Spector protégé who started out as a session pianist but quickly graduated to status as rock's A-list arranger, working with Neil Young, the Rolling Stones, and TIM BUCKLEY. Though his ambitions as a recording artist were extinguished with the poor sales of his 1972 opus *St. Giles Cripplegate*, he gained new renown as a soundtrack composer; movies as diverse as *Performance*, *One Flew over the Cuckoo's Nest*, and *An Officer and a Gentleman* bear his spectral imprimatur. *Check out that awesome* Nitzsche *arrangement on Springfield's "Expecting to Fly."*

Nuggets. Landmark anthology LP of obscurish 60s "punk" singles by one-hit-wonder garage bands, compiled in 1972 by Lenny Kave, a scrawny, prototypical rock nerd who would shortly thereafter be a prime mover in the 70s punk movement as the guitarist for the Patti Smith Group. *Early Nirvana combined Beatles-esque songcraft with* Nuggets *abandon.*

Parks, Van Dyke. Campy, southern-born, half-pint composer-lyricist best known for being tapped by BRIAN WILSON to write the words to the Beach Boys' aborted *Smile* album. Though Parks's bizarre Joycean, free-associative lyrics served him well on his own albums (such as the Rock Snob orchestral-pop favorites *Song Cycle* [1968] and *Discover America* [1972]), his baroque tendencies (including the deathless line, "Columnated ruins domino" in the song "Surf's Up") alienated the other Beach Boys and exacerbated tensions within the group. Parks and Wilson reteamed on the 1995 album *Orange Crate Art*.

Parsons, Gram. Southern, Harvard-educated, trustafarian pretty-boy who invented country rock by bringing his high-lonesome tastes to bear on his one album as a Byrd (1968's *Sweetheart of the Rodeo*, considered the first country-rock LP). Parsons and fellow Byrd Chris Hillman went on to form the Flying Burrito Brothers. A hard-livin' soul who favored tightfitting Nudie suits custom-decorated with pictures of naked girls and marijuana leaves, he greatly impressed Mick Jagger and Keith Richards (inspiring them to write "Wild Horses"), and recorded two Rock Snob–ratified solo albums, *GP* and *Grievous Angel*, before dying of a morphine-and-alcohol overdose in a motel in Joshua Tree, California, in 1973 at the age of 26.

Penn, Dan, and Spooner Oldham. Memphis-based songwriting duo invariably praised for being "real soulful for white boys." Their 1960s hits include "Do Right Woman Do Right Man," "Dark End of the Street," and "You Left the Water Running." Penn and Oldham have lately hit the road as performers, doing a *Storytellers*-like set of their oldies, plus some new songs. The raggedy-looking Spooner Oldham, whose funny name Rock Snobs like to utter just for the sheer frisson of it, is also an in-demand session keyboardist.

Perry, Lee "Scratch." Mercurial, kooky, formerly forgotten reggae shaman (born in 1936) who has enjoyed new recognition since being pronounced cool by ageless Rock Snob collective the Beastie Boys in the early 1990s. As a producer and as the front man for his own band, the Upsetters, Perry was, in the 1960s and 70s, a prime exponent of Jamaica's swashbuckling "dub" remix genre. Though his gargantuan output is as hard to penetrate as the quasi-mystical pronouncements he gives to interviewers from his home in Switzerland, he now plays to packed houses of young hipsters, few of whom actually know any of his songs.

P-Funk. Catchall term used to encompass the multifarious output of two no-longer-extant 1970s funk–R&B collectives, Parliament and Funkadelic, that were both founded by ex-hairdresser George Clinton. Parliament began its life as a doo-wop act but progressed to elaborate concept albums about outer space; live shows featured musicians in diapers along with a giant "mother ship" descending from an enormous denim cap. The rockier Funkadelic made LSD–tinged music that Clinton devised to be "too black for white folks and too white for black folks." Clinton tours today with veterans of both bands as the P-Funk All Stars.

Pixies, the. Boston-based 1980s alterna-band whose formula—
grunged-up pop that alternated between quiet verses and loud
choruses—was transmuted into platinum sales in the 1990s by the
grungy likes of Nirvana. (See also THE REPLACEMENTS.) The Pixies'
chubby lead singer, Black Francis (né Charles Kitteridge III), still
plays the club circuit solo as Frank Black; tough-gal bassist Kim
Deal disappeared from sight after enjoying initial success with her
boisterously poppy band the Breeders.

Power-pop. Record-reviewer term for Beatles-esque music made
by intelligent-dork bands that, though they've given it the old college try, can't actually muster the songcraft, cleverness, vocal
agility, or production ingenuity of the Beatles. First applied to
early-70s acts such as the Raspberries and Badfinger (the latter
group actually being McCartney protégés), and subsequently given
a new lease on life with the 90s advent of such bands as Jellyfish and
the Apples in Stereo. *The first song on the new Apples in Stereo album
shimmers with pure* power-pop *exuberance.*

Replacements, the. Shambolic 80s guitar band from Minnesota
whose plaid-shirted, raspy-throated leader, Paul Westerberg, was a
profound influence on both the grunge movement and the more
recent "modern rock" travesties of the Goo Goo Dolls. Westerberg
broke up the band in 1990 due to poor sales and has subsequently
alienated his fan base by "going soft."

Rhino Records. Juggernaut reissue label launched out of a Los
Angeles record shop in the late 70s. One of the first labels to divine
the commercial appeal of kitsch, oddities, and forgotten gems.
Rhino astutely assembled several compilation series of period pop,
such as the *Have a Nice Day!* series of 70s hits, the *Golden Throats*
series of celebrity debacles (Shatner sings "Mr. Tambourine
Man"!), and more tasteful assemblages of soul and lounge. Major
deals with Atlantic Records and Turner Entertainment enable this
good-taste clearinghouse to resell you every pop-culture memory
you've ever had.

Rickenbacker. Distinctively jangly-sounding, California-manufactured electric guitar associated with mid-60s pop in general and the "Mr. Tambourine Man"–era Byrds in particular. Retro-pop acts from Tom Petty to the Rembrandts (the *Friends* theme song) have long found the Rickenbacker—particularly in its 12-string incarnation—efficacious in evoking an era of "quality pop," much as harpsichords evoke the court of Queen Elizabeth. *The plangent chime of McGuinn's Rickenbacker embodied the jingle-jangle optimism of mid-1960s California.*

Roland 808. Primitive yet cherished drum machine introduced by the Roland company in 1980. The user-friendly "808" combines metallic, artificial top-end sounds with a distinctive bass drum whose amniotic *whoomp* is the closest thing electronic dance music has to a trademark sound à la the RICKENBACKER's jangle. *The bottom end on that track is heav-ee, that's got to be an* 808 *kick in there.*

Seminal. Catchall adjective employed by rock writers to describe any group or artist in on a trend too early to sell any records. *The Germs were a* seminal *L.A. punk band: David Johansen, who fronted the* seminal *glam-rockers the New York Dolls . . .*

Spence, Skip. Canadian-born musician and acid casualty who, like ROKY ERICKSON, is often held up as a North American answer to SYD BARRETT. Spence played drums for Jefferson Airplane before achieving greater fame as a guitarist for the psychedelic band Moby Grape. After quitting the Grape and sojourning for a time at New York's Bellevue Hospital, Spence retired to Nashville, where, wearing pajamas, he recorded a bunch of dithering, fried-brain song fragments, out of which was constructed the 1969 album *Oar.* Though it sank without a trace upon its release, *Oar* was subsequently re-released in 1991, and today is held up by overeager Rock Snobs as a lost classic. Spence, to his credit, professed before his death in 1999 that he was, in a friend's words, "mildly puzzled by all the hoopla surrounding *Oar.*"

Stax/Volt. Composite term for two Memphis-based soul labels of the 1960s. Stax Records and its subsidiary, Volt, whose releases, by the likes of Sam & Dave, Otis Redding, and Rufus Thomas, provided a rawer, grittier counterpart to the more polished black pop of Motown. Rock Snobs are particularly enamored of Stax/Volt's crack house band, Booker T. and the MGs, and its equally adept horn section, the Mar-Keys. *When I saw all those great Stax/Volt players backing up Belushi and Aykroyd, I didn't know whether to laugh or cry.*

Stooges, the. Filthy-sounding, drug-addled late-60s–early-70s band fronted by charismatic, self-mutilating singer Iggy Pop, né James Osterberg. The Stooges' primal, three-chord rock and Pop's naughty, nihilistic lyrics (on such songs as "I Wanna Be Your Dog" and "Your Pretty Face Is Going to Hell") helped form the template for punk. *Degenerate drummer seeks like-minded fuckups to jam and kick ass like* the Stooges.

Television. Late-70s guitar band lumped into the New York punk movement by dint of connections to the CBGB's scene (Blondie, Talking Heads, Ramones) but actually wont to do unpunk things such as play eight-minute songs featuring noodly guitar duels between second banana Richard Lloyd and ornery, beanpole-ish front man Tom Verlaine (whose ex-girlfriend Patti Smith described his playing as sounding "like a thousand bluebirds screaming"). Considered by Rock Snobs to be more important than any other New York band of the era, despite having released just two albums, 1977's *Marquee Moon* and 1978's *Adventure* (plus an obligatory 1990s reunion album).

Thompson, Richard. Wry, bearded singer-songwriter-guitarist and veteran of SEMINAL British folk group the Fairport Convention; unaccountably deified by rock critics for his intelligent yet ultimately tedious albums. Thompson provided the template for a slew of younger, similarly overpraised troubadours such as Freedy Johnston, Vic Chesnutt, and Ron Sexsmith (whose next album is being produced by STEVE EARLE).

Tropicalia. Term describing both a 1968 compilation of avant pop released in Brazil and the subsequent movement it inspired. Mixing Brazilian rhythms with Anglo-American songcraft and hippie flourishes, Tropicalia—and its foremost practitioners, such as the Rock Snob cult fave Tom Ze—gained new currency in the late 90s thanks to youthful champions such as Beck, who included a song called "Tropicalia" on his album *Mutations.*

Walker, Scott. Morose crooner, born Noel Scott Engel in Ohio, who first achieved success as part of the Walker Brothers, a 1960s teenybop trio (not actually brothers) that scored a hit with BURT BACHARACH and Hal David's "Make It Easy on Yourself." Walker's lasting Rock Snob appeal comes from the string of solo albums he made in the late 60s and early 70s, which are worshiped in his adopted homeland of Great Britain. Setting his ridiculously vibrato'd, Vegas-worthy wail against Weill-esque orchestral arrangements, he became the dark knight of schlock. In 1995, Walker released an impenetrable, Trent Reznor–influenced comeback album entitled *Tilt.*

Webb, Jimmy. Oklahoma-born, Los Angeles-based songwriter currently enjoying a BURT BACHARACH–like renaissance after years in too-soft-for-these-times exile. The author of such 1960s cocktail-pop classics as "MacArthur Park" and "Up, Up and Away," Webb recently played a few feel-good reunion dates with Glenn Campbell, who scored Top 10 hits 30-odd years ago with Webb's "Wichita Lineman" and "By the Time I Get to Phoenix."

Wilson, Brian. Mentally fragile Beach Boys leader. While revered by normal people for the catchiness and ingenuity of such hits as "I Get Around" and "California Girls," Wilson is revered by Rock Snobs more for his sensitive orchestral-pop masterwork, *Pet Sounds,* and for the ambition and general way-outness of its unfinished follow-up, *Smile*, the unraveling of which sealed his repute as a misunderstood genius forever persecuted by his own demons and "the Man."

Wrecking Crew. Crack team of 60s-era Los Angeles session musicians whose number included drummer Hal Blaine, bassists Carol Kaye and Ray Pohlman, keyboardists Larry Knechtel and Leon Russell, saxophonist Steve Douglas, and guitarists Jerry Cole and Tommy Tedesco. Often summoned at odd hours to execute the tricky, ambitious arrangements of Phil Spector, BRIAN WILSON, and JACK NITZSCHE.

Zimmy. Insiderist nickname for Bob Dylan, favored by shut-in Dylanologists in their painstaking discussions of their godhead's oeuvre, derived from Dylan's actual surname, Zimmerman. *Man, Blood on the Tracks is just a harrowing document of Zimmy's divorce.*

RICHARD MELTZER

Third Spud from the Sun

Cameron Crowe Then and Now

In the merry sequence of things, Cameron Crowe was the third of a conspicuous trio of teenage rock-crit wanna-bes, junior spuds from the gitgo, whose paths crossed mine in the early 1970s.

The biggest cheesepuff of the bunch, if also initially the most ambitious, Jon Tiven began publishing the mimeo rag *New Haven Rock Press* during his sophomore year of high school. To look at the damn thing now, a single staple holding 20-some off-white pages together, it might be tough to figure how something so lame and ugly managed to endure the three-four years it did, but when mommy and daddy foot the bills, merit is inconsequential. Having grown up in the mansion where that spooky pic *The Other* later got shot, he made no bones about being what could be loosely termed a rich kid—*upper middle class* we today would call him—but without the "finish" his class would typically afford him: a dumb little, poor little, u.m.c. dipshit, younger than his years. *Ein Kind* without much *Wunder*.

On weekends down from Connecticut, crashing sometimes at Nick Tosches' pad or mine, he brought along Tupperwares full of homecooked crap—his mother didn't trust Manhattan food. Back then, with the drinking age in New York still 18, nobody ever got asked for I.D., and Nick and I would always try to get him drunk.

22

He'd order some wimp drink like a sloe gin fizz, and we'd tell him, "Jon, this bar has a two-drink minimum." He'd get another, and then we'd hand him some bullshit like "The custom here is to *make your own bar*"—raise a forearm to your chin and drink around it (haw!)—and like a monkey he'd go for it. (Never met another 16'er so slowww on the draw.)

When he stayed at my place, he'd have my girlfriend take him to neighborhood fop stores—"boutiques"—where he'd shop for the sorts o' things rock stars wore: satin, velvet, "English cut." (Even girl-things with darts were okay if he could imagine Procol Harum wearing them.) He was one thudding *fool* for platform footery.

Finally, his parents sprung for a room at the New York Hilton, giving him occasion to invite this gal he met at a Nick party up for some room service *plus*, later claiming they'd whooped and he'd come 13 times ... say what? ... which led us to believe he'd never even jerked off.

If Tiven's 'zine had truly reflected his misadventures as a neo-phyte simp, an amateur's apprentice, that would've been one thing, but all it did was blend the same old shit ("With this album, Elton is performing to his potential ... *5 stars*") with a painful preadoles-cent cuteness ("Oatmeal Harv" was his favorite pseudonym). Issue after issue, nothing in the *New Haven Rock Press* spoke even generi-cally of (or from) the "outrageousness of youth"—or the center of grav of its goofy enthusiasm. With an abiding Junior Achievement blandness, it sought merely to coalesce with the least anarchic, least invigorating aspects of the burgeoning rock media, to simulate "rockmag" status and in so doing score mailings of promo albs, tick-ets to Rod Stewart in Yonkers ... oh goody.

Hey—the groovy myth of Everyperson a writer/publisher be damned: 99.9 percent of *all* 'zines—then, now, ever—are lame, tame, and insipid. As fate would have it, though, one of the *great* vanity rock sheets of all time was a contemporary of the *NHRP*. The progeny of a core of young hellions from the Bronx and Queens (only slightly older than Tiven himself) who would later morph into the proto-punk band the Dictators, *Teenage Wasteland Gazette* could usually be counted on to make a fine mess. Both personally and ideologically, *TWG* regarded Tiven as a doofus and made him its designated enemy. "The *New Haven Rock Press*," wrote editor Andy Shernoff, "really sucks my noodle. If I see another fuckin review by Jon Tiven I will take action. I challenge Tiven to any form of competition he wants. I prefer 12 oz. gloves but he may want GOLF (they have a lotta country clubs in N. Haven). Eat five-iron, limey lover!"

When I told Shernoff that once, after Tiven had split our apartment, my girlfriend and I found a load of doodoo in the crapper, unflushed, but *no toilet paper*, an occurrence we were hard put to explain, he devoted a full page to the incident, closing with the following hypotheses:

"1) Mr. Tiven may have used his hand.

"2) Mr. Tiven may collect used toilet paper.

"3) In an economy move Mr. Tiven may have eaten his toilet paper.

"4) It is a well-known fact that citizens of the well-to-do suburbs of the 'nutmeg' state maintain a live-in maid. One of the doodies of such a maid is to wipe the heinies of family members. Possibly Mr. Tiven is too young & immature to be trained to do the deed himself."

I haven't seen Jon since '76, but on evidence it would seem he made it through adolescence. Dunno 'bout the years between, but lately he's producing records by B.B. King, Wilson Pickett, and writing songs for aging blues and soul people—ain't life funny? The only thing I've heard is Buddy Guy's "Heavy Love": too heavy for a man to bear alone, he could use a little *help*, see? (Still makin' with the *cutesy*.) I leave it to soul music aficionado Kevin Kiley to fill out the picture:

"He ruined Pickett's comeback CD with shit arrangements, REAL BAD production, GARBAGE songs written by him and his fucking wife, and bad playing in general. I hate most of today's records. Even my old favorites' new records suck, due to crummy 'modern' production techniques. I may be a dinosaur, but I know

what the shit SHOULD sound like, and Tiven ain't got a fucking
CLUE!

"At the Luther Ingram benefit in Memphis last year he was a self-
absorbed prick, and a real asshole namedropper. He played guitar
there with Mack Rice and Swamp Dogg. He brought his own guitar,
one of those stupid-looking things with a whacky headstock (how
do you come to MEMPHIS to play at a SOUL show without a
fucking FENDER?!), he overplayed with a rock tone that had
NOTHING to do with soul music, and fucked up one of Swamp's
tunes, even though there were CHARTS!

"There was a birthday party for Rufus Thomas. Everyone was
smiling, laughing, having a good time. Tiven had his dour, 'gotta
look cool' mug on. He seemed taken aback that I didn't know his
name. During our entire conversation, he rarely looked at me, but
was instead surveying the happenings around the room. He had finished a CD on Sir Mack Rice, and I asked what kinda stuff was on it.
'You'll just have to wait to hear it.' It was like he was thinking,
'Leave me alone, I'm too cool, I don't want to miss anything by talking to YOU.' What a rude, condescending mother-fucker!"

For almost 30 years, the single word which might best fit the
Gestalt of *NHRP*'s "Los Angeles correspondent," Danny Sugerman,
the face he's with extreme volition worn for the world, is SLEAZE.
The night I met him, at an L.A. party in '72, the first thing he told
me was "My father works for the Mafia, and I'm a heroin addict"—
uttered with a great deal of teenage pride, like *Can you top* either *of
these?* Two cool.

I've never known the veracity of boast number one, nor of number two vis-à-vis *then*, but in the lead story of *Methadone Today*, Volume III, Number 4 (www.tir.com/~yourtype/v3_n04.htm), Danny
waxes loud and long on select details of his *eighteenth* detox attempt. A tour-de-force combo of personal confession (the bitter—
ouch—Truth) and whole-cloth William Burroughs, of empiricism
and giddy egoism (nothing in the closet 'bout me-me-ME),
"Delayed Onset Withdrawal" is the first thing I've read by the guy
since 1980.

Sleaze, and if there's another word, maybe *Jim*, y'know Morrison—he's made great hay of their ten- (or was it five?) minute relationship. Though others who were there insist that when the Doors still included Jim, before he took his death cab to Paris, young Danny's bond to the Lizard King was no more, no less, than to lurk about the band office seeking ways to be "useful," opening fan mail and perhaps going out for donuts, and while I've heard two of the three living Doors mention in passing that the growed-up Danny made their skin crawl, the dude has by sheer tenacity parlayed the lurk and its aftermath into an official calling card as "long-time Doors associate."

In 1980, he fleshed out and flavored Jerry Hopkins' stab at a Morrison bio, something variously described as a skeleton of research and a flawed ms. that had been lying around unpublishable for years. The result was *No One Here Gets Out Alive*, a ponderous and despicable piece of celebrity fluff, heavy on the "dark side" (ooh, Jim was *such a bad boy*) and including a cameo by a kid named "Danny." When it came out, he phoned to beckon me into the night: "Let's celebrate Jim." Uh, thanks but no-thanks . . . I'd rather walk my schnauzer.

In my subsequent review, I wrote: "Hey, this book stinks. I don't wanna really play its game, but one error in particular really irks my recollective whatsis. I was there at the 'infamous' Singer Bowl show of '68 and all I gotta say's Jim was wearing brown leather (not black) and if 'hundreds of teenagers were bleeding' at concert's-end (p. 195) then I guess it must've been menstrual or out in the parking lot because it certainly wasn't within proximity of the stage. Little things like that (including bogus alternate death scenarios and the scumbait sham of coddling the myth that Jim—like Paul—might still be alive) would be enough to make the cognoscenti puke if not for the trail of vom independently left in the wake of the BOOK AS IDEA." Idea? Oh, something about the intrinsic—inseverable—connection between genius and perversion, or creativity and excess . . . or something.

Since then he's had his hand in another two or possibly three Doors books, plus a Guns N' Roses book . . . say, that's really branching out. I think the word for this is "rock-sploitation," evincing an entrepreneurial, as opposed to strictly journalistic, agenda. (When, to cover the release of Oliver Stone's *The Doors*, a European TV crew was dispatched to L.A., he wasn't deemed a relevant enough "journalist" to bother interviewing.)

For a glimpse at another of his entrepreneurial fortés—rock manager—check out *Please Kill Me*, where on p. 251 Ron Asheton tells a good'un 'bout the time Danny left his "charge," a fucked-up Iggy Pop (wearing a dress), to fend for himself when three surf louts began pounding him outside a David Bowie show, leaving him bloody and minus a couple teeth on the pavement in Hollywood.

Last I heard about Danny he was living with Fawn Hall—remember her? (What a *perfectly* corrupt universe.)

For whatever reason(s), Danny didn't make it to the first and only mass gathering of the U.S. rockscribble crowd, known to history, generally and simply, as "The Rockwriters Convention," Memphis '73, but Tiven was there, as was San Diego's Cameron Crowe. By sucking up to John King, marketing director for Ardent Records—a subsidiary of Stax, which underwrote the whole silly event—Tiven had a major hand in putting together the guest list, guaranteeing a sizable 'zine contingent. Since the National Rock Writers Association, as Stax had dubbed the throng, was an org of no card-carrying members, nor even of cards, to be among the chosen 140-plus signified equal parts much and nothing. Given the basic unreality of the affair, its dream-within-a-dream sound and fury, all intimations of pecking order were foolish and fruitless (the rock-crit "profession" being all of five-six years old anyway).

Still and all, a couple things about Cameron set him down a peg from even the rank and file of 'zine greenhorn dust-suckers. Unless he had an *NHRP* affiliation that no one was aware of (S.D. correspondent-*designate?*), he for all intents & purps was not even a—how you say?—*symbolically* employed writer-in-training, most likely just someone Tiven knew, or knew of, through the teen-auxiliary grapevine. While hardly the sole unaffiliated writeboy at the convention, or the only one who had yet to earn a dime from writing, he was for damnsure, in more ways than one, the YOUNGEST such being in attendance: 16, maybe only 15, a goony-goofy gosh-oh-gee KID, blowing on a goddam kazoo. Or maybe an ocarina.

Recorder? Something. Playing Name This TV Themesong with anyone who would sit still for 30 seconds, not really that tough a score on a bus full of stationary writefolk en route to a Budweiser brew tour—playing it with, to, and at us . . . *Bewitched* . . . *The Flintstones* . . . *Father Knows Best* . . . *The Jetsons* . . . give the boy a bubble gum cigar!

Which ain't quite the same as leading with your own chin, or wearing a lampshade on your head, or actually demanding, *Pay attention, dammit*—hey, he wasn't *that* assertive—but the Cameron I met on the bus was certainly more forward—sassy—cheeky—than "William Miller," the sullen little cocksucker standing in for him in this flick he's got out now, *Almost Famous*. More cheerful and outgoing, he wurn't no self-conscious smallfry (taller than me, and I was 28). Why he would go and turn himself into a solemn sawed-off goody-goody geek—someone *less* bearable than he was at that age— is a mystery. 'Cause in '73 he was, well, bearable. (More, at any rate, than either Tiven or Sugerman.)

In the months following the convention, he wrote for the *San Diego Door* and *Creem* (at the time edited by former San Diegan Lester Bangs, who'd also been on the Bud bus), before eventually landing in *Rolling Stone*. When people I meet these days find out I once myself wrote for the fugging *Stone*, they ooh and ahh, then I tell 'em, "Sure, but fortunately I've had the good sense to never stick my penis in a garbage disposal." It's debatable whether the *Stone* had ever been a class venue for the *writing* of rockwriters—appearing in its pages was basically always about visibility and money. Well before there was anything like a rockwrite style sheet—a by-the-numbers for dealing with this thing-called-rock, a throbbing what-sem that for a while remained relatively nascent-and-nasty—in the rock/underground/counterculture press at large, *Rolling Stone* had one in spades. Heavy-handed editors—the meanest in the biz— would routinely (as a matter of policy) alter your text without consulting you; delete entire paragraphs if they contained the itsiest allusion to people or things the "fact checker" of the day was having trouble finding backup on; try to coerce you out of positions you'd taken on favored musical celebs. By the time Cameron showed up, the paper was little more than a highwater marker for self-effacing, slave-drudge careerism: the most conspicuous place, nationally, to have your copy butchered, your ideas reshaped to fit the moment's market-driven party line.

Salon.com has called *Almost Famous* "a sweet-natured paean to the '70s, a time when . . . editors at magazines like *Rolling Stone* told their staff to write the truth and damn the consequences"—what a hoot! First of all, there were no other mags "like" the *Stone*, but the only "truth" it sought was a sprinkling of sensationalism ("Dead Busted in N.O.—Set-Up Suspected"). Another review claims that the *Stone* in those days ran "more exposés than puff pieces." Gimme a break: the *Stone* INVENTED the rock 'n' roll puff piece.

Rolling Stone in the '70s was, as it remains today, a TRADE PAPER, a record industry HYPE SHEET, a promulgator of mass compliance in the Consumer Sector, a principal factor in the dumbing, maiming, and calming down of the public's taste for a rock-roll beast that had once indeed been not only wild & crazy but GENUINELY ANARCHIC. (Radical!—with or without the superadding of topical content.) The very idea, as nearly every review has put it, of the film's "poking fun" at *Rolling Stone* . . . whew. Would you have "poked fun" at Nixon for killing two million Southeast Asians? Hey, folks: *Rolling Stone* is not some venerable institution in need, from time to time, of a good-natured lampoon or two. Like MTV to follow, it has for a longgggg time been one of the big things GRAVELY WRONG WITH THE WORLD.

Jimmy Olsen incarnate, the youthsome Mr. Crowe accepted the *R.S.* style sheet implicitly, in all likelihood worked very hard, but essentially got and kept the gig when it was discovered that rock stars, such a sensitive lot, were less intimidated by him than by actual functional grownups, who had the disconcerting habit of asking grownup questions. He would never, for inst, have *thought* to ask Jimmy Page, as interviewers already had, whether the guitarist, pre-

Led Zeppelin, had in fact "done" a certain Linda E., famous for later marrying Someone Big—done her (he'd privately boasted) with a PICKLE. Cameron's writeup of Led Zep demonstrated his ability to fill pages as glibly as the next bozo, and a tad more affably to boot. Y'know: cheerfully. But it offered scarcely a hint of the service-with-a-smile he would provide the Singer-Songwriter gang in the years ahead—as its advocate, mouthpiece, interlocutor, shill . . . its virtual publicist and "man inside" the *Stone*.

Ah, the gang: I knew it well. I'd had an encounter with one of its thugs, see, and in the process got tossed by said mag for telling what was it?, oh yes, the truth. This was '72. After several false starts, Jackson Browne finally had an album out, which seemed a good occasion to bring to light some interesting hokum from his past— I'd known the mutha since '67. So I did the first feature on him for *Rolling Stone* or anywhere else—a rave, for crying out loud, and he freaking *hated* it, thought it made him look "too punk." And what might be so wrong with that? Before twelve people knew who the fuck he was, he was like some weird-isn't-the-word cross between the Young Marble Giants, say—or from a later universe: Cat Power—and Byron or Shelley. On his first visit to New York, he backed up (and horizontal-danced with) the fabulous NICO, had a connection to Lou Reed and the Warhol crowd, blah blah blooey. So I talked all this stuff up—what the hey—it was what I thought would make him MOST APPEALING. And he's so upset he gets Asylum Records prez David Geffen to call the *Stone* and have me booted, good riddance, don't come back.

Four years later, I was eating at South Town Soul Food in L.A. when Jackson walked in with gang-sister number one Linda Ronstadt. Not wanting her exposed to my cooties, he motions for her to stay put, struts over, sits down, and in less than a minute explains to me *how it is*. "We singer-songwriters"—he always relished being part of something (but imagine *calling* yourself such hogwipe)— "feel we get a *better shake* from this Cameron kid . . . he never *challenges us* . . . accepts *our* side of the story . . . we don't have to *worry* what he'll say . . . no offense, but . . ." I.e., writers exist to write-about-musicians, bub . . . so go wash dishes or something.

To some extent, Lester Bangs was prob'ly cheated by posterity when he got pigeon-holed in stone as a punk-rock scribbler, more or less, but at least there's some oompah to that. Just dig it if your rockwrite credential consisted to an inordinate degree of your coverage of Jackson, Linda, and related twaddle—a subset of the rock mainstream which by the mid '70s was almost Exhibit A of how far rock had sunk, how far it had gone in the direction of ceasing-to-be. Not to mention the decidedly SOFT edge (and LIGHT weight) implicit in such a number: being *that* kind of rockwriter . . . yow. (Where's the existential reverb in that one?)

Anyway, after a tour of *Stone* duty had given him enough chops to deal with non-rock matters, Cameron wrote *Fast Times at Ridgemont High*, a youth-demographic pile of pulp which few people in L.A. ever seriously considered—re his contention (and his publisher's marketing premise)—a work of non-fiction. Like had Cameron, by now in his twenties, actually gone back to school, where he impersonated (and passed for) a student? Not v. many thought so. Which is fine, who cares, but anyhow I haven't read it, nor did I see the '82 film of the same name (for which he got both script and "novel" credit), nor have I seen any of the later cinematic thingies he's written, directed, or produced, except for the current monstrosity.

I'm probably not the person to judge his oeuvre, but *Almost Famous*, which he wrote, directed, *and* produced, and which purportedly draws its content from the dawn's early light of his own rockwrite apprenticeship, strikes me as insufferable dogmeat, coming from the same neverneverland (w/ the *briefest* shot of nipples thrown in) as a bad week's episode of *Happy Days*. A first-string ditz based on the auteur's MOTHER provides plot annoyance throughout (hey, she's a *player*). Has there been such parental non-exclusion in an alleged rock film since *Bye Bye Birdie*? All-age sentimental slop: the sort of film that if it wasn't *nominally* a rock film you'd bring in violins to ensure, and intensify, audience submission at every emotional checkpoint. The scene towards the end where the William kid wags a finger at the guitarist (whose music he so-o-o respects) for mistreating the groupie (who respects *and* loves the bloke), thus triggering plot resolutions that culminate in fame and fortune for both (and vicarious gratification for the groupie), is something Ron Fucking Howard wouldn't put in one of *his* dogmeat films. And the actual "rock" soundtrack? Well, the FIRST TWO TUNES are the Chipmunks' Xmas single and Simon & Garfunkel's "America"—ye gods. (Don't wanna turn off the grandmas.)

Aside from all the references to *Creem* and *Rolling Stone*, and the recurrent presence of Lester Bangs as dramatis persona, *Almost Famous* is clearly a fiction film. It would be kind of absurd to try and extract from it anything *specifically* autobiographical re its director's own historical past, and/or his present retrospect on such biz, but shoot—long as we're here—let's go for it. To wit: Does Cameron Crowe, former rockwriter, have the self-awareness to grasp the true basis of his early career? (Do the Jimmy Olsens—cub reporters for Dotted-Line Central—even in retirement realize they were once dupes and decoys of the first water?) Possibly not, but by recasting the setup from the p.o.v. of an *utter* bumpkin/child/innocent, by using the b/c/i as a model of generic reporterly *integrity*, by going SO wide of the personal-historical mark—assuming, of course, the guy *remembers* anything pre–*Ridgemont High*—the frigging movie registers on *my* shit detector (don't know 'bout yours) as a willful act of evasion. A gross cultural-personal "lie."

All this poppycock with little William as "the enemy"—someone bands have reason to fear!—feels suspiciously like what in football parlance you'd call the ol' misdirection play. Sure, you bet—the mid-'70s Cameron, like most of his colleagues, did at times have to wear down or slip under bands' defenses in pursuit of et cetera, yet even after repeated encounters manymost of his targets *welcomed* his amiable crit-cum-hype. Compared to the rest of the write pack, even after he'd grown a bit, he remained inherently harmless. The millennium Cameron, meanwhile, would like us to view li'l Will as anything *but* harmless: a tough little bulldog dead-set on "getting the story" (when, in any case, "story" and "truth" are separate domains of the journaloid firmament).

But like so what. A shitty movie suggested by an unaffecting (if "successful") life. They make 'em all the time.

What's troublesome is the movie's use of Lester. I won't even complain about Philip Seymour Hoffman, who after makeup and coaching isn't totally *un*like Lester—he's just not especially *like* him. Did they get the mustache right? Well, he only had one about a tenth of the time ('70–'83) that I knew him. Cigarettes? If in his lifetime he sometimes smoked, he was hardly a smoker (drank far more bottles of Romilar—full bottles—than he smoked individual cigs). (If you want an actor's version of somebody quitelike Lester, personally like him in significant mammal ways, rent Gus Van Sant's first feature, *Mala Noche*. Tim Streeter is Lester to a *T*. And not too far afield—don't laugh—is Smiley Burnette, the comic sidekick in old Gene Autry films.)

And why *not* use Lester? A dab of Lester will add a touch of class—certainly of interest—to virtually any proceeding. (A little 'll go a long way.) But for Cameron to have him bouncing around as the movie's roving "disclaimer"—a guy who'd rather listen to the Stooges than the Eagles; who knows the difference between commodity and culture—is BAD FAITH, pure and simple. At least that's what Sartre would call it.

What's laughable—and downright insidious—is Cameron actually believes Lester "influenced" him. He's said so in a score of interviews. *Lots* of folks are claiming he influenced them, like this third-rate gossip at the *L.A. Times*, Patrick Goldstein. When he wrote full-tilt, Lester was a STAND-UP IDEOLOGUE, a man on a total-assault LIFE MISSION—not some careerist cluck lockstepping to the illusions of payday and acclaim. Conviction and contention oozed out of him like they did from any front-line '50s Beat poet. He influenced the likes of Cameron and Patrick about as much as he influenced Clinton and Reagan.

The dictionary def.: "(1) To affect or alter by intangible means; sway (2) To have an effect on the condition or development of; modify"—'s a matter of cause/effect. To have caused (if he did) budding young Cameron to perform acts *not* in kind: is that influence? As far as rockwriters go, the whole last 30 years of 'em, with the exception of Metal Mike Saunders (from Arkansas—you prob'ly never heard of him), Lester influenced NO ONE. He was the end of a line—believe it!—not the beginning of one. Even "inspired" would be too strong a word, too active. At best, Cameron and his ilk *received* inspiration, or let's put it this way: *perceived* what they received to *be* inspiration. From bad faith to blind faith . . .

Fuggit.

In all probability (and with all due respect), on the *hottest* writing day of the rock phase of his professional life, Mr. C. Crowe was not one of rock-crit's TOP TWENTY-FIVE figures (list available upon request). He was simply one of the era's more readable hacks—a cheerful, good-natured hack, but still a hack—one about whom the best *and* worst that can be said is he was benign. As in: he didn't cause cancer, nerve damage, birth defects, or ingrown toenails. But in the merry scheme of things, considering the range of hands, dealt and undealt, some if not all of us have lived, embraced, fought, raved, and died for, what the bloody, bleeping hell is BENIGN?

If you go and see his stupid flick, please keep that question in mind.

SPUDS. They're there to keep the rest of us honest.

So don't y'fall down on the job, y'hear?

I Like It
Warm and Fuzzy

Danger is corny. So why's Tabb trying to sell it to me? We're sitting in a bar and Tabb, by way of complimenting my recently defunct band, is expressing his incredulousness at my band's lack of danger-ous content. As in: isn't it fucked up that I dig your band, which was so puzzlingly undangerous. So I go: Tabb, what is this danger you speak of? And he tells me about how *really* good music makes one want to break stuff. Aaarrgh, danger!

Oh, come on. Danger is a shell game. Danger is a sham. Black clothes? Slimming. Heroin? Imparts a warm and fuzzy feeling. A warm and fuzzy feeling! Wanting to break stuff? What a dumb way to interpret an emotional response to music. Now, you won't find a guy more likely to link the continued existence of Western culture with the presence of AC/DC than me. I know from the evil feeling. But this danger stuff is just really dumb. And don't be telling me that the danger response *is* the evil feeling. Tabb proceeds to list the top three bands of All Time: the Beatles, the Ramones, Nirvana. (And to his list I say: begins with an H and ends with an oh hum.) I don't think he's even trying to tell me the Beatles provide danger content, but apparently the Ramones and Nirvana make him want to break stuff. "Smells Like Teen Spirit" had loads of evil feeling, but—and perhaps this is just my personal failure—I don't feel threatened by a guy in a holey cardigan who enjoyed a drug that made him feel warm and fuzzy. And the Ramones? The band that covered "California Sun," right?

Danger is another noun on the list of baby-boomer indulgence-nouns, which includes other punk rock standards like *sellout* and hippie notions like *progressive*. (Look, bub, music doesn't *progress*—it's not a fucking technology. New sounds can be found—very very rarely—but not new feelings.) You remember the baby boomers, right? The guys who fucked up show business for everybody, so that now if you want to be a singer when you grow up you have to want to be the messiah? Who imparted to pop music the totally ludicrous notion that to be anything near real you have to write your own material? Billie Holiday didn't. Hank Williams didn't write "Lovesick Blues." The history of R&B—a lot of current history, too—is of traditional songwriter, arranger and singer in separate camps. Sure I dig the Beatles. But does everybody have to be them?

(Let me just make a most hypocritical aside to my lawyer, manager and Warner/Chappell rep: don't worry, I'm not trying to subtly hint at a career change here. Let them songwriting revenues come in! Who's your boy?)

I just read that *Please Kill Me* book, the oral punk-rock history one. I love me some punk rock. And there's nothing I enjoy more than talented people getting pilled up and falling down, often violently. But I'm just not getting what exactly the danger is. That is, unless you're, like, real close to the front and Iggy actually falls on you. Richard Lloyd—whose music, I'm afraid, I'm totally unfamiliar with—says, about drug use, in an addendum to *Please Kill Me*, "I mean, some people climb Mount Everest . . . I took things that made you do that without going anywhere . . . You can look at it as adventuring." Yes, you can. I sure did when I was a kid in the suburbs and had no access to drugs. But when I did get them, guess what I found? A warm and fuzzy feeling.

Let me just say that I can't really front here: for one thing, I pretty much design my music to be undangerous. I like it to have big fat superlow frequencies that cause a palpable physical tingle, and which make people want to fuck. For another thing, I have a long history of critics having trouble with this rather calculated lack of scariness. I remember reading something on *Addicted to Noise*, about a Knitting Factory show, in which the reviewer was highly, pointedly annoyed at my band for lacking any trace of what she called "sex and death." Sex and death! (Just as a sidebar, I know a number of folks who got quite thoroughly laid at that show. Well, okay, not *at* it. And at the time I smoked like three packs a day. I've since quit, which no doubt makes me doubly undangerous.)

A guy wrote a *Spin* review, way back in the way back, actually lambasting me for not even trying to sound black when I sang. His point was something like: well, Ad-Rock avoids his whiteness by getting all whiny and raceless, Beck avoids his whiteness by shticking on his nonblackness, but this guy, why, he's just *white*. The writer really had a problem with the vocals—they made him uncomfortable. He actually said something to the effect of this would be quite the decent record, if it weren't for the vocals.

Now, here is something that actually might be kind of dangerous: those who get their little danger thrill in music by having an intense fantasy relationship with black people—the myth of the big black superhero rapper guy. Dangerous, as in, dangerous to their mental health—I don't think the standard-issue white rock critic longing to be the scary black man on the CD has absolutely anything to do with anything remotely related to actual black people in the world. But, boy, do they get mad when white people take up with the elements of rap music, thus fucking up their high. It remains cool—as in, no stigma—to make fun of white people for rapping. Twelve years after Faith No More, dude, look, it's just not all that bizarre.

I was struck by the recent controversy when Mike Rubin and Mark Dancey did a cartoon piece about the Insane Clown Posse for *Spin*. They actually tried to link the band with minstrelsy (a guy at an upright piano sings "way down upon the swanee ribber" in one panel), and made hay out of the fact that ICP were playing Detroit and their fans were all white people from the suburbs. This was illustrated with a map of Michigan with "Detroit" in oo-scary lettering, with a barbed-wire fence surrounding it. Does it have to be pointed out that pretty much *any* band—rap bands definitely included—playing Detroit are drawing mostly white kids from the suburbs? Unfortunately, ICP are boobs and went on a Detroit radio station, calling upon their fans to attack Rubin and Dancey. Deeply stupid though that is, I have to say, if I were chumped by self-loathing writers using me as an externalized target for their fear of themselves—who pretty much believe, with a straight face, that musical miscegenation should be mocked so others won't attempt it—I wouldn't react rationally, either.

This kind of nonsense is still going on. The April 27 *Rolling Stone* contains a Douglas Wolk review of the LaFace artist Pink that starts: "Pink is twenty-year-old Alecia Moore's hair dye of choice and, for that matter, her skin color." Never mind that Gwen Stefani—associated with ska, an older black genre than Pink's triplet-heavy contemporary r&b, which I guess makes it okay—sports the same race/coif combo in the same issue. Never mind that Pink's label was founded and is run by black people working in the same genre as she. Black musicians are cool with the girl, but the fucking critic points out her race like it actually means something.

Tabb, thankfully, doesn't have a rich fantasy life in which he's Redman. At least, as far as I know. But this danger stuff? He's not budging. He really thinks that the desire to inflict damage on private property is the righteous response to melodic stimuli. Then Giorgio Gomelsky, who we're drinking with, turns around and totally busts his argument up, winding it back to the Crusades and working his point up through the centuries. Tabb keeps trying to interject, but Giorgio won't let him, laying on another century of evidence every time he tries. Ooh, *face*, Tabb.

But Giorgio doesn't have much time for *my* argument, either, and shuts me up by telling me that the architects of rock music were making something because they had nothing else to express what they were feeling. I still don't buy it, but Giorgio has been in music since the 60s in London. To the cat that's seen it all, Tabb and I are *both* just a couple of punks.

N. R. KLEINFIELD

Guarding the Borders of the Hip-Hop Nation

He waited until the bus was ready to leave before squeezing up front to address the passengers. The Greyhound was going from Chicago to Indiana. It was winter. The sky was suffused with gray.

He surveyed the bunched rows of seats. There were only 19 passengers, most of them young, most of them black. Billy Wimsatt was white. It was an audience that made him especially comfortable.

He held aloft a slender book. "I wrote this book," he said over the chitter of talk. "It's pretty good. It normally sells for $12. On this bus, I'll sell it for $5, and you can read it along the way free."

It was called "No More Prisons," and was about incarceration and philanthropy and hip-hop, always hip-hop, for hip-hop was the everlasting undertone to his life. He was a writer and activist, and over the years his work had made him something of a minor cult figure in the hip-hop world, a white man with unusual credibility among blacks deeply protective of their culture. He was an unbudgeable optimist, convinced he could better the world by getting whites and people of other races to talk together and work together. He spent most of his time on the road, on a yearlong tour of several dozen college campuses, preaching his message. Now the bus was taking him to Earlham College in eastern Indiana.

Some passengers gave grudging looks of curiosity. What gives with this guy? Six people beckoned for copies. One woman gave hers back after 15 minutes, opting for sleep. A man behind her bought one. A woman said she'd take one, too. "Cool," Mr. Wimsatt said. He gave her a big smile and a hug.

Billy Wimsatt was 27, still clinging to the hip-hop life. He didn't look terribly hip-hop, and not because he was white. He was balding and brainy-looking, with an average build and an exuberant nature.

He was born as rap music was being invented by blacks and Latinos in the South Bronx. What began as party music became their cry of ghetto pain and ultimately their great hope for a way out. And as hip-hop—not just rap music but fashion, break-dancing, graffiti and the magazines that chronicle it all—blossomed into the radiant center of youth culture, Billy Wimsatt and lots of white kids found in it a way to flee their own orderly world by discovering a sexier, more provocative one.

Like many young hip-hop heads, he regarded hip-hop, with its appeal to whites and blacks, as a bold modern hope to ease some of the abrasiveness between the races. Hip-hop, as he saw it, endowed him with cultural elasticity, allowed him to shed the privilege of whiteness, to be as down with blacks as with whites. For a long time, he felt black in every respect but skin color, he says, which was why he had been able to get away with that much-noticed article seven years ago in *The Source*, a magazine considered one of the bibles of hip-hop.

It was a withering critique of "wiggers," whites who try too hard to be black so they will be accepted. Soon, he argued, "the rap audience may be as white as tables in a jazz club." In the last paragraph, which *The Source* cut from the final version, he warned black artists that the next time they invented something, they had better find a way to control it financially, because whites were going to steal hip-hop.

"And since it's the 90s," he concluded, "you won't even get to hear us say, 'Thanks, niggers.'"

Yes, Billy Wimsatt seemed about as authentically hip-hop as a white guy could get. But as he slid into the complexities of adulthood, he said, he often found himself wondering if that was enough, unsure which culture was truly his. He had drifted a long way from his black hip-hop roots. Now, on these unsettled grounds, he was far from certain he could stay true to his ideas.

A Believer on the Brink

On a clangorous Manhattan sidewalk, Elliott Wilson stopped to study the bootleg rap tapes splayed on a street vendor's blanket. Music emanated from a portable stereo.

"Some dope stuff here," Mr. Wilson, a gangly, light-skinned young black man with inquisitive eyes and a contagious laugh, said approvingly. The bargains got him pumped up. He peeled off a five-dollar bill and bought "Opposite of H2O" by Drag-On.

Elliott Wilson had never met Billy Wimsatt, but their lives had traced similar trajectories across the hip-hop landscape. As a writer and editor, he too had spent much of his adult life thinking about hip-hop. And not just hip-hop, but race and hip-hop. Race was unavoidable in hip-hop—what with all those black rappers idolized by white teen-agers—and like Billy Wimsatt, Elliott Wilson was preoccupied with that conjunction and what it meant in his own life.

Which culture was his was not Elliott Wilson's worry. Hip-hop had inspired him to believe that, precisely because he was black, he could achieve what whites simply assumed was theirs by birthright—a gainful life over which he asserted control.

When he read Mr. Wimsatt's "wigger" article, he and a black friend were beginning their own hip-hop publication, *Ego Trip*. They saw it as a brash challenge to the established, white-owned magazines like *The Source*. Bubbling with assurance, Mr. Wilson had judged the "wigger" article amusing; for all its ridicule of whites, he had still considered it "a white boy's perspective on hip-hop." He certainly hadn't seen it as a prophecy of personal doom.

Now, he sometimes had to wonder. He was closing in on 30, trying to hold fast to his own idea of the hip-hop life. He had watched with anger and growing pessimism as *Ego Trip* folded and whites asserted ever-greater control over the hip-hop industry. Recently, he had become editor of a promising hip-hop magazine, *XXL*. It was white-owned. And so he wondered if he was selling out, if he would ever become what he wanted on his own terms. Was hip-hop his story, the black man's story, after all? Did hip-hop unite the races or push them further apart?

A White Boy Confined in His Skin

Growing up in Chicago, Billy Wimsatt remembers, he believed the only way he could have a good life was to be black.

His own life felt proscribed. He was an only child. There was rarely music in the house, just the droning news stations. He saw an awful lot of "Nova" on PBS. He was to avoid the unsavory black neighborhoods.

Yet, he recalls, black children seemed to roam freely. They seemed to grow up faster. In fourth grade, his teacher asked if anyone baby-sat. A black girl's hand shot up. Incredible. Black girls were mature enough to baby-sit. He says he longed to live in the projects.

Where he lived was the integrated neighborhood of Hyde Park, in a perfectly diverse six-flat: two white families, two black, two mixed. His father taught philosophy of science at the University of Chicago. His mother was sort of a perpetual student.

At his mostly white private school, he was not especially popular. He imagined becoming a computer programmer, a scientist, an astronaut. Then, in sixth grade, a black kid told him to listen to a rap song, "Jam On It." "It was like a message from another world," he said.

Increasingly, he disconnected from a white culture that he equated with false desires. He had jumped out of his container, he said, "like spilled milk." After sixth grade, he persuaded his parents to transfer him to a largely black public school. The cool kids, he noticed, wore fat sneaker laces, favored gold jewelry, did graffiti. He began shoplifting fat laces, fake gold jewelry and markers and selling them to hip-hop heads.

He started break-dancing on the streets. And at 13, he began sneaking out at night and riding the trains with black and Latino friends, bombing the city with spray paint. Upski was his chosen tag. From then on, little Billy Wimsatt became Upski, one of Chicago's most prolific graffiti artists.

His frazzled mother, dogged by insomnia, would discover him gone at 2 A.M. She barred his graffiti crew from the house (one of them even burglarized the place), sent him to a psychiatrist, threatened military school. When he persisted, his parents plunked him back in private school. But he barely associated with white classmates, he says. Hip-hop had cloaked him in a new identity.

Astonishingly, and much to the dismay of many older people who abhorred its defiant attitude, its frequent misogyny, violence and vulgarity, hip-hop culture was becoming a great sugar rush for young people of all races. Before long, rap would eclipse country and rock to become America's top-selling pop-music format. And whites would be the ones buying most of those rap albums—a full 70 percent.

For many, even most, young whites, hip-hop was ultimately a hobby, to be grown out of in good time. For Upski, it became a cause, especially as the late 80s gave rise to politically conscious rappers like Public Enemy, with its peppery blend of black nationalism and rebellion. "Once it became a pretty full critique of American life—race, politics and political hypocrisy—that's when it really registered with me," he said.

A Black 'Leader of the Nerds'

Elliott Wilson grew up in the Woodside Houses project in Queens, the oldest of three brothers. His mother was of Greek and Ecuadorean roots; his father, a printer from Georgia, was black. Elliott was very light-skinned, and his hair was different from the black kids'. When it came to skin color, he picked up some mixed messages.

He was 5 when his father told him: "You're going to be judged by who your father is. I'm black. So you're black. Accept it before you get hurt." And he did, he said: "I felt like the black man from the jump."

He also spent a lot of time with his father's mother. She was tough, and she had friends of all races. She called white people crackers, but told Elliott, "Never trust a black person darker than you."

Attending predominantly white schools, self-conscious about his looks, he never really fit in, he says, recalling that time now. The black and white students didn't mix much, and while the black football players were cool, he was no football player. Instead, he befriended the outcasts.

"I wanted to be a cool kid and I wasn't," he said. "But I didn't want to sacrifice who I was to fit into the system. I'd rather create my own system. I wasn't going to be a fake. So I was the leader of the nerds."

His parents sheltered him from the influence of the streets. He watched a lot of television. He loved "Happy Days" and "Good Times," admired Howard Cosell and imagined becoming a sportscaster. In high school, he says, he increasingly felt himself an outsider. His grades, always good, fell.

But there was hip-hop. Hip-hop was cool, and his growing love of it made him begin to feel cool. His parents bought him a set of Technics 1200 turntables and a mixer. On weekend nights, while classmates were out on dates, he would be home taping the hip-hop shows off the radio.

When he listened to Public Enemy, he began to shake his head knowingly. For young Elliott Wilson, unaware of so much, the group's powerful lyrics of oppression and rage, especially the album "It Takes a Nation of Millions to Hold Us Back," were an awakening to what it meant to be black in America. He got a Public Enemy jacket, with the group's logo on the back: a black man in the cross hairs of a gun.

He became more aloof. He no longer said hello to white people, even family friends, unless they greeted him first, he now says. They asked his parents, What's gotten into Elliott?

He went to La Guardia Community College—in part because Run of Run-DMC had gone there to major in mortuary science— and then to Queens College. He began writing for hip-hop publications. One day first semester, he had an interview with Kool G. Rap. School felt irrelevant. He walked out of class and never returned. He entrusted his fate to hip-hop, and hip-hop breathed possibility into his life.

"If I came out of school without hip-hop, I wouldn't have thought of owning my own business and having power," he said. "As a person of color, to be legit, you think you have to be a worker for someone. Hip-hop made me believe."

But hip-hop was full of bizarre crosscurrents. When he saw white kids simulating his behavior, he got annoyed. It was one thing if they had grown up in the culture. But those well-to-do young whites who tried to appropriate hip-hop for themselves, he says, were simply insecure "image chameleons."

Right here was the enigma of hip-hop: The black rappers certainly weren't preaching integration, inviting whites into their homes. They were telling their often dismal stories, the pathologies they felt had been visited on them by a racist system they yearned to escape. But so many white kids were turning that on its head. They wanted to live life large, the way the rappers did.

A Reason for Rhymes

The phone rang. Dog got it: "He here. We here. I'll hit you back later. You gonna be in the crib?"

It was afternoon. Like a lot of aspiring rappers, Dog and his friend Trife were living life small, passing time in Dog's rampantly messy apartment in Brooklyn's Clinton Hill section. Passing time was what they did most days. They played games, gossiped, drank Hennessy, chewed over the future. Weekends, they went bowling. They were 23, young black men seeking sanctuary from the streets by rhyming their lives.

With their friends Po and Sinbo, they had formed a rap group, Wanted and Respected. Dog's closet was stuffed with recording equipment; his specialty was creating the beats. He made some slim money doing tapes for kids with their own rap dreams ($100 a tape) and selling shirts on the street. The group had played a few clubs, always gratis. Others shuttled in and out, but life weighed on the composition: members kept getting jailed, and one had been killed.

Dog and Trife had followed a trajectory of intense poverty and outlaw life. Dog's grandmother basically raised him—a dozen relatives packed into a three-bedroom place. Trife grew up with his mother, an R & B singer, and seven others in the nearby projects; he still lived there with her.

They had belonged to a gang called the Raiders, they said, selling drugs and doing other things that landed them in prison. If a white person came into their neighborhood, they said, they robbed him. They all packed guns. "It was bad as Beirut," Dog said. Trife said he still sold drugs, and some of the others did dubious things.

A few years ago, they gravitated to rap, embracing it the way so many poor blacks have long embraced basketball. But it was better. There were more slots. And it seemed to demand less talent. "You don't even have to sing well," Dog said.

"Music is my sanity," Trife said. "If I wasn't doing this, I'd probably be doing 25 to life."

Dog laughed. "If it weren't for rap, I'd be dead."

Many older blacks felt rap denigrated their race. They hated the constant use of "nigga" in the songs. Dog and Trife shrugged this off. Rap was raw and ugly, but that was their lives, they said. Rap was a blunter truth.

Dog found it curious that whites—suburban mall rats, college backpackers—bought most rap records. "White people can listen to rap, but I know they can't relate," he said. "I hear rap and I'm saying, 'Here's another guy who's had it unfair.' They're taking, 'This guy is cool, he's a drug dealer, he's got all the girls, he's a big person, he killed people.' That is moronic."

Later, Dog said: "Hip-hop is bringing the races together, but on false pretenses to make money. Look at Trife. He's got two felonies. That means he's finished in society. But he can rap. His two felonies, in rap, man, that's a plus."

"It's messed up," Trife said. "In hip-hop, I'm valid when I'm disrespected."

Trife recited some lyrics he had written:

You can't walk in my shoes,
If you ain't lived my life.
Hustling all day, clapping out all night.

The Cool Rich Kids' Movement

The road to Earlham was speckled with billboards for Tom Raper RV's, the Midwest's largest RV dealer. The trees were sheathed in glass from the freezing rain.

Earlham, a small Quaker college, was predominantly white, marginally into hip-hop. Upski was to give a talk, accompanied by a hip-hop group, Rubberoom.

Upski had dropped out of Oberlin College in his junior year. He had only reluctantly gone to college at all. He spent more time doing graffiti and reading magazines than going to class. He wrote an anonymous column for the black paper that scathingly denounced white people. He had a hip-hop radio show: "Yo, this is live from Chicago." Many people thought he was black.

Even so, he says, he was sporadically queasy about his hip-hop moorings. He knew his infatuation with blacks could be taken different ways. He could be accepted as credible, or taken as exploitative.

"That is the great fear of blacks," he said. "'Oh, you'll be fascinated with us, and then go back to dominating us and you'll be better at it because you'll have inside information.'" When he had shown drafts of his writings about race to a black classmate at Oberlin, she had slipped them back under his door and stopped talking to him.

He committed himself to journalism and activism. As he put it, "I saw it as my job to get white people to talk about race."

In 1994, a year after his influential "wigger" article, he self-published "Bomb the Suburbs"—part memoir of a white man's life in hip-hop, part interviews with hip-hop figures, part treatise on race and social change. It sold an impressive 23,000 copies. The gangsta rapper Tupac Shakur declared it "the best book I read in prison."

Upski hitchhiked around the country, promoting the book, pushing his views on racial cohesion, further cementing his eccentric renown. "I thought white people would start listening to and liking black people," he said, but ultimately, he was discouraged.

He refocused. He would become a social-change agent, motivating whites to be activists. Last fall, he published "No More Prisons" and began the "Cool Rich Kids' Movement." He would coax cool rich kids to give money to the cause. He started the Active Element Foundation and, with an ally, a well-to-do white woman, also started a group, Reciprocity, that paid him a modest salary. This year, he began his college tour.

At Earlham, before a mostly white audience, Upski said: "The thing that drives me is getting to know people and making relationships across race and class, which doesn't happen so much in America. Some of the stuff I'm going to say is going to sound heavy, and you're going to say, 'Let me go smoke some weed and chill.'"

He bounced around the room, his manner that of the motivational speaker. He said: "My goal today is to encourage you to accept the best and worst things about yourself." He talked about how they were too comfortable in this school, and how he had been "saved" by transferring to a black school after sixth grade. And then Rubberroom performed, and a lot of people left and the remaining ones danced. Upski danced.

Upski had brought along a copy of *Stress*, a small hip-hop magazine published by people of color. Upski told the students to read this, not the white-owned magazines.

He used to write for *XXL*, a fledgling magazine with a white owner and publisher. In 1997, the original black editor and black staff quit after being refused an ownership stake. There were innuendos of racism, but whether it was just business or race depended on the vantage point. Upski, however, swore never to work for *XXL* again.

After all, there were always ways for a smart white guy to make money.

Agonizing at the Monkey Academy

When the editor's job at *XXL* was offered to him last August, Elliott Wilson was put in a delicate spot. He was broke. In college, he accepted a flurry of credit cards and bought all the "fly" clothing. Now he owed $8,000.

He remembers thinking about how blacks needed to think more like whites. "We have a short expectancy in life," he said. "So we go for the quick buck. That's why kids sell drugs. That's why they rob. We don't feel we can be on a five-year plan to success."

The *XXL* job came with excellent pay—low six figures. But talk of racial tension stained the place. He asked himself, he said, could blacks think he was selling out? First, he had to discuss it with the *Ego Trip* collective. He went over to the Monkey Academy.

Two rooms in a Chelsea basement, the Monkey Academy was a shrine to hip-hop. Roosting on a shelf was a "Talking Master P" doll ("Make 'em say uhhh") and a memento from Puff Daddy's 1998 birthday gala. Rap posters adorned the wall: Snoop Doggy Dogg, RZA, Jungle Brothers.

Ego Trip was five young men of color with ambitions of hip-hop entrepreneurship: Mr. Wilson, Sacha Jenkins, Jeff Mao, Gabriel Alvarez and Brent Rollins. They saw race as a depressive undercurrent to everything, and it was the focus of their scabrous humor. "We're always talking about the blacks and the whites," Mr. Wilson said. "That's the way me and my boys are."

The very name Monkey Academy reflected their saucy attitude. As Mr. Jenkins explained it: "Call me paranoid, but when I meet with white people, I feel that with their eyes they're calling me monkey. So why not wear that proudly? Everyone in hip-hop wants to use the N-word, so why not take it to the next level? Call us monkeys." They especially liked to trace their understanding of society to the "Planet of the Apes" movies, where the light-skinned orangutans controlled the dark gorillas.

Several years ago, the group published *Ego Trip*, which they saw as a magazine about race disguised as a hip-hop magazine. They invented a white owner, one Theodore Aloysius Bawno, who offered a message in each issue, blurting his bigoted views and lust for Angie Dickinson. His son, Galen, was a Princeton-educated liberal who professed common cause with blacks. But in truth, he was an unaware bigot, as Mr. Wilson says he feels so many young whites are.

So much of the hip-hop ruling class was white. As Mr. Wilson put it, *Ego Trip* wanted "to strike at all the black magazines that are white-owned and act as if they're black." It was a small irony that *Ego Trip*'s seed money of $8,000 came from a white man, but at least he was a passive partner.

Though it gained a faithful following, *Ego Trip* stayed financially wobbly. No new investors came forth; the collective suspected the reluctance had to do with skin color. *Ego Trip* gasped and expired.

Now its founders scrambled with day jobs and worked on projects like "*Ego Trip*'s Book of Rap Lists" and a companion album. Hip-hop Web sites were proliferating, and they hoped to start one, too. They said they wanted to hear the roar of money, on their terms. "Black people create, but we don't reap the benefits," Mr. Wilson said. "We get punked and pimped. If we were white boys, we'd all be rich by now."

On that August day, he recalls, he sat on the couch, his emotions in an uproar. He had to wonder: was he now going to work for a true-life Ted Bawno? The others, he says, expressed a dim view of the *XXL* offer: "They were feeling I was pimping."

Not long before, he had been music editor of *The Source*. One duty was to rate new albums, on a scale of one to five "microphones." When he gave three microphones to "Corruption" by Corrupt, he says, the white publisher, David Mays, increased it to three and a half without telling him. When he confronted Mr. Mays, he concluded that the publisher did not respect him. Mr. Mays wouldn't give his side, but as Mr. Wilson tells it, he quit over half a microphone.

He felt strongly, he recalls, that he had to help himself. He no longer saw hip-hop as a great equalizer. "Who because of hip-hop now believes, 'I've seen the light, I'm going to save the blacks'?" he would say.

Sure, there was something positive in white kids' idolizing black rappers, but "what's going to happen when these white kids lose their little hip-hop jones and go work for Merrill Lynch?" he said.

What should he do? Months later, he remembers the confusion, the vectors of his life colliding. His throat tightened and he began to cry. He went to the bathroom of the Monkey Academy and composed himself. The message left hanging in the air from the others was, Do what you got to do.

As a black man, how many opportunities would come his way? He had this unslaked desire to prove his mettle. He took the job.

Tapping the Unconscious Biases

Upski went to the laundermat. Shaking in detergent, he talked about how he was a bundle of contradictions, subject to irrational racist phantasms for which he had no cogent defense. "I have patterns like every other white guy that I'm not very aware of that play out as racist," he admitted. He laughed at racist jokes. Walking down the street at night, he felt threatened if he saw a shabbily dressed black man. "I frequently feel I have more of a level of comfort and trust with white people," he said.

He talked differently to black friends ("Yo . . . That's wack . . . Peace, brother."). It infuriated his white girlfriend, Gita Drury. "I'll say to him, 'Do you know you're talking black now? Can you talk white, because that's what you are,'" she said. "I think it's patronizing." When he got on the phone, she could detect at once the caller's race. When he talked black, she would wave a sign at him: "Why are you talking like that?"

She saw this episodic behavior in other ways: "If we walk down the street and a black person walks by, he will give this nod, raise his chin a bit. He wouldn't do it with a white guy. I'll say, 'Oh, you have to prove to a black person that you're down.'"

Not long ago, Upski recalled, he spoke about race at a prominent college along with a black friend. He was paid twice as much as his friend. He spoke longer, but not twice as long. He never told his friend.

Sometimes, he said, he believed that black people were dumber than whites. Sometimes he felt the opposite. Now, as the washers ended their cycles, he hauled the wet clothes to the dryers. A stout black woman stood beside an empty cart. He asked if she was using it. She stared at him, bewildered. He asked again. Nothing.

Exasperated, he simply grabbed the cart and heaped it with his clothes.

Later on, he said: "When that happened, part of my gut reaction was, 'This is a black woman who has limited brain capacity, and it fits my stereotype of blacks having less cognitive intelligence.'"

Would a white woman have understood?

"It's dangerous for me to even say that," he said. "But that's what I thought."

Embarrassed by Rap's 'Babies'

The strip club was scattered with patrons with embalmed looks, solemnly quaffing their beverages. Elliott Wilson pulled up a stool beside a dancer. A fistful of dollars flapped from a rubber band curled around her wrist, the night's rewards.

Strip clubs, in particular this one in Queens, had a powerful hold on him. Though rap was his music, he said, he liked to unwind here rather than at a hip-hop club. There, everyone wanted something. Here, no one wanted anything but his money. "I'm not caught up in me and Puffy having each other's cell phone numbers," he said.

He had conflicted feelings about rap and rappers. "A lot of rappers rap about sex and violence, because people are interested in it," he said. "But it's art. It's poetry. If a rapper says, 'Kill your mother' in a song, it doesn't mean kill your mother. You can't take anything at face value." The real-life violence and arrests of rappers were something else. "Rappers are babies," he said. "They don't know how to balance their success and their street life. When I hear about Jay-Z this and Puffy that, I'm embarrassed to be part of the profession."

Mr. Wilson and his friend Gabe Alvarez shared an apartment in Clinton Hill, next to Fort Greene, a gentrifying neighborhood promoted by Spike Lee before he moved to the Upper East Side.

"Part of it's good and part isn't," Mr. Alvarez said. "You go a block over and there're the drug dealers."

"It's like the classic black neighborhood," Mr. Wilson said. "The liquor store, the bodega. I want good restaurants. I don't want to live in the 'hood. Who wants to live in the 'hood?" He wanted to move to Park Slope.

It was not his thing to go out of his way to patronize black businesses. It was fruitless, he said. He had seen that so much in hip-hop. "There's always a white man somewhere making money," he said. "You can't avoid the white man. My going to a black barber or something doesn't do anything."

Upski Meets Dog and Trife

Upski had gone to get his hair cut at the black-owned Freakin U Creations. He only went to black barbers, and part of his manifesto was to direct at least half his money to minority stores. Fort Greene afforded plenty of possibilities. All in all, though, he found the neighborhood imperfect, already too gentrified. His girlfriend lived there, so he did. He had lived in a black neighborhood in Washington. He said he felt he belonged either in a rich white neighborhood, where he could persuade residents to integrate, or in the true 'hood, where he could organize. He mused about moving to East New York.

Upski chatted with one of the owners, Justice Cephas. Two young black men waited their turn. Mr. Cephas was a hip-hop promoter on the side and was working with their group. They were Dog and Trife.

Upski said, "Don't take anything off the top."

Dog studied Upski's pate and said, "What's there to take off?"

Upski laughed. He asked how they felt about whites' moving into the neighborhood.

"Five years ago, I would have beaten you up just for sitting in that barber chair," Dog told him.

"Oh," Upski said.

"But I've matured," Dog said.

Later, though, he talked about how he was still deeply bitter toward white people. No white person had ever done anything positive for him, he said. As he remarked of whites: "I've never been with you. Why would I want to be with you now?"

Trife added, "If you're not my people now, you're not my people down the line."

Dog and Trife had told Upski about their group, Wanted and Respected. Trife's older brother had started a record label, Trife-Life Records, and they were working on its first album. They hoped to sell it on the street, create some buzz. All the while, Trife said later, he was thinking, "What is this white guy doing in this barbershop?"

Upski smiled. These young men, he said, reminded him of the black friends he used to run with in Chicago. If he were younger, he mused, he might want to run with them.

The Beatles Parallax

Inside Elliott Wilson's *XXL* cubicle was a computer, a stereo and a table strewn with rap albums. The music was on—loud.

His eyes scanned the screen—copy for the next issue. He fiddled with it. "I'm adding curse words," he said. "Putting in ain'ts. Making it more hip-hop."

The publisher, Dennis Page, came in with his beneficent smile. "Hey, man, we doing O.K.?"

"Yeah."

Mr. Page peeked over his shoulder at the screen. He nodded: "That's dope."

They went on like that, bantering.

Mr. Wilson called his boss D.P.G.—Dennis Page Gangsta, after Snoop Doggy Dogg's crew, the Dogg Pound Gangstas. Mr. Wilson had given D.P.G. an inscribed copy of "*Ego Trip*'s Book of Rap Lists." He wrote, "I don't care what people say, I know your favorite color is green."

It was how he felt about the relationship. They were both there for the money, he said.

Dennis Page was 46. He had the black walk, the black talk. His father had run a liquor store in Trenton, and Mr. Page had hung around with black kids and absorbed their ways. Now, he says, he has no real black friends. He admits he's been called a wigger. "I feel stigmatized by black people in hip-hop who feel I'm exploiting them," he said. "I don't feel I'm exploiting. It's a business. The record companies are white-owned. But I feel I take more heat. Certain black people feel that white people shouldn't even buy hip-hop albums, no less write about it. I'm not saying a black man can't buy a Beatles record."

XXL was just going monthly, and its circulation, which it gave as 175,000, was still far below the leading magazines'—*Vibe* sold more than 700,000 copies, *The Source* 425,000. *XXL* had been heavily political, clearly aimed at blacks. To build up the white audience, Mr. Page and Mr. Wilson agreed to tone it down, focus it almost entirely on the music.

"My magazine isn't some white-boy magazine, though," Mr. Wilson said. "It's black, too. I'm not sacrificing what *XXL* stands for." Even so, he added, "it can't be totally black if a white man is signing the check."

'I Preach to Mess Up'

Tuesday dawned muggy. It started badly and got worse. Upski was addressing about 250 students at Evergreen College in Olympia, Wash. Maybe 10 weren't white.

He had gathered a panel of half a dozen students. One, Evelyn Aako, was black. Introducing her, he said: "I don't know her very well, but she's black. And she's going to talk about issues of being black on campus."

Ms. Aako gave him an arch look. "That was very weird," she recalled thinking. "Like I was a little dark object."

As Upski began talking, the white audience got defensive. One student said: "Why do we have to talk about race? Why can't we talk about how we're alike?"

Ms. Aako was getting disgusted. Finally she told Upski: "I've been sitting here with an uncomfortable feeling in my stomach about how you introduced me. I felt tokenized and on display. This follows a tradition where black people serve as entertainment for white people. That's not what I do."

Upski said: "I screwed up. But what can we do? The world is screwed up."

Some white students were looking irritated. One said: "Can't we hear Upski talk? We can talk about race later."

A black student said: "What do you mean later? We never talk about race."

Some whites left. Virtually all the students of color followed. Before leaving, Ms. Aako said, "It's not my job to educate you."

Later, Upski sounded no less confident of his ability to stimulate change. But perhaps, he said, he needed to refine his approach.

"I think the main thing that keeps white people from growing is they're afraid to look bad," he said. "So I preach to mess up. One of my blind spots at Evergreen was that Evelyn wasn't going to trust me, that black people and white people, we're still at war."

Increasingly, he said, he was questioning his own evolution. Here he was intent on helping blacks, and spending most of his time in white culture. He had had a string of black girlfriends, but now he was with a white woman. A few years ago, probably two-thirds of his friends were black and Latino. Now it had flip-flopped.

Hip-hop itself had moved away from political and racial talk and for the most part sold excess and riches, women and violence. So much of hip-hop, he said, was self-denigrating, imitative and shallow. It was candy.

"One of the things I have the least respect for about parts of black culture," he said, "is there's so much pain and insecurity that it gets medicated by aping the worst aspects of white culture."

He talked about how so many of his old black and Latino graffiti friends hadn't survived hip-hop too well. One got locked up for fire-bombing a car. Another fell from a fire escape while trying to rob an apartment. He is now a paraplegic, drinking away his life, Upski said.

And yet, Upski had to admit, he was cruising along. His girl-friend, Ms. Drury, had inherited money, though they lived modestly. He didn't earn a lot, but he didn't worry. Until recently, he never took cabs and rarely ate out; he called it flaunting privilege. But now he was traveling more in white circles where everyone took cabs and ate out. So he did, too. And, he acknowledged, he liked it.

"The part of Billy that wanted to be black for a good part of his youth, that's fading," Ms. Drury said. "One of the issues in our relationship is he's a chameleon. The thing with Billy, he wants to be liked."

He had always cared so much about how he looked through black eyes, he said. Now his success depended on how he looked through white eyes. He had always dressed poorly and now he owned three suits. Where was he going? he wondered. As you got older, holding onto your hip-hop values seemed a lot harder if you were white.

Traps and Trappings of Success

Elliott Wilson climbed the stairs to the basketball court. The old guys were already there. The doctor had told him he had high blood pressure, a real slap in the face. "I've got the black man's disease," he joked.

Who knew the factors, but he had never eaten properly. He was also feeling the pressure of his job, he said. A friend who had been editor of *The Source* said the same thing happened to him.

His doctor put him on medication, urged exercise. So he had begun playing full-court basketball three mornings a week. There was an early crowd of young guys, but Mr. Wilson wasn't ready for them. He played with a bunch of white guys, some in their 50s and 60s, and one black guy in his 70s. He hit some baskets and missed some. He changed and headed for *XXL*.

He had now edited four issues. The first one, with DMX on the cover, had outsold any previous issue. He felt he was making a mark, he said. He had his disputes with Dennis Page, but they got along. His *Ego Trip* comrades felt proud of him.

He was making such good money, more than three times what Upski made, but somehow, he said, that wasn't the point. What he really wanted to do was to "take *The Source* out in a year or two," then expand the reaches of *Ego Trip*. Still, there were always seeds of self-doubt.

"Do I feel secure?" he said. "No. Because I'm black and I have bad credit. Having bad credit in this country is like being a convict. You don't have a prosperity mind-set when you're a person of color. You have something, you always feel someone is going to take it. You're always on edge, wondering what next."

'I Just Want the Money'

Dog twirled the dials and gave Trife the signal to start. In the tiny apartment, Dog and Trife and Sinbo and Po were rehearsing for their album, the one they hoped might be destiny's next chosen one.

Scrizz, Trife's brother and the C.E.O. of Trife-Life Records, was listening like a jittery father. With no product yet, Trife-Life was not a paying job for him. His background, like that of the others, was drugs and crime. At the moment, he was out on bail while fighting an assault charge.

Wanted and Respected started in on its song "All the Time." Golden bars of light streaked through the windows. Scrizz tapped his foot. He, too, had a got-to-happen mentality. He didn't much care who bought the album, white or black, but he knew where the money was. "I just want them to eat it up," he said. "I just want the money."

It came down to that. A group of young black guys in Brooklyn rhyming their lives, betting on a brighter tomorrow sponsored by white kids' money.

Dog turned up the music. They cleared their throats and kept rapping.

RIAN MALAN

In the Jungle

Once upon a time, a long time ago, a small miracle took place in the brain of a man named Solomon Linda. It was 1939, and he was standing in front of a microphone in the only recording studio in black Africa when it happened. He hadn't composed the melody or written it down or anything. He just opened his mouth and out it came, a haunting skein of fifteen notes that flowed down the wires and into a trembling stylus that cut tiny grooves into a spinning block of beeswax, which was taken to England and turned into a record that became a very big hit in that part of Africa.

Later, the song took flight and landed in America, where it mutated into a truly immortal pop epiphany that soared to the top of the charts here and then everywhere, again and again, returning every decade or so under different names and guises. Navajo Indians sing it at powwows. The French favor a version sung in Congolese. Phish perform it live. It has been recorded by artists as diverse as R.E.M. and Glen Campbell, Brian Eno and Chet Atkins, the Nylons and Muzak schlockmeister Bert Kaempfert. The New Zealand army band turned it into a march. England's 1986 World Cup soccer squad turned it into a joke. Hollywood put it in *Ace Ventura: Pet Detective*. It has logged nearly three centuries' worth of continuous radio airplay in the U.S. alone. It is the most famous melody ever to emerge from Africa, a tune that has penetrated so deep into the human consciousness over so many generations that one can truly say, here is a song the whole world knows.

Its epic transcultural saga is also, in a way, the story of popular music, which limped, pale-skinned and anemic, into the twentieth century but danced out the other side vastly invigorated by transfusions of ragtime and rap, jazz, blues and soul, all of whose bloodlines run back to Africa via slave ships and plantations and ghettos. It was in the nature of this transaction that black men gave more than they got and often ended up with nothing.

This one's for Solomon Linda, then, a Zulu who wrote a melody that earned untold millions for white men but died so poor that his widow couldn't afford a stone for his grave. Let's take it from the top, as they say in the trade.

Part I: A Story about Music

This is an African yarn, but it begins with an unlikely friendship between an aristocratic British imperialist and a world-famous American Negro. Sir Henry Brougham Loch is a rising star of the British Colonial Office. Orpheus McAdoo is leader of the celebrated Virginia Jubilee Singers, a combo that specializes in syncopated spirituals. They meet during McAdoo's triumphant tour of Australia in the 1880s, and when Sir Henry becomes governor of the Cape Colony a few years later, it occurs to him that Orpheus might find it interesting to visit. Next thing, McAdoo and his troupe are on the road in South Africa, playing to slack-jawed crowds in dusty villages and mining towns.

This American music is a revelation to "civilized natives," hitherto forced to wear starched collars and sing horrible dirges under the direction of dour white missionaries. Mr. McAdoo is a stern old Bible thumper, to be sure, but there's a subversively rhythmic intensity in his music, a primordial stirring of funk and soul. The African brothers have never heard such a thing. The tour turns into a five-year epic. Wherever Orpheus goes, "jubilee" music outfits spring up in his wake; eventually, they penetrate even the loneliest outposts of civilization.

One such place is Gordon Memorial School, perched on the rim of a wild valley called Msinga, which lies in the Zulu heartland, about 300 miles southeast of Johannesburg. Among the half-naked herd boys who drift through the mission is a rangy kid named Solomon Linda, born 1909, who gets into the Orpheus-inspired syncopation thing and works bits of it into the Zulu songs he and his friends sing at weddings and feasts.

In the mid-Thirties they shake off the dust and cow shit and take the train to Johannesburg, city of gold, where they move into the slums and become kitchen boys and factory hands. Life is initially very perplexing. Solly keeps his eyes open and transmutes what he sees into songs that he and his homeboys perform a cappella on weekends. He has songs about work, songs about crime, songs about how banks rob you by giving you paper in exchange for real money, songs about how rudely the whites treat you when you go to get your pass stamped. People like the music. Solly and his friends develop a following. Within two years they turn themselves into a very cool urban act that wears pinstriped suits, bowler hats and dandy, two-tone shoes. They become Solomon Linda and the Evening Birds, inventors of a music that will later become known as *isicathamiya*, arising from the warning cry *"Cothoza, bafana"*—"Tread carefully, boys."

These were Zulus, you see, and their traditional dancing was punctuated by mighty foot stompings that, when done in unison, quite literally made the earth tremble. This was fine in the bush, but if you stomped the same way in town, you smashed wooden floors, cracked cement and sometimes broke your feet, so the whole dance had to be restrained and moderated. Cognoscenti will recall Lady-smith Black Mambazo's feline and curiously fastidious movements onstage. That's treading carefully.

In any event, there were legions of careful treaders in South Africa's cities, usually Zulu migrants whose Saturday nights were devoted to epic, beer-fueled bacchanalias known as "tea meetings." These were part fashion show and part heroic contest between rival a cappella gladiators, often with a stray white man pulled off the street to act as judge and a cow or goat as first prize. The local black bourgeoisie was mortified by these antics. Careful treaders were an embarrassment, widely decried for their "primitive" bawling and backward lyrics, which dwelled on such things as witchcraft, crime and using love potions to get girls. The groups had names like the Naughty Boys or the Boiling Waters, and when World War II broke out, some started calling themselves "'mbombers," after the dive-bombing Stukas they'd seen on newsreels. 'Mbombers were by far the coolest and most dangerous black thing of their time.

Yes! Dangerous! Skeptics are referred to "Ngazula Emagumeni" (on Rounder CD 5025), an early Evening Birds track whose brain-rattling intensity thoroughly guts anyone who thinks of a cappella songs as smooth tunes for mellow people. The wild, rocking sound came from doubling the bass voices and pumping up their volume, an innovation that was largely Solomon's, along with the high style and the new dance moves. He was the Elvis Presley of his time and place, a shy, gangly thirty-year-old, so tall that he had to stoop as he passed through doorways. It's odd to imagine him singing soprano, but that was usually his gig in the group: He was the leader, the "controller," singing what Zulus called *fasi pathi*, a blood-curdling falsetto that a white man might render as first part.

The Evening Birds were spotted by a talent scout in 1938 and taken to an office building in downtown Jo'burg. There they saw the first recording studio in sub-Saharan Africa, shipped over from England by Eric Gallo, a jovial Italian who started in the music business by selling American hillbilly records to working-class Boers. Before long be bought his own recording machine and started churning out those Dust Bowl ditties in local languages, first Afrikaans, then Zulu, Xhosa and what have you. His ally in this experiment was Griffith Motsieloa, the country's first black pro-ducer, a slightly stiff and formal chap whose true interests were clas-sical music and eisteddfods, in which polished African gentlemen entertained one another with speeches in highfalutin king's English. Motsieloa was appalled by the boss's cultural slumming, but what could he do? Gallo was determined to sell records to blacks. When Afro-hillbilly failed to catch on, they decided to take a chance on some *isicathamiya*.

Solomon Linda and the Evening Birds cut several songs under Motsieloa's direction, but the one we're interested in was called "Mbube," Zulu for "the lion," recorded at their second session, in 1939. It was a simple three-chord ditty with lyrics something along the lines of "Lion! Ha! You're a lion!" inspired by an incident in the Birds' collective Zulu boyhood when they chased lions that were stalking their fathers' cattle. The first take was a dud, as was the second. Exasperated, Motsieloa looked into the corridor, dragooned a pianist, guitarist and banjo player, and tried again.

The third take almost collapsed at the outset as the unrehearsed musicians dithered and fished for the key, but once they started cooking, the song was glory bound. "Mbube" wasn't the most remarkable tune, but there was something terribly compelling about the underlying chant, a dense meshing of low male voices above which Solomon howled and scatted for two exhilarating minutes, occasionally making it up as he went along. The third take was the great one, but it achieved immortality only in its dying seconds, when Solly took a deep breath, opened his mouth and improvised the melody that the world now associates with the words:

In the jungle, the mighty jungle, the lion sleeps tonight.

Griffith Motsieloa must have realized he'd captured something special, because that chunk of beeswax was shipped all the way to England and shipped back in the form of ten-inch 78-rpm records, which went on sale just as Hitler invaded Poland. Marketing was tricky, because there was hardly any black radio in 1939, but the song went out on "the re-diffusion," a land line that pumped music, news and "native affairs" propaganda into black neighborhoods, and people began trickling into stores to ask for it. The trickle grew into a steady stream that just rolled on for years and years, necessitating so many re-pressings that the master disintegrated. By 1948, "Mbube" had sold in the region of 100,000 copies, and Solomon Linda was the undefeated and undefeatable champion of hostel singing competitions and a superstar in the world of Zulu migrants.

Pete Seeger, on the other hand, was in a rather bad way. He was a banjo player living in a cold-water flat on MacDougal Street, in

Greenwich Village, with a wife, two young children and no money. Scion of wealthy New York radicals, he'd dropped out of Harvard ten years earlier and hit the road with his banjo on his back, learning hard-times songs for people in the Hoovervilles, lumber camps and coal mines of Depression America. In New York he joined a band with Woody Guthrie. They wore work shirts and jeans, and wrote folk songs that championed the downtrodden common man in his struggle against capitalist bloodsuckers. Woody had a slogan written on his guitar that read, "This machine kills fascists." Pete's banjo had a kinder, gentler variation: "This machine surrounds hate and forces it to surrender." He was a proto-hippie, save that he didn't smoke reefer or even drink beer.

He was also a pacifist, at least until Hitler invaded Russia. Scenting a capitalist plot to destroy the brave Soviet socialist experiment, Pete and Woody turned gung-ho overnight and started writing anti-Nazi war songs, an episode that made them briefly famous. After that, it was into uniform and off to the front for Pete, where he played the banjo for bored GIs. Discharged in '45, he returned to New York and got a gig of sorts in the public-school system, teaching toddlers to warble the half-forgotten folk songs of their American heritage. It wasn't particularly glorious, the money was rotten, and on top of that, he was sick in bed with a bad cold.

There came a knock on the door, and, lo, there stood his friend Alan Lomax, later to be hailed as the father of world music. Alan and his dad, John, were already famous for their song-collecting forays into the parallel universe of rural black America, where they'd discovered giants like Muddy Waters and Lead Belly. Alan was working for Decca, where he'd just rescued a package of 78s sent from Africa by a local record company in the vain hope that someone might want to release them in America. They were about to be thrown away when Lomax intervened, thinking, "God, Pete's the man for these."

And here they were: ten shellac 78s, one of which said "Mbube" on its label. Pete put it on his old Victrola and sat back. He was fascinated—there was a catchy chant and that wild, skirling falsetto was amazing.

"Golly," he said, "I can sing that." So he got out pen and paper and started transcribing the song, but he couldn't catch the words through all the hissing on the disc. The Zulus were chanting, "*Uyimbube, uyimbube,*" but to Pete it sounded like *awimboowee,* or maybe *awimoweh,* so that's how he wrote it down. Later he taught "Wimoweh" to the rest of his band, the Weavers, and it became, he says, "just about my favorite song to sing for the next forty years."

This was no great achievement, given that the Weavers' late-Forties repertoire was full of dreck like "On Top of Old Smoky" and "Greensleeves." Old Pete won't admit it, but one senses that he was growing tired of cold-water flats and work shirts, and wanted a proper career, as befitting a thirtysomething father of two. He landed a job in TV, but someone fingered him as a dangerous radical, and he lost it before it even started. After that, according to his biographer David King Dunaway, he fell into a funk that ended only when his band landed a gig at the Village Vanguard. Apparently determined to make the best possible impression, Pete allowed his wife to outfit the Weavers in matching blue corduroy jackets—a hitherto unimaginable concession to showbiz.

The pay was $200 a week, plus free hamburgers, and the booking was for two weeks only, but something unexpected happened: Crowds started coming. The gig was extended for a month, and then another. The Weavers' appeal was inexplicable to folk purists, who noted that most of their songs had been around forever, in obscure versions by blacks and rednecks who never had hits anywhere. What these critics failed to grasp was that Seeger and his comrades had managed to filter the stench of poverty and pig shit out of the proletarian music and make it wholesome and fun for Eisenhower-era squares. Six months passed, and the Weavers were still at the Vanguard, drawing sellout crowds, even the odd refugee from the swell supper clubs of Times Square.

One such figure was Gordon Jenkins, a sallow jazz cat with a gigolo's mustache and a matinee idol's greased-back hairstyle. Jenkins started out by arranging for Benny Goodman before scoring a hit in his own right with an appalling piece of crap, "I'm Forever Blowing Bubbles." Now he was arranging for Frank Sinatra and was also musical director at Decca Records. Jenkins loved the Weavers, returning night after night, sometimes sitting through two consecutive shows. He wanted to sign them up, but his bosses were dubious. It was only when Jenkins offered to pay for the recording sessions himself that Decca capitulated and gave the folkies a deal.

Their first recording came out in June 1950. It was "Goodnight Irene," an old love song they'd learned from their friend Lead Belly, and it was an immediate click, in the parlance of the day. The flip side was an Israeli hora called "Tzena, Tzena, Tzena," and it clicked too. So did "The Roving Kind," a nineteenth-century folk ditty they released that November, and even "On Top of Old Smoky," which hit Number Three the following spring. The Weavers leapt from amateur hootenannies to the stages of America's poshest nightspots and casinos. They wore suits and ties, Brylcreamed their hair, appeared on TV and pulled down two grand a week. Chagrined and envious, their former comrades on the left started sniping at them in magazines. "Can an all-white group sing songs from Negro culture?" asked one.

The answer, of course, lay in the song that Seeger called "Wimoweh." His version was faithful to the Zulu original in almost all respects save for his finger-popping rhythm, which was arguably a bit white for some castes but not entirely offensive. The true test was in the singing, and here Seeger passed with flying colors, bawling and howling his heart out, tearing up his vocal cords so badly that by the time he reached age seventy-five, he was almost mute. "Wimoweh" was by far the edgiest song in the Weavers' set, which is perhaps why they waited a year after their big breakthrough before recording it.

Like their earlier recordings, it took place with Gordon Jenkins presiding and an orchestra in attendance. Prior to this, Jenkins had been very subdued in his instrumental approach, adding just the occasional sting and the odd swirl of strings to the Weavers' cheery singalongs. Maybe he was growing bored, because his arrangement of "Wimoweh" was a great Vegasy explosion of big-band raunch that almost equaled the barbaric splendor of the Zulu original. Trombones blared. Trumpets screamed. Strings swooped and soared through Solomon's miracle melody. And then Pete cut loose with all that hollering and screaming. It was a revolutionary departure from everything else the Weavers had ever done, but *Billboard* loved it, anointing it a Pick of the Week. *Cash Box* said, "May easily break." *Variety* said, "Terrific!"

But around this time *Variety* also said, FIVE MORE H'WOODITES NAMED REDS and CHAPLIN BEING INVESTIGATED. It was January 1952, and America was engaged in a frenzied hunt for Reds under beds. The House Un-American Activities Committee was probing Hollywood. *Red Channels* had just published the names of artists with commie connections. And in Washington, D.C., one Harvey Matusow was talking to federal investigators.

Matusow was a weaselly little man who had once worked alongside Pete Seeger in People's Songs, a reddish organization that dispatched folk singers to entertain on picket lines and in union halls. He had undergone a change of heart and decided to tell all about his secret life in the communist underground. On February 6th, 1952, just as "Wimoweh" made its chart debut, he stepped up to a mike before HUAC and told one of the looniest tales of the entire McCarthy era. Evil reds, he said, were "preying on the sexual weakness of American youth" to lure recruits into their dreaded movement. What's more, he was willing to name names of Communist Party members, among them three Weavers—including Pete Seeger.

The yellow press went apeshit. Reporters called the Ohio club where the Weavers were scheduled to play that night, demanding to know why the Yankee Inn was providing succor to the enemy. The show was called off, and it was all downhill from there. Radio stations banned their records. TV appearances were canceled. "Wimoweh" plummeted from Number Six into oblivion. Nightclub owners wouldn't even talk to the Weavers' agents, and then Decca dropped them too. By the end of the year they'd packed it in, and Pete Seeger was back where he'd started, teaching folk songs to kids for a pittance.

So the Weavers were dead, but "Wimoweh" lived on, bewitching jazz ace Jimmy Dorsey, who covered it in 1952, and the sultry Yma

Sumac, whose cocktail-lounge version caused a minor stir a few years later. Toward the end of the decade, it was included on *Live From the Hungry I*, a monstrously popular LP by the Kingston Trio that stayed on the charts for more than three years (178 weeks), peaking at Number Two. By now, almost everyone in America knew the basic refrain, so it should've come as no particular surprise to find four nice Jewish teenagers popping their fingers and going *ah-weem-oh-way, ah-weem-oh-way* in the summer of 1961.

The Tokens were clean-cut Brooklyn boys who had grown up listening to DJs Alan Freed and Murray the K, and the dreamy teen stylings of Dion and the Belmonts and the Everly Brothers. Hank Medress and Jay Siegel met at Lincoln High, where they sang in a doo-wop quartet that briefly featured Neil Sedaka. Phil Margo was a budding drummer and piano player, also from Lincoln High, and Mitch Margo was his kid brother, age fourteen. One presumes that girls were already casting eyes in their direction, because the Tokens had recently been on TV's *American Bandstand*, decked out in double-breasted mohair suits with white shirts and purple ties, singing their surprise Top Twenty hit, "Tonight I Fell in Love."

And now they were moving toward even greater things. Barely out of high school, they landed a three-record deal with RCA Victor, with a $10,000 advance and a crack at working with Hugo Peretti and Luigi Creatore, ace producers for Sam Cooke, Frankie Lymon and many, many others. These guys worked with Elvis Presley, for God's sake. "This was big for us," says Phil Margo. "Very big."

The Tokens knew "Wimoweh" through their lead singer, Jay, who'd learned it from an old Weavers album. It was one of the songs they'd sung when they auditioned for "Huge" and "Luge," as Peretti and Creatore were known in the trade. The producers said, "Yeah, well, there's something there, but what's it about?" "Eating lions," said the Tokens. That's what some joker at the South African consulate had told them, at any rate.

The producers presumably rolled their eyes. None of this got anyone anywhere in the era of "shooby doo" and so on. They wanted to revamp the song, give it some intelligible lyrics and a

contemporary feel. They sent for one George David Weiss, a suave
young dude in a navy-blue blazer, then making a big name for himself in grown-up music, writing orchestrations for Doris Day, Peggy
Lee and others. The Tokens took him for a hopeless square until
they discovered that he'd co-written "Can't Help Falling in Love
With You" for Elvis Presley. That changed everything.

So George Weiss took "Wimoweh" home with him and gave it a
careful listen. A civilized chap with a Juilliard degree, he didn't
much like the primitive wailing, but the chant was OK, and parts of
the melody were very catchy. So he dismantled the song, excised all
the hollering and screaming, and put the rest back together in a new
way. The chant remained unchanged, but the melody—Solomon
Linda's miracle melody—moved to center stage, becoming the tune
itself, to which the new words were sung: "In the jungle, the mighty
jungle. . . . "

In years to come, Weiss was always a bit diffident about his revi-
sions, describing them as "gimmicks," as if ashamed to be associated
with so frothy a bit of pop nonsense. Token Phil Margo says that's
because Weiss wrote nothing save thirty-three words of doggerel,
but that's another lawsuit entirely. What concerns us here is the
song's bloodline, and everyone agrees on that: "The Lion Sleeps
Tonight" was a reworking of "Wimoweh," which was a copy of
"Mbube." Solomon Linda was buried under several layers of pop-
rock stylings, but you could still see him beneath the new song's
slick surface, like a mastodon entombed in a block of clear ice.

The song was recorded live in RCA's Manhattan studios on July
21st, 1961, with an orchestra in attendance and some session players
on guitar, drums and bass. The percussionist muted his timpani,
seeking that authentic "jungle drum" sound. A moonlighting opera
singer named Anita Darian practiced her scales. Conductor Sammy
Lowe tapped his baton and off they went, three Tokens doing the
wimowehs, while Jay Siegel took the lead with his pure falsetto and
Darian swooped and dived in the high heavens, singing the haunting countermelodies that were one of the song's great glories. Three
takes (again), a bit of overdubbing, and that was more or less that.
Everyone went home, entirely blind as to what they'd accomplished.

The Tokens had been mortified by the new lyrics, which struck them as un-teen and uncool. Hugo and Luigi were so casual that they did the final mix over the telephone, and RCA topped them all by issuing the song as the B side of a humdrum tune called "Tina," which sank like lead.

Weird, no? We're talking about a pop song so powerful that Brian Wilson had to pull off the road when be first heard it, totally overcome; a song that Carole King instantly pronounced "a motherfucker." But it might never have reached their ears if an obscure DJ named Dick Smith in Worcester, Massachusetts, hadn't flipped the Tokens' new turkey and given the B side a listen. Smith said, "Holy shit, this is great," or words to that effect, and so his station, WORC, put "The Lion Sleeps Tonight" on heavy rotation. The song broke out regionally, hit the national charts in November and reached Number One in four giant strides.

Within a month, a cover by someone named Karl Denver reached Number One in England, too. By April 1962 it was topping the charts almost everywhere and heading for immortality. Miriam Makeba sang her version at JFK's last birthday party, moments before Marilyn Monroe famously lisped, "Happy birthday, Mr. President." Apollo astronauts listened to it on the launchpads at Cape Canaveral, Florida. It was covered by the Springfields, the Spinners, the Tremeloes and Glen Campbell. In 1972 it returned to the charts, at Number Three, in a version by Robert John. Brian Eno recorded it a few years later.

In 1982 it was back at Number One in the U.K., this time performed by Tight Fit. R.E.M. did it, as did the Nylons and They Might Be Giants. Manu Dibengo did a twist version. Some Germans turned it into heavy metal. A sample cropped up on a rap epic titled "Mash Up da Nation." Disney used the song in *The Lion King*, and then it got into the smash-hit theatrical production of the same title, currently playing to packed houses around the world. It's on the original Broadway cast recording, on dozens of kiddie CDs with cuddly lions on their covers and on an infinite variety of nostalgia compilations. It's more than sixty years old, and still it's everywhere.

What might all this represent in songwriter royalties and associated revenues? I put the question to lawyers in several countries, and they scratched their heads. Around 160 recordings of three versions? Fourteen movies? A half-dozen TV commercials and a hit play? Number Seven on Val Pak's semi-authoritative ranking of the most-beloved golden oldies, and ceaseless radio airplay in every corner of the planet? It was impossible to accurately calculate, to be sure, but no one blanched at $15 million. Some said $10 million, some said $20 million, but most felt that $15 million was in the ballpark.

Which raises an even more interesting question: What happened to all that loot?

Part II: A Story about Money

"It was a wonderful experience," said Larry Richmond, hereditary president of The Richmond Organization. He was talking about his company's "wonderful efforts" to make sure that justice was done to Solomon Linda. Larry was in Manhattan, and I was in Johannesburg, where it was 2 A.M., so I said, "Hold it right there. I'll come see you." I hung up, started packing, and a few days later, I walked into TRO's HQ, a strangely quiet suite of offices on West Nineteenth Street.

The dusty old guitar in the waiting room was a relic of a long-gone era. Back in the Forties, when TRO was young, eager songwriters streamed in here to audition their wares for Larry's dad, Howie Richmond, the firm's founder. If he liked the songs, he'd sign 'em up, transcribe 'em and secure a copyright. Then he'd send song pluggers out to place the tunes with stars whose recordings would generate income for the composer and the publisher, too. At the same time, salesmen would be flogging the sheet music, while bean counters in the back office collected royalties and kept an eye out for unauthorized versions.

In its heyday, TRO was a music-publishing empire that spanned the globe, but it was forced into decline by the Seventies advent of savvy rock & roll accountants who advised clients to publish themselves, which was fairly easy and doubled their songwriting income, given that old-style publishers generally claimed fifty percent of royalties for their services. By 1999, TRO was little more than a crypt for fabulously valuable old copyrights, manned by a skeleton crew that licensed old songs for TV commercials and movies.

Larry Richmond was an amiable bloke in an open-necked shirt and beige slacks. We drank coffee and talked for an hour or two, mostly about social justice and TRO's commitment to the same. There were stories about Woody Guthrie and Pete Seeger, the famous radical troubadours in TRO's stable. There was a story about the hospital in India to which the Richmonds made generous donations. And finally, there were some elliptical remarks about Solomon Linda and TRO's noble attempts to make sure that he received his due. I was hoping Larry would give me a formal interview on the subject, but first I had to get some sleep. That was a mistake. By the time I'd recovered, he had retreated into the labyrinth of his voice-mail system, from which he would not emerge.

So there I was in New York, with no one to talk to, I called music lawyers and record companies, angling for appointments that failed to materialize. I wandered into *Billboard* magazine, where a veteran journalist warned that I was wasting my time trying to find out what any song had ever earned and where the money had gone. But I'd come a long way, so I kept looking and, eventually, figured some of it out.

The story begins in 1939, when Solomon Linda was visited by angels in black Africa's only recording studio. At the time, Jo'burg was a hick mining town where music deals were concluded according to trading principles as old as Moses: Record companies bought recordings for whatever they thought the music might be worth in the marketplace; stars generally got several guineas for a session, unknowns got almost nothing. No one got royalties, and copyright was unknown. Solomon Linda didn't even get a contract. He walked out of that session with about one pound cash in his pocket, and the music thereafter belonged to the record company, which had no further obligations to anyone. When "Mbube" became a local hit, the loot went to Eric Gallo, the playboy who owned the company. All Solomon Linda got was a menial job at the boss's packing plant, where he worked for the rest of his days.

When "Mbube" took flight and turned into the Weavers' hit "Wimoweh," Gallo could have made a fortune if he had played his cards right. Instead, he struck a deal with Howie Richmond, trading "Mbube" to TRO in return for the dubious privilege of administering "Wimoweh" in such bush territories as South Africa and Rhodesia. Control of Solomon Linda's destiny thus passed into the hands of Howie and his faithful sidekick, one Al Brackman.

Howie and Al shared an apartment in the Thirties, when they were ambitious young go-getters on Tin Pan Alley. Howie was tall and handsome, Al was short and fat, but otherwise, they were blood brothers with a passion for night life and big-band jazz. Following World War II, Howie worked as a song promoter before deciding to become a publisher in his own right. He says he found a catchy old music-hall number, had a pal write new lyrics and placed the song with Guy Lombardo, who took it to Number Ten as "Hop Scotch Polka." Howie was on his way. Al joined up in 1949, and together they put a whole slew of novelty songs on the hit parade. Then they moved into the burgeoning folk-music sector, where big opportunities were opening up for sharp guys with a shrewd understanding of copyright.

After all, what was a folk song? Who owned it? It was just out there, like a wild horse or a tract of virgin land on an unconquered continent. Fortune awaited the man bold enough to fill out the necessary forms and name himself as the composer of a new interpretation of some ancient tune like, say, "Greensleeves." A certain Jessie Cavanaugh did exactly that in the early Fifties, only it wasn't really Jessie at all—it was Howie Richmond under an alias. This was a common practice on Tin Pan Alley at the time, and it wasn't illegal or anything. The object was to claim writer's royalties on new versions of old songs that belonged to no one. The aliases may have been a way to avoid potential embarrassment, just in case word got out that Howard S. Richmond was presenting himself as the author of a madrigal from Shakespeare's day.

Much the same happened with "Frankie and Johnny," the hoary, old murder ballad, and "The Roving Kind." There's no way Al Brackman could really have written such songs, so when he filed royalty claims with the performing-rights society BMI, he attributed the compositions to Albert Stanton, a fictitious tunesmith who often worked closely with the imaginary Mr. Cavanaugh, penning such standards as "John Henry" and "Michael Row the Boat Ashore." Cavanaugh even claimed credit for a version of "Battle Hymn of the Republic," a feat eclipsed only by a certain Harold Leventhal, who copyrighted an obscure whatnot later taken as India's national anthem.

Leventhal started out as a gofer for Irving Berlin and wound up promoting concerts for Bob Dylan, but in between, he developed a serious crush on the Weavers. In 1949, he showed up at the Village Vanguard with an old friend in tow—Pete Kameron, a suave charmer who was scouting around for an entree into showbiz. Leventhal performed some introductions, and Kameron became the Weavers' manager. Since all these men knew one another, it was natural that they should combine to take charge of the band's business affairs. Leventhal advised; Kameron handled bookings and tried to fend off the redbaiters. Howie and Al took on the publishing, arranging it so that Kameron owned a fifty-percent stake. The Weavers sang the songs and cut the records, and together they sold around 4 million platters in eighteen months or so.

Toward the end of 1951, these men found themselves contemplating the fateful 78-rpm record from Africa and wondering exactly what manner of beast it could be. The label read "MDUBE," BY SOLOMON LINDA'S ORIGINAL EVENING BIRDS, but it had never been copyrighted. Anything not copyrighted was a wild horse, strictly speaking, and wild horses in the Weavers' repertoire were usually attributed to one Paul Campbell. The Weavers' version of "Hush Little Baby" was a Paul Campbell composition, for instance. The same was true of "Rock Island Line" and "Kisses Sweeter Than Wine," tunes the folkies had learned from Lead Belly at Village hoots and rewritten in their own style.

On the surface of things, Paul Campbell was thus one of the most successful songwriters of the era, but of course the name was just another alias used to claim royalties on reworked songs from the public domain. "Mbube" wasn't public domain at all, but it was the next best thing—an uncopyrighted song owned by an obscure foreign record label that had shown absolutely no interest in protecting Solomon Linda's rights as a writer. So the Zulu's song was tossed in among the Weavers' wild horses and released as "Wimoweh," by Paul Campbell.

As the song found its fans, money started rolling in. Every record sale triggered a mechanical royalty, every radio play counted as a performance—which also required payment—and there was always the hope that someone might take out a "sync license" to use the tune in a movie or a TV ad. Al, Howie and Kameron divided the standard publisher's fifty percent among themselves and distributed the other half to the writers—or in this case, the adapters: Pete Seeger and the Weavers. Solomon Linda was entitled to nothing.

This didn't sit well with Seeger, who openly acknowledged Solomon as the true author of "Wimoweh" and felt he should get the money. Indeed, Seeger had been hassling his publishers for months to find a way of paying the Zulu.

"Originally they were going to send the royalties to Gallo," Seeger recalled. "I said, 'Don't do that, because Linda won't get a penny.'" Anti-apartheid activists put Seeger in touch with a Johannesburg lawyer, who set forth into the forbidden townships to find Solomon Linda. Once contact was established, Seeger sent the Zulu a $1,000 check and instructed his publisher to do the same with all future payments.

He was still bragging about it fifty years later. "I never got author's royalties on 'Wimoweh,'" Seeger said. "Right from '51 or '52, I understood that the money was going to Linda. I assumed they were keeping the publisher's fifty percent and sending the rest."

Unfortunately, Solomon's family maintains that the money only arrived years later, and even then, it was nothing like the full writer's share Seeger was hoping to bestow. We'll revisit this conundrum in short order, but first, let's follow the further adventures of "Wimoweh," which fell into the hands of RCA producers Hugo and Luigi, by way of the Tokens, in the summer of 1961. In addition to being act producers and buddies of Presley's, these men were wild-horse breakers of the very first rank. They'd put their brand on a whole herd of them—"Pop Goes the Weasel," "First Noel," you name it. They even had "Grand March from Aida," a smash hit for Giuseppe Verdi in the 1870s.

As seasoned pros, these guys would have checked out the "Wimoweh" composer of record, Paul Campbell, and discovered that the name was an alias and that his *oeuvre* consisted largely of folk songs from previous centuries. They seemingly leapt to the obvious conclusion: "Wimoweh" was based on an old African folk song that didn't belong to anyone. As such, it was fair game, so they summoned George Weiss, turned "Wimoweh" into "The Lion Sleeps Tonight" and sent it out into the world as a Weiss/Peretti/Creatore composition. They did exactly the same thing four months later with "The Click Song," a Xhosa tune popularized in America by Miriam Makeba: Weiss cooked up some more doggerel about jungle drums and lovelorn maidens, the Tokens sang it, and it landed in record stores as "B'wanina," another "composition" by the same trio.

But they had made a mistake. "The Click Song" was indeed a wild horse that had been roaming Africa for centuries, but "Mbube" was an original: the subject of a U.S. copyright taken out by Gallo in '52 and subsequently traded to TRO in the "Wimoweh" deal. When "The Lion Sleeps Tonight" began playing on America's radios, Howie Richmond instantly recognized its bloodline and howled with outrage. He set his lawyers on the Tokens and their allies, and what could they say? It must have been deeply embarrassing, but what the heck—Howie was on first-name terms with Hugo and Luigi, and was deeply respectful of Weiss' lyrical talents. He would be willing to forget the whole thing—provided the publishing rights to "Lion" came back to him.

Within a week there was a letter on Howie's desk acknowledging infringement, and urgent settlement talks were underway. Why urgent? Because "The Lion Sleeps Tonight" was soaring up the charts, and the Weiss/Peretti/Creatore cabal would have been desperate to avoid a dispute that might abort its trajectory. This put Richmond and Brackman in a position to dictate almost any terms they pleased. They didn't have a contract with Solomon Linda, but there was nothing to prevent them from making demands on his behalf. They could even have forced Luigi, Hugo and Weiss to settle for a smaller adapters' cut and allocated everything else to the Zulu, but this probably would have soured an important business relationship. They weren't legally obliged to Solomon, and so they allowed the three men they were later to describe as "plagiarists" to walk away with 100 percent of the writer's royalties on a song that originated in Solomon Linda's brain.

And why not? It was no skin off their noses. TRO received the full fifty-percent publisher's cut. Huge and Luge and Weiss were happy. The only person who lost out was Solomon, who wasn't even mentioned in any document: The new copyright described "Lion" as "based on a song by Paul Campbell."

The paperwork was finalized on December 18th, 1961, just as the song commenced its conquest of the world's hit parades. "The Lion Sleeps Tonight" was Number One in the States on Christmas Day and reached South Africa two months later, just in time to bring a wan smile to the face of a dying Solomon Linda. He'd been ailing since 1959, when he lost control of his bowels and collapsed onstage. Doctors diagnosed kidney disease, but his family suspected witchcraft.

If true, this would make Solomon a victim of his own success. Sure, he was nothing in the world of white men, but "Mbube" made him a legend in the Zulu subculture, and to be a legend among "the people of heaven" was a pretty fine destiny, in some respects. Strangers hailed him on the streets, bought him drinks in shebeens. He was in constant demand for personal appearances and earned enough to afford some sharp suits, a second bride and a windup gramophone for the kinfolk in mud huts back in Msinga.

A thousand bucks from Pete Seeger aside, most of his money came from those uproarious all-night song contests, which remain a vital part of urban Zulu social life to this day. Most weekends, Solly and the Evening Birds would hire a car and sally forth to do battle in distant towns, and they always came back victorious. Competitors tried everything, including potions, to make their voices hoarse and high like Solomon's, but nothing worked. The aging homeboys would take the stage and work themselves into such transports of ecstasy that tears streamed down Solly's face, at which point the audience would go wild and the Evening Birds would once again walk off with first prize—sometimes a trophy, sometimes money, sometimes a cow that they slaughtered, roasted and shared with their fans as the sun came up. Blinded by the adulation, Solomon wasn't particularly perturbed when his song mutated into "The Lion Sleeps Tonight" and raced to the top of the world's charts.

"He was happy," said his daughter Fildah. "He didn't know he was supposed to get something."

Fildah is Solomon's oldest surviving child, a radiant woman who wears beads in her hair and a goatskin bangle on her right wrist, the mark of a *sangoma*, or witch doctor. Her sister Elizabeth works as a nurse in a government clinic, but she announced, giggling, that she is a *sangoma* too. A third daughter, Delphi, had just had surgery for arthritis, but she was also, under her sisters' direction, using ancestral medicine—a plant called *umhlabelo*, apparently. Elizabeth thought a water snake might be useful, too, and wondered where she could obtain such a thing. Though they live in an urban slum, they are deeply Zulu people, down to the cattle horns on the roof above the kitchen door—relics of sacrifices to the spirits of their ancestors. Only Elizabeth spoke fluent English, but even she didn't flinch at the talk of witchcraft.

Their aunt Mrs. Beauty Madiba was the one who brought it up. A sweet old lady in her Sunday best, she remembered meeting Solomon in the late Forties, when he started to court her sister Regina. The singer was at the peak of his career then and had no trouble raising the ten cattle their father was asking as the bride price. The wedding feast took place in 1949, and Regina went to live in Johannesburg. Beauty joined her a few years later and had a ringside seat when Solomon was brought down by dark forces.

"People were jealous, because all the time, he won," she explained. "They said, 'We will get you.' So they bewitched him."

Elizabeth muttered something about renal failure, but she agreed there was something odd about the way her father's disease refused to respond to treatment. He grew so sick that he had to stop singing. By the time "The Lion Sleeps Tonight" was released, he had been in and out of the hospital constantly, and on October 8th, 1962, he died.

Everyone sighed. Rival a cappella groups were to blame, growled Victor Madondo, a burly old warrior whose father had sung alto in the Evening Birds. "They were happy, because now they could go forward nicely."

But they went nowhere. Solomon was the one whose influence lived on, becoming so pervasive that all Zulu male choral singing came to be called "Mbube music." Ethnomusicologists dug up the early Birds recordings, and Solomon was posthumously elevated to godhead—"one of the great figures in black South African music," according to professor Veit Erlmann, of the University of Texas. Latter-day Mbube stars like Ladysmith Black Mambazo sent gifts to this very house when they made it big, a tribute to the spirit of a man they venerated. And then I came along, asking questions about money.

It soon became clear that the daughters had no understanding of music publishing and related arcana. All they knew was that "people did something with our father's song outside" and that monies were occasionally deposited in their joint bank account by mysterious entities they could not name. I asked to see documents, but they had none, and they were deeply confused as to the size and purpose of the payments. "Mr. Tucker is helping us," they said. "Mr. Tucker knows everything."

Raymond Tucker is a white lawyer with offices in a grand old colonial mansion on the outskirts of downtown Jo'burg. On the phone, he explained that Pete Seeger and TRO contacted him at some point in the mid-1960s, asking him to act as a conduit for payments to Solomon's widow. Tucker was honored to help out, he said. As we spoke, he flipped through his files, assuring me that the royalty payments that came in were "pretty regular, with proper accounting" and "totally and absolutely aboveboard."

Solomon's daughters didn't contest this, but they were surprised to learn that their mother had received royalties back in the Sixties. Solomon Linda's widow, Regina, was an illiterate peasant with no job and six children to feed. Her husband's death, in 1962, was a catastrophe beyond reckoning. She brewed and sold beer in a desperate attempt to make ends meet. Her girls walked to school barefoot, took notes on cracked bits of slate and went to bed hungry. Critical Zulu death rites went unperformed for years, because the family was too poor to pay a *sangoma* to officiate.

"This house, it was bare bricks," said Elizabeth. "No ceiling, no plaster, no furniture, just one stool and one coal stove." Her eldest brother left school and started working, but he was murdered by gangsters. Her second brother became the breadwinner, only to die in an accident, whereupon Delphi took a job in a factory to keep the family going. "There was suffering here at home," said Elizabeth. She thought that the money "from outside" arrived only after 1980. Her sisters agreed. That was when they erected a tombstone for their father, who had rested in a pauper's grave since 1962. That's how they knew.

I asked Tucker if I could see his files, but he balked, citing his client's confidentiality. I obtained a letter of introduction from the daughters and called to discuss it, but he slammed down the phone. I wrote a note, pointing out that the daughters were legally and morally entitled to information. In response came a series of letters reminding me that he had nothing to do with the calculations of royalties and accusing me of misrepresenting myself as a "white knight" when I was clearly just a devious muckraker intent on "writing an article for your own gain." "I have absolutely no intention of cooperating to assist in your exploration," he sniffed, saying that he would speak only to a lawyer.

Defeated on that front, I sent an e-mail to Larry Richmond, asking him to clarify the size and nature of TRO's payments to Solomon's family. "It will take some time to review your letter," he wrote back. "I hope to get back to you in due course." Months passed, but nothing happened, so I appealed to Harold Leventhal, the grandfatherly figure who had once managed the Weavers' affairs. "You're in a void," he said, sounding sympathetic. "All you can do is describe it, or you'll never finish your story." A wise man would have heeded his advice, but I plodded onward until someone took pity and provided some key documents to me. Ambiguities remained, but at least I found out why the Americans were so coy about making disclosures: It looked as if Solomon's family had been receiving just 12.5 percent of the writer's royalties on "Wimoweh," along with a tiny fraction of those from "The Lion Sleeps Tonight."

The payments on "Lion" were coming out of "performance royalties," jargon for the bucks generated when a song is broadcast. The sums in question averaged around $275 a quarter in the early Nineties, but who are we to raise eyebrows? Solomon's family was desperate and grateful for the smallest blessing. The money "from outside" enabled his widow to feed her children and educate the two youngest, Elizabeth and Adelaide. After Regina's death in 1990, Raymond Tucker set up a joint bank account for the daughters in which small sums of money continued to materialize from time to time. It was never very much, but it was enough to build a tin shack in their back yard and rent it out for extra money, even enough to start a little shop at the front gate. In American terms, their poverty remains appalling, but in their own estimation, this was a happy ending—until I showed up, and told them what might have been.

Part III: The Annals of a Curious Lawsuit

It's November 1991 in a bland conference room in the American Arbitration Association's New York headquarters. At the head of a long table sit three veteran copyright lawyers who will act as judges in these proceedings. Ranged before them are the warring parties: the entire cast of the 1961 "Lion Sleeps Tonight" plagiarism contretemps, either themselves or their legal representatives.

Hugo Peretti died a few years back, but fortune has smiled on the rest of the guys since last we saw them. Howie Richmond published the Rolling Stones and Pink Floyd for a while and is now rich beyond wild imaginings. His sidekick Al Brackman (who got ten percent of all Howie's deals) is rich too, and putters around in boats on weekends and winters at his second home near San Diego. Luigi Creatore has retired to Florida on the proceeds of his many hit records, and George Weiss is a successful composer of movie scores and musicals.

So why are they spending time cooped up here, flanked by lawyers? It's another long story.

In the fall of 1989, just as the initial copyright on "The Lion Sleeps Tonight" was about to expire, Howie and Al were notified by George Weiss that he and his fellow writers would dispense with TRO's publishing services in the renewal term unless they were paid a handsome bonus. Failing this, they would renew the "Lion" copyright in their own names and thereafter publish the song themselves, thus cutting Howie and Al out entirely and pocketing their fifty-percent share. The publishers were incensed, pointing out that "Lion" would never have existed if they hadn't allowed Weiss and Co. to "plagiarize" the underlying music, "Mbube" and "Wimoweh." To which the "Lion" team responded, in effect, how can you accuse us of stealing something you gave us in 1961? The fight went to court in 1990 and wound up in this arbitration months later—a band of rich white Americans squabbling over ownership of the most famous melody ever to emerge from Africa.

The music industry is riveted, because these men are pillars of the showbiz establishment. Al sits on the board of the Music Publishers' Association. Howie founded the Songwriters Hall of Fame. George Weiss is president of the Songwriters Guild of America and a tireless champion of downtrodden tunesmiths. As such, he can't possibly state that "The Lion Sleeps Tonight" infringes on the work of a fellow composer, and so he doesn't. Sure, he says at the hearing, the Tokens "threw the music together" using a "few themes they knew from this Weavers' record," but so what? Weiss said he'd been told that "Wimoweh" was just Pete Seeger's interpretation of "an old thing from Africa," so they hadn't really plagiarized anyone. To prove his point, Weiss produces the liner notes of an old Miriam

Makeba record in which "Mbube" is described as "a familiar Zulu song about a lion hunt."

TRO counters by presenting a yellowing affidavit in which the Zulu swears that "Mbube" was wholly original. At this juncture Weiss backs down, saying, in essence, "Gee, sorry, all this is news to me," and the hearing moves on to the real issue, which is the validity of the 1961 contract between TRO and the "Lion" trio. Drawn up in a spirit of incestuous back-scratching, the contract allows the Weiss parties free use of "Wimoweh" and "Mbube" in "The Lion Sleeps Tonight," with no royalty provisions for the author of the underlying songs. Some observers now find it a bit curious that TRO should start shouting, "Hold on! Our own contract's inaccurate! The underlying music never belonged to them! They can't just take it!"

Apparently worried that they might not be taken seriously, the men from TRO now depict themselves as the righteous defenders of Solomon Linda's heirs, openly accusing their rivals of "greed." "The defendants seek to deprive Mr. Linda's family of royalties," declares Larry Richmond, directing the brunt of his attack at George Weiss. The president of the Songwriters Guild should be "protecting the poor families of songwriters," he says, not robbing them. In the face of these accusations, the Weiss parties say that if they win the case, they'll give a share to Solomon's estate. The publishers then raise the ante, declaring that the family is rightfully entitled to up to a half of the enormous "Lion" spoils.

Amazing, no? If TRO had enforced such a distribution in 1961, Solomon's daughters might be millionaires, but nobody informed them that this dispute was taking place, so there was no one to laugh (or cry) on their behalf.

The arbitrators weren't very impressed, either—they awarded "The Lion Sleeps Tonight" to Weiss and Co., with the agreed proviso that they send "ten percent of writers' performance royalties" to the family. The order came into effect on January 1st, 1992, just as the song set forth on a new cycle of popularity. That year, a new recording of the song hit the Japanese charts. Pow Wow's version made Number One in France, in 1993. Then someone at Disney wrote a cute little scene in which a cartoon wart hog and meerkat pranced together, singing, "In the jungle, the mighty jungle. . . ." The song had been used in at least nine earlier movies, but *The Lion King* turned into a supernova. Every kid on the planet had to have the video and the vast array of nursery CDs that went with it. The Tokens' recording bounced back onto the U.S. charts, and Disney vocal arranger Lebo M's version (on *The Lion King: Rhythm of the Pridelands*) was the centerpiece of an album that went gold.

George Weiss could barely contain his glee. "The song leads a magical life," he told reporters. "It's been a hit eight or nine times but never like this. It's going wild!" The great composer came across as a diffident fellow, somewhat bemused by his enormous good fortune. "The way all this happened was destiny," he said. "It was mysterious, it was beautiful. I have to say God smiled at me."

I was hoping to talk to Weiss about God and Solomon Linda, but his lawyer said he was out of town and unavailable. On the other hand, he was visible in the *New York Times'* Sunday magazine last August, which ran a spread on his awesome retreat in rural New Jersey. I drove out to Oldwick and found the place—an eighteenth-century farmhouse in a deer-filled glade, with a pool and a recording studio in the outbuildings—but Weiss wasn't there. Maybe he was in Santa Fe, where he maintains a hacienda of sorts. Maybe he was in Cabo San Lucas, Mexico, where he and his wife were building a house on a bluff overlooking the sea. I gave up, returned to my hotel and wrote him a letter. Weiss faxed back almost immediately, saying he was "distressed" to hear that Solomon had been shabbily treated in the past. "As you can see," he continued, "none of that was our doing. While we had no legal obligation to Mr. Linda whatsoever, when we gained control of our song, we did what we thought was correct and equitable so that his family would share in the profits."

A nice gesture, to be sure, but what did "Lion" earn in the Nineties? A million dollars? Two? Three? Ten? And what trickled down to Soweto? Judging from the tattered scraps of paper in the daughters' possession, ten percent of the writer's performance royalties amounts to about $20,000 over the decade. Handwritten and unsigned, the notes appeared to be royalty statements, but there was no detailed breakdown of the song's overall earnings, and Weiss' business people declined to provide one, despite several requests.

Twenty grand was nice money in Soweto terms, but split several ways it changed little or nothing. Solomon Linda's house still had no ceiling, and it was like an oven under the African summer sun. Plaster flaked off the walls outside; toddlers squalled underfoot; three radios blared simultaneously. Fourteen people were living there, sleeping on floors for the most part, washing at an outdoor tap. Only Elizabeth was working, and when she moved out, most of the furniture went with her. Last time I visited, in January, the kitchen was barren save for six pots and a lone Formica table. Solomon's youngest daughter, Adelaide, lay swooning under greasy bedclothes, gravely ill from an infection she was too poor to have properly treated. A distant relative wandered around in an alcoholic stupor, waving a pair of garden shears and singing snatches of "Mbube." Elizabeth put her hands to her temples and said, "Really, we are not coping."

All the sisters were there: Fildah, with her *sangoma*'s headdress swathed in a bright red scarf; Elizabeth and Delphi in their best clothes; Adelaide, swaying back and forth on a chair, dazed, sweat pouring down her gaunt cheekbones. I'd come to report back to them on my adventures in the mysterious overseas, bringing a pile of legal papers that I did my best to explain. I told them about Paul Campbell, the fictitious entity who seemed to have collected big money that might otherwise have come their way, and about Larry Richmond, who wept crocodile tears on their behalf in a legal proceeding, that might have changed their destiny, if only they'd been aware of it. And, finally, I showed them the letter in which George Weiss assured me that the amounts his underlings were depositing into the bank account of their mother, "Mrs. Linda" (who had been dead and buried for a decade), were a "correct and equitable" share.

The daughters had never heard of any of these foreigners, but they had a shrewd idea of why all this had happened. "It's because our father didn't attend school," Elizabeth said. "He was just signing everything they said he must sign. Maybe he was signing many papers." Everyone sighed, and that was that.

Part IV: In Which a Moral Is Considered

Once upon a time, a long time ago, a Zulu man stepped up to a microphone and improvised a melody that earned many millions. That Solomon Linda got almost none of it was probably inevitable. He was a black man in white-ruled South Africa, but his American peers fared little better. Robert Johnson's contribution to the blues went largely unrewarded. Lead Belly lost half of his publishing to his white "patrons." DJ Alan Freed refused to play Chuck Berry's "Maybellene" until he was given a songwriter's cut. Led Zeppelin's "Whole Lotta Love" was lifted from Willie Dixon. All musicians were minnows in the pop-music food chain, but blacks were most vulnerable, and Solomon Linda, an illiterate tribesman from a wild valley where lions roamed, was totally defenseless against sophisticated predators.

Which is not to say that he was cheated. On the contrary, all the deals were perfectly legal, drawn up by respectable men. No one forced him to sell "Mbube" to Eric Gallo for ten shillings, and if Gallo turned around and traded it at a profit, so what? It belonged to him. The good old boys of TRO were perfectly entitled to rename the song, adapt it as they pleased and allocate the royalties to nonexistent entities. After all, they were its sole and uncontested owners. Solomon was legally entitled to nothing. The fact that he got anything at all seemed to show that the bosses were not without conscience or pity.

So I sat down and wrote long letters to George Weiss and Larry Richmond, distancing myself from pious moralists who might see them as sharks and even suggesting a line of reasoning they might take. "The only thing worse than exploitation," I mused, "is not being exploited at all." And then I enumerated all the good things old Solomon gained from making up the most famous melody that ever emerged from Africa: one pound cash, a big reputation, adulation and lionization; several cool suits, a windup gramophone, a check from Pete Seeger and a trickle of royalties that had spared his daughters from absolute penury. "All told," I concluded, "there is a case to be made against the idea that Solomon Linda was a victim of injustice."

I sat back and waited for someone to make it. I waited in vain. Months passed. Seasons changed. This article was completed and edited and about to go to press, but I was haunted by the thought that I'd missed something, so I sent a final appeal to the publishing honchos in America. And, lo, Howie Richmond got back to me, saying that he wanted to accept responsibility for some "gross errors." The blame for this "tragic situation," he continued, lay with a long-dead Gallo executive, who had never provided written proof that "Mbube" was Solomon's creation.

Beyond that, Howie insisted that TRO had paid "semiannual royalties" to Solomon "since the first commercial success of 'Wimoweh'" in 1951. But a document he provided to back his claim indicated that regular payments (aside from at least one, Pete Seeger's check, in the 1950s) commenced at least eleven years later. He said Pete Seeger never profited from his adaptation, then said that Seeger had indeed received a cut, but that it "may have been paid to nonprofit institutions" and/or passed on to Solomon's widow.

But what the hell, Howie's heart seemed to be in the right place. He wanted to fly me to California to work out a grand scheme of atonement. Then I received a call one morning from Solomon Linda's daughter Elizabeth, who said thugs had barged into her new house a few nights earlier, terrorized her family at gunpoint and looted her possessions. Her front door was still hanging off its hinges, and so she couldn't leave to check out a rumor she had heard from her bank. I investigated on her behalf and called back an hour later. "Money is pouring into your account from America," I said. "Nearly $15,000 in the last ten days." This was a fortune in local terms, an awesome mountain of cash. Elizabeth said nothing for a long time. I couldn't be sure, but I thought she was crying.

The windfall arose from use of "Wimoweh" in a U.S. TV commercial for a hotel. A big chunk of money had gone at first to Pete Seeger, who'd turned it back. It seemed he'd been receiving royalties on the song all along.

"I just found out," he tells me on the phone. "I didn't know."

MONICA KENDRICK

This Wreckage Was No Accident

The Complete Fun House Sessions

A seven-CD box set chronicling the making of a 36-minute album—was this really necessary? Back in 1970, with Elektra footing the bill for the casual slaughter of oxide particles and brain cells alike, it's not shocking that they recorded everything and taped over nothing, but it's still freak weather that every scrap from those sessions survived, not to mention that someone actually put this out.

You know before you put your money down that *1970: The Complete Fun House Sessions* isn't going to be a study in delicate studio science, like the four-CD *Pet Sounds* set from 1997. My first guess, which turned out to be way off, was that it would be more like the first disc of the 1995 Velvet Underground box set, which to hardcore VU geeks is one of the funniest comedy records ever made and to anyone else is mostly unlistenable.

The label responsible for *The Complete Fun House Sessions* is Rhino Handmade, a specialty division of Rhino that produces very limited editions for sale exclusively over the Internet. Late last year they guesstimated that there were 3,000 people out there to whom this monstrosity would be absolutely, immediately, urgently necessary despite the price tag: $119.98 plus shipping and handling. Upon learning that it would exist, I decided I'd pay for my copy by signing myself up to write about it—or at least that's how I rationalized doing what I knew I was going to do anyway, just as an alcoholic insists that he's going to the liquor store to buy cat food and toilet paper.

It turns out that 3,000 was an overguesstimation—the set is still available—but among the diehards word spread quickly. Not long after it came out, I was chatting with someone at a local record label, and he said that one of the heads of said label had been playing it incessantly in the office—in fact, it was going right then, as we spoke. A filmmaker friend told me that disc two, with its 17 takes of "Loose," was quickly becoming one of his favorite records ever. When my copy finally arrived, I took it to my editor's office. She snatched it out of my hand, put disc four, which includes 14 takes of "T. V. Eye," into her tinny boombox, and pointed her browser to www.rhinohandmade.com. As she typed in her credit card number and shipping address, I watched powerlessly, feeling like an enabler. A week or two later, during a visit to New York, over the vaguely Stoogey shriek and clatter of the subway, a friend asked me, "So is that *Fun House* box really any good?" In the tone I reserve for breaking bad news, I said, "I'm afraid so," and he sighed with briar-patch resignation.

Most of these people are not rich by any stretch, but once food, clothing, and shelter are accounted for, their thoughts turn next and naturally to finding more of the sort of rock 'n' roll that pushes all the pleasure buttons at once. And no record has ever activated the head-banging mechanism or stimulated that dirty little brain in the hips with more ruthless effectiveness than *Fun House*. All three of the Stooges' studio albums are classics, with sufficient charms to speed up to a stroke the savage breast. The first album represents the climb of the curve, in which a young band allows outside influences to fill the spaces not yet grown into—hence the chilly European weirdness of John Cale and Nico, who lurk in the wings like Gomez and Morticia Addams. The third album represents the downward slide, during which a powerful band inexplicably allows outside influences to hobble its power—hence David Bowie's prissy, timid production, which Iggy finally corrected in a 1998 remix.

But the second album, *Fun House*, is the pure, uncut zenith of cocky, hairy, sticky Stoogeness, the product of extraordinary Detroit delinquents under the influence of Chicago blues, free jazz, Antonin Artaud, ultraviolent cartoons, horny women, and the kind of drugs they just don't make anymore. For these seven songs, Iggy played the id-savant better than any other closet intellectual before or since, and he and the band spurred each other to reach that perfect climactic confluence of sex-lust, power-crave, and violence-terror that rock 'n' roll has to work its way through before coming out of Chapel Perilous to nab its Holy Grail. "I feel aw-rahht!" he howls and yowls and barks, over and over and over and over, until he can't possibly feel all right at all and the words lose meaning and Ron Asheton worries the riff like a dog with a dead bird and Steve Mackay on sax is ululating and squawking overtime just to catch up.

On the original LP, the two sides are the two halves of the best bad trip you ever had: the serious rockers are on side one, the gibbering freak-outs on side two. The CD, with no stop-and-flip, sweeps you along on a wild ride with no place to get off. The only thing that's better than *Fun House* is *The Complete Fun House Sessions*, because there's so much more of it. Anybody who only wants a little bit of *Fun House* has failed to fully appreciate it.

Once you've gotten the objet d'rawk in the mail, opened it up and spread it out on the table and set it spinning in the CD drive, the full magnitude of what the Stooges did begins to reveal itself. Disc one features seven takes of "1970," interspersed with early takes of "Loose," "Down on the Street," "Fun House," "T. V. Eye," and a song that didn't make the album, "Lost in the Future," which leads us to epiphany number one: There's a tendency among fans to believe, or to want to believe, that the perfect punk record is a document of a singular moment of sloppy intensity, a moment that, in its scriptural perfection, could have happened only once. Lightning never strikes twice in the same place, right? Inspiration can't be commanded to repeat itself, right? Speaking in tongues is more about the whims of God than the preparations of the individual, right?

Wrong. If you thought Iggy's vocal gymnastics sounded grueling on the official take of "1970," listen to him try it again and again here. He tests out infinitesimal variations on the rhythm and phrasing, feeling for the G-spot between the beat and the sax. Take three: "I feel aw-raht! I feel aw-raht! I feel all-rawt!" Take four: "Ah veel all-rot! Ah veel all-ROT!" Take five: "Aie feel! Aw-raaght! AI PHEEL AL RAIIIIIT!" Iggy may have been the very antithesis of a jock, but he was the ultimate athlete, pushing himself—and pulling the band—into the red every time.

This is what separates great music from pretty good music: the sense that the players have exceeded themselves, pushed themselves beyond what they'd previously known was possible, taught themselves something they didn't even know they didn't know, made it physical, made it spiritual, made it stick. This is why most of the CDs that come into my possession, from all corners of the musical universe, are a million times more tedious than 17 straight takes of "Loose." Nice changes, nice harmonies, nice solos, nice ass, whatever, but where's the cry to God? Where's the eureka when years of agonizing over the same equation finally yields up a secret of the universe? Where's the yee-haw when the General Lee goes airborne?

Give me the rough drafts of genius over the finished product of not-genius any day. Take disc four, which contains three more takes of "Loose" (they still hadn't gotten it quite right) but is mostly devoted to "T. V. Eye"—which is on my short list of flawless rock 'n' roll songs, a vicious cycle of lust and adrenaline able to withstand decades of overplay. In Legs McNeil and Gillian McCain's oral history of punk, *Please Kill Me*, Iggy explains that the title has nothing to do with the idiot box: T. V. here stands for twat vibe, as in, she's got a twat-vibe eye on me. In its final version, it's a perfect hunter-and-hunted table-turning frenzy, but the buildup is pretty hot too. The first take is at a slightly slower tempo, and when Iggy screams "now RAM IT—RAM IT—RAM IT!!" it sounds like he's coming on to the band. On take four Asheton, whose evil repetitive riff drives the song, turns in a solo that would have sounded fantastic on an Amboy Dukes record but isn't quite what was being gone for, and Iggy's vocalese—stuttering, growling, coughing, hacking—registers as commentary. They already knew that wasn't the take they were going to use, but they finished it anyway, just to see what else might happen.

Actually, for the most part the tracks don't differ significantly from the ones that made the final cut. The variations are there, but they're usually a matter of refining a tempo, timing a break perfectly, landing a syllable in just the right spot, trying out one lyric over another. In many cases it seems like an alternate take would've sufficed as well as the one that ended up on the original release. But it's the creative process you couldn't hear until now that makes the record a life-affirming masterpiece: OK, now put your head through that wall one more time. *Fun House* is a perfect articulation of the inarticulate, of that frustrating point where our most urgent needs and desires ram up against the language barrier and reel with heavenly dizzy idiocy. You can't put that into words, but you can put it into rock 'n' roll.

Neil Young on a Good Day

Follow the crack of the Liberty Bell as far as the eye can see and there he is, alone on a park bench in the middle of Philadelphia, as obscure as he wants to be. "Getting a little vitamin D," he says when I reach him, and lifts his face to the first sun either of us has seen after 15 hours on a bus, riding the interstate through the night and into this afternoon.

He's as obscure as he wants to be—except for all those tour buses parked on the other side of the square, his in particular, with the tops of two '49 Buick Roadmasters erupting through the roof and a license plate that reads POCAHONTAS. For a while we talk about the allure of the road ("I like it," he says, "I mean, I miss my family, but. . . . " and then shrugs, a concession not an apology), the music he listens to ("I don't play that much pop these days, mostly Beethoven, Wagner"), about his recent CD, "Silver and Gold" (his first studio recording in four years). We talk about the eight-disc archival box set he's preparing for release this fall, covering his ascent from obscurity in the mid–60s to 1972, when he had *Billboard*'s No. 1 album of the year; and the two tours he's staging, one on his own and one with three old friends, who, 30 years ago, were the biggest band in America.

Time has finally cornered him long enough to monumentalize him, it seems; but we'll see. Once he wrote songs with titles like

"Journey Through the Past"—barely conscious efforts to conquer the present and cheat the future—and he has always given a very good impression of a man running from his place in musical history as if it were a tomb. When we make our way to the hotel where the bus is parked, a fan works up the nerve to ask for an autograph, but Neil Young says, "No, I don't do that," and walks right on by, breaking his stride not even a little.

Until I actually step on board, everyone assures me the Pocahontas is a sanctuary never breached. Back beyond the special well designed for Ben, his 21-year-old son with cerebral palsy who watches the highway from his wheelchair, Young sprawls on his huge bed. "I was playing in a club in Fort William," he begins, "and we're doing a song called 'Farmer John,' and toward the end of it we started jamming. . . . "

This is way back. This is back in the autumn of 1964 with a band called the Squires, in Canada, where Young was reared in the little town of Omemee with its "blue, blue windows behind the stars" and where at the age of 3 he slipped into a nearby lake and nearly drowned. This is back before his early days as part of a Motown band with Rick James, back before his long exodus to L.A. in a hearse looking for Stephen Stills, whom he would find only at the last minute in a Sunset Strip traffic jam, before they formed Buffalo Springfield. This is before "After the Gold Rush" and "Harvest" put him on the map in the early 1970s, and before the subsequent 28 albums that have kept him on and off the map ever since.

This is way back, before a crumbling spinal disc in 1971 and before the epilepsy, which still haunts him onstage. This is before the afternoon he fired his lead guitarist for an uncontrolled heroin problem that took the guitarist's life that very night, and before the subsequent music that Young recorded in a tequila-flooded exorcism of grief and guilt. This is before the Thermidor of late-70s punk, when one rock icon after another fell before its guillotine of cultural relevancy, and Young was the one 60s artist not only spared by the revolution but also embraced as a kindred spirit.

This is back before the nitwitted lawsuit filed against him in the 80s by the head of his record label, David Geffen, for not making true "Neil Young" records, before the 90s, when Kurt Cobain quoted him in his suicide note, before he became the only artist in the year 2000 that one could possibly imagine sharing a concert bill with, say, Merle Haggard on the one hand and Nine Inch Nails on the other.

This is back before he became rock's Man That Time Forgot, making music at once primordial and futuristic, homegrown and surreal, traditional and insurrectionist, beguiling and cataclysmic—before he became, with his distinctive voice and racked Mojave-storm guitar, a one-man vortex for folk, country, blues, psychedelia, grunge, electronica, symphonic sweep, metallic squall.

Way back, playing "Farmer John" when he wasn't yet 20, Young remembers, the music got really wild. "I had never played like that before. We were just slamming it. We played the song without the song, we played what the song was about," and in that moment his musical identity was born. If rock has always been driven by two impulses, the utopian and the anarchic, many of its most enduring figures have straddled the two: Chuck Berry, Elvis Presley, John Lennon, Bob Dylan, Jimi Hendrix, Neil Young. It's the utopian Neil whose records people buy in droves. But with songs like 1995's sonic Imax "I'm the Ocean," or the brilliant "Powderfinger," about a young frontier boy killed in an explosion of survivalist pride and madness ("Then I saw black, and my face splashed in the sky"), it's the anarchic Neil who howls into the zeitgeist and alters it.

He likes it when the zeitgeist howls back. With Crazy Horse, a band just cacophonous and primal enough to capture "Farmer John" on record with Young a quarter-century after Fort William, he makes a point of recording around a full moon, when "a lot of mechanical things go wrong, technical difficulties, things that usually work don't work." And in the congenitally enlightened company of Crosby, Stills and Nash, unabashed utopians who have always sounded a little funny singing "Down by the river I shot my baby," Neil Young is Baader-Meinhof: when he performs "Rockin' in the Free World" in Philadelphia, it seems he simply won't let go of the song, until it becomes clear the song won't let go of him. As the lights glide across the audience, 60,000 people stand slack-jawed at the sight, except for a few zombies in the front row who go the entire show without responding at all until finally, just to get a reaction, Young lies flat on the stage in front of them playing all the more dementedly. "A whorish move," he allows sheepishly the next morning on the bus, "but. . . . "

From out of the conflict between utopia and anarchy has emerged moral ambiguity and complexity. In 1970, when he wrote "Ohio" following the murder of four students by National Guardsmen at Kent State University, his rage was more instinctive than political: "My lyrics get personal about it," he acknowledges. "I'm singing: 'What if you knew her and saw her dead on the ground? How could you run when you know?'" But that anger was also answered a few years later by "Campaigner," when alone among major spokesmen for the counterculture he expressed compassion for a disgraced president who lost everything ("Even Richard Nixon has got soul"); and conspicuously over the years he has refused to adopt any ideological line. At one time or another he has supported Ronald Reagan and Jesse Jackson. His ideal ticket in 2000 is Gore-McCain.

The utopia of his early music succumbed to anarchy most spectacularly during an unhinged 1973 tour that was his rude answer to superstardom. The shows would routinely climax with Young screaming, "Wake up!" at his audiences as the 60s crashed down around him in a rain of dead junkies; now, at the back of the Pocahontas, all he can manage to say of the period is, "I'm glad I made it through it," before a pall settles over the interview. Whenever Young "tried to get away from success," his manager, Elliot Roberts, remarks of the period, "it just turned into a bigger success," which wasn't just confusing but mortifying, since success wasn't particularly subtle about its human toll. Young went on to chronicle the deaths of the people around him in a series of anti-drug songs— "The Needle and the Damage Done," "Tired Eyes," "Tonight's the Night"—that were all the more authoritative for the way they were reportorial rather than judgmental, never denying for a moment the attraction of excess and darkness.

"I just didn't like people telling me what to do," he explains almost offhandedly. "I didn't like people telling me if I made more records like 'Harvest,' I would be successful. That's when I came up with the concept of destroying what I created in order to move on. I wanted to do what I called audio verite."

He pauses and looks out the window. "At a certain point, trained, accomplished musicians"—which is to say, not him—"hit the wall. They don't go there very often, they don't have the tools to go through the wall, because it's the end of notes. It's the other side, where there's only tone, sound, ambience, landscape, earthquakes, pictures, fireworks, the sky opening, buildings falling, subways collapsing. . . . When you go through the wall, the music takes on that kind of atmosphere, and it doesn't translate the way other music translates. When you get to the other side, you can't go back. I don't know too many musicians who try to go through the wall." He stops for a moment. "I love to go through the wall," as if you ever doubted it for a moment.

In the collective memory of his longtime audience, he may forever be the brooding figure reclining alone in the shadowy gatefold of "After the Gold Rush." But in fact virtually everyone who has ever known him attests to his humor—sometimes zany, sometimes wry, mischievous. Over six feet tall, he has an easy yet determined stride that encompasses all his contradictions: zen yet a little obsessive, open yet a little unapproachable, lurching toward his ambitions yet held back by his wariness of having to explain himself.

During a disgruntled taping with Crosby, Stills and Nash of "Storytellers," the VH-1 series in which songwriters relate the stories behind their songs, he paces the small stage like a caged animal and cracks, "I thought the song was supposed to tell the story." And when I bump into him in a hotel lobby one afternoon after failing to pin him down for an interview, and he assures me, "I'm really not avoiding you, I'm just waiting until I feel more alert," personally I feel quite certain he's avoiding me. But I'm in the curious position of respecting him all the more for it.

Similarly, though the archival box set—the first of four planned—seems truly imminent, it has been delayed by Young so many times in so many different incarnations over the last decade that his own record company will believe it only when it finally

reaches the stores, and maybe not then. His career is cratered with
last-minute flip-flops and bailouts on myriad album releases and
interviews and tours and reunions. "I've left some charred paths
behind me," he admits.

The line between such capriciousness and outright manipulation
can be hazy. Years ago, Elliot Roberts was just a 22-year-old from
the Bronx managing Buffalo Springfield when Young abruptly
stopped a rehearsal one afternoon to demand Roberts be fired on
the spot. "I was shocked," Roberts recalls. "It blew my mind." For
days he wandered L.A. stunned, trying to figure out what hit him,
only for Young to appear suddenly one night at 2 A.M. to explain he
was leaving the band and wanted Roberts to manage him.

"Oh, he had plotted it all out," Roberts now laughs. "I thought,
Wow, cool—this guy is as devious as I am." To those who have
watched him over the years, Young comes off as a mastermind of
unpredictability. But sometimes he can appear less integrated and
more genuinely divided against himself than people think. The
utopian-anarchic "schizophrenia" (Young's word) of his music
reveals both a Spontaneous Neil and a Control-Freak Neil, each
real and each peering over the other's shoulder, each trying to correct the other's misjudgments, each averting the other from perceived disaster.

There is no better example of this than the recent misadventures
of Young's authorized biographer. After signing a contract with both
Young and Random House, Jimmy McDonough, a journalist, spent
eight years writing, researching and interviewing more than 300
people, all with Young's cooperation. But when McDonough delivered a manuscript at the end of 1998, Young suddenly—according
to the publisher—"sabotaged" the book by withholding his approval
of it, and Random House dropped the biography.

In the Young camp, nobody will comment for the record about
why he killed the project. But the unofficially stated reason—that
McDonough submitted the book to Random House before submit-
ting it to Young and thereby breached the contract, betraying
Young's trust—sounds flimsy, a technical end run around an agreement that granted McDonough wide editorial freedom with the sole

exception of the privacy of Young's immediate family, which neither side in the dispute cites as an issue. One can hardly discount the possibility that Neil Young is just being his ruthlessly whimsical self again. McDonough is now suing him for $1.8 million.

The melodrama of Neil Young's early life reached critical mass in November 1978 with the birth of his second son—by his wife, Pegi—and the subsequent realization that, like Young's first son, Zeke, by the actress Carrie Snodgrass, Ben had cerebral palsy.

Zeke's case is mild (he is 27 and works as a sound engineer on a number of his father's projects), but Ben is a quadriplegic. Young would later recount walking out of the hospital and "looking at the sky, looking for a sign, wondering: What did I do? There must be something wrong with me." But cerebral palsy is a twist of fate, not of genetics—Young's daughter, Amber, doesn't have the disease. If all this weren't overwhelming enough, not long after Ben's birth, Pegi was found to have a brain tumor, from which, at the time, she had only a 50–50 chance of recovering.

So in the early 80s, the man whose obsession with his music was supposedly all-consuming set the music aside to devote himself to his family. "There were a lot of thoughts in my mind at that time," he says now, "that I wasn't ready to share with the world," and the matter of Ben's health was so personal that in 1982, when Young released a strange album called "Trans" with electronically distorted vocals, few knew it grew out of an effort to communicate with his speechless son by computer. During the rest of the decade, Young's music seemed at loose ends on a series of recordings that in hind-sight appear redeemed as stylistic explorations of an artistic identity in turmoil—out of which ultimately emerged one of his best albums, "Freedom," in 1989. He then spent the 90s making one important record after another.

One afternoon in Philadelphia, when we had once again sched-uled an interview and he had once again vanished, I found out he had gone to a school for children with cerebral palsy. Along with Pegi, Young is a major supporter of such a school in California, and during tours he often arranges for young people with the disease to see the shows. I was annoyed that I hadn't been with him to get the scene at the school for the story; in true Neil Young fashion, it even happened during a full moon, when an elevator at the school suddenly malfunctioned and the singer hovered for several precarious minutes between floors. But then it occurred to me that 99 out of 100 rock stars would have jumped at the chance to drag me along and put their humanitarianism on display, and that like so much else with Young, maybe this was private, too.

And sometimes, you know, he just wings it. Sometimes it's not a matter of a personal code (which he obviously has), or a Machiavellian ploy (of which he's clearly capable); it's a matter of impulse. Standing in the middle of a shopping-center parking lot on the highway to Cleveland, waiting for the bus to refuel, Young is talking about spending some time with his family after the tour on the volcanic Big Island of Hawaii, when a young woman pulls up in a pickup truck. She leans over and rolls down the window on the passenger side, and on her face is the disbelief of her own eyes. "Are you who I think you are?" she asks.

"Who do you think I am?" he says.

"Are you Neil Young?"

"Yeah," he finally answers.

Suspended between astonishment and opportunity, she sputters, "Would you sign your name for me?"

She scrambles to find something for him to write on—a beer coaster, a highway map, a gas receipt. There's a pause that seems longer than it probably is, and who knows what he's thinking; of course I'm remembering the autograph hound outside the hotel in Philadelphia. Now this woman in a pickup truck on her way to get her kid from school maybe, or coming home from a job waiting on tables, in the middle of a Wal-Mart parking lot that everybody knows is nowhere, happens to peer through her windshield to see, standing over on a small square of grass waiting for his dog to relieve himself, the full-moon genius of rock 'n' roll. And then she makes two decisions: the first, to have faith in what her eyes tell her; and the second, to confront it.

"Sure," he says. He steps up to the truck, leans in and scrawls his name on whatever she has offered him, a gut reaction to the purity of her wonder; and then as she drives away, with a story she'll tell for the next 50 years, he goes back to contemplating volcanoes and the sea, and the tropical winds where utopia and anarchy converge.

As he now seems eternally young, in earlier days Young was old before his time. "I'm getting old," he sang in his most famous song, "Heart of Gold," written when he was 24. In Phoenix, after another show, as the others in the band celebrate with friends backstage, Young sits alone in a dark, hushed room with a few candles burning low nearby, nursing his back with an ice pack; he seems every one of his 54 years. Earlier onstage he lost himself in a deranged "Down by the River" as he had with "Rockin' in the Free World" in Philadelphia, the Man That Time Forgot shredding time to ribbons. But back here in the dark he's the Man That Time Remembers, and it's remembering him in his lower back.

So for a while we make small talk that he probably finds more awkward than his graciousness allows him to admit. And then I finally leave, after he has just "slammed" one more time through the wall of age, the wall of fear, the wall of passion, to the end of the night. As if you ever doubted it for a moment, he loves to go through the wall, beyond the end of notes.

LORRAINE ALI

West Bank Hard Core

"Rubber bullets to dirt/ Tear gas to glass/ Air force to
Hamas/ Bombin' civilians, raising death to the millions/
We get the hundreds so u's get the billions"
—Ata, 15

"You better check yourself before you wreck yourself!" Seventeen-year-old Fathi Khaleq is rhyming as he steps away from a fight between groups of teens in the West Bank town of Ramallah. The American-born Palestinian struts down a narrow alleyway just off the main drag of this bustling Arab city, an abundance of heavy pendants clanking around his neck as he passes shops selling roasted nuts, plastic flowers, and prayer beads. "These are my boyz," says Fathi, pointing to his Palestinian-American friends in tow. "My niggas, my *A-raabs*."

Though we're just 12 miles and one Israeli checkpoint north of Jerusalem, they speak to each other in a variety of American dialects: heavy Brooklynese, nasal Mid-western slang, and Southern drawl, all mixed with Arabic phrases and throaty intonations. Looking like kids from an L.A. street gang in their baggy camouflage pants, oversized jackets, and Nike sneakers, the youths soon shuffle towards another altercation—this time a man has barricaded himself in a presumably stolen car and Palestinian police are trying to pry him out. A crowd gathers, civilians begin kicking the vehicle and, finally, a plain-clothed Palestinian Authority officer starts waving his ancient machine gun in the air. The teens watch the scene unfold until blond-haired, blue-eyed Ata announces in an impassive New Jersey accent, "Betta step back 'cause they gonna start shootin'."

Tension is something you just live with in Israel: Jews fight with Jews, Arabs fight with Arabs, and they both fight with each other. It's nothing new to these Palestinian teens, Muslim kids who were raised in America's inner cities (Fathi in Cleveland; Ata, 15, in Newark, New Jersey; Emad, 18, on the West Bank of New Orleans), then shipped here by concerned parents to finish out their high school years. They are the children of Arab shop owners, wholesalers, and cab drivers, parents who feared the bad influence of America. They were sent to Ramallah to avoid gangs, drugs, and premarital sex. Many of the approximately 2,500 Palestinian students who have been imported to the West Bank from America stay with extended family, aunts and uncles who teach them about Islam, push them to speak Arabic fluently, and immerse them in their Palestinian heritage. But these young Palestinians also hold tight to their own culture. Hip-hop culture.

It's a natural fit for kids who grew up ensconced in urban America. Rap has always been a voice of the disenfranchised, and now, as young men regarded as second-class citizens in Israel, these Palestinian-Americans take up its traditions, busting freestyle raps and dreaming of becoming as famous as Tupac Shakur. They twist hip-hop lingo to their own needs, making it a language of empowerment, using racial epithets like "A-raabs" in the same way Dr. Dre calls his homies "niggas."

Here in Ramallah, they call their group of friends the Madina Clique, and use nicknames like Kert Daddy (Fathi), Brixx (Ata), Sunshine (Emad), Mighty 'Mad (Ahmad), and Big Mo (Mohammed). The dark-complected Fathi is usually in charge, planning where he and his formidable if passive sidekick, Mohammed, should hang, and often correcting the wise-cracking Ata with lines like "Dude, don't be an idiot." The half-Arab, half-Polish Ata is low-key, edgy. The similarly light-skinned Emad is polite, accommodating. The group sticks together, their golden hair making them look more like tourists in the West Bank than Palestinian residents. Walking down the street, they try to top each other with their best freestyle rhymes: *"I'm just a Palestinian/ tryin' to come up on a million,"* raps Fathi. *"I'm a disaster at its peak/ I'm only spittin' rhymes cause at night I can't sleep."*

Since word has gotten out that a journalist and a photographer are here to do a story on Ramallah's rappers, our group has grown from five to 20 teenage boys. And all this surging testosterone attracts attention. Old men in head scarves stare, young men in off-brand jeans and cheap acrylic sweaters sneer (occasionally imitating the teens' English with gibberish), while passing women in *mendeel* head scarves keep their eyes firmly focused on the empty space ahead of them. The teenagers seem unfazed. They drop lines by rapper DMX (*"I don't give a fuck about you niggas!"*) and mock unaware passersby by busting out high-pitched, Eminem raps.

"I wanna be a famous rapper," proclaims Fathi once we've settled inside the Mocha Rena Café, a hangout for American-Palestinian teens. "I wanna tell everyone about me, who I am, what I am. I also wanna drive a Benz and wear Armani."

His friend Alla exclaims, "Nigga, that'd be sick."

This could be a scene between any two white suburban kids in America who jack "black" lingo and dress off MTV's Top 10, but it's not. Most of these Palestinian-Americans grew up in economically depressed areas of the U.S., and learned first-hand about the underlying tension that drives their heroes like DMX and Tupac Shakur. But it's unlikely that their raps will ever see the light of day in Israel. Local record labels like Hed Arzi barely even serve up Israeli rap, and when they do, it's typically the sort of hip-hop lite produced by the group Saback Semech. It's hard to imagine the labels putting out Ata's raps about anti-Arab racism: *"Rubber bullets to dirt/ Tear gas to glass/ Air force to Hamas/ Bombin' civilians, raising death to the millions/ We get the hundreds so u's get the billions."*

The teens of Ramallah wanted to get their story out so badly that Fathi's entire school donated nearly 800 shekels (about $200) for him to record one song at a studio in town. A visiting Palestinian kid from England who could DJ and produce laid down the beats, while Fathi, Morad Faieh (aka Solo), and Mohammed Joseph (aka Mumbles) launched into creamy, G-funk-style rhymes: *"PLO-style kamikaze, we don't give a shit about nobody/ Meet my lyrical team, camouflaged in green/ I swear to the holy book, I'm crazier than Saddam/ Catch bullet rounds in the knee/ Advice from the Arab posse, nigga you need to quit 'cause when the West is in the house we most definitely come equipped, motherfucka."*

Then Fathi drops in, his voice gravelly, the style harder and more straight-ahead: *"Yo, pass the microphone my way/ I'll show you how it's done, Arab superstars crashing in like thunder, representing PLO from here to Lebanon."*

Later, Fathi shrugs, "I've got a lot more rhymes, but what am I gonna do with them?"

The girls strolling by in their chunky platform shoes and dark lipstick hardly seem to notice. Right here, on Jerusalem's trendy Jaffa Street, machine-gun wielding Israeli soldiers are searching a pack of Palestinian kids. They pad them down for weapons and check ID cards. The soldiers are almost as young as the teens, making for a double dose of male tension, muscle-flexing, and, ultimately, humiliation.

Fathi says he and his friends are frequently stopped and checked for weapons, even while hanging out by the city's only McDonald's. "It's not just the police. We get it when we try to get into clubs, too," says Fathi. "You're old enough to get in and have all the qualifications, but they look at your name on the ID and it's an Arabic name, and it's like, 'Sorry, invitation only.' It's like back in the Fifties in the States for blacks. They tell me it's a private party, and I see a bunch of Israelis I know, and they're getting in. At first I'd wild out and end up fighting and not getting in the club. Now I lay low—I got a lot of people I know that hook me up. But people get in fights all the time."

There are few opportunities for Palestinian youth in the Occupied Territories. Kids grow up without phones, plumbing, or electricity, yet can see encroaching Jewish settlements, complete with satellite TV, playgrounds, and fully stocked supermarkets. The new Palestinian checkpoint into Ramallah is telling: Though the area recently opened up to limited Palestinian self-rule, funds are so low that the checkpoint looks like a taco stand—all corrugated tin and wood—compared to the white-painted cement kiosks of the Israelis. "Yeah," says Ata, "we get the dirt roads and they get the highways."

A parent's decision to send a child to Israel or the tumultuous West Bank for his own good might seem absurd. A notorious hotbed of political inequality and racial tensions, the West Bank and Gaza Strip have been Occupied Territories under tight Israeli rule since 1967, home to bloody battles with Israeli settlers, crushing military curfews, and human rights violations. It was from here, in the 1990s, that CNN telecast images of Palestinian boys throwing rocks at heavily armed Israeli soldiers during the *Intifada*—the Palestinian uprising. But for those accustomed to the battle zones of inner-city Detroit, Chicago, and other American cities, where new Arab immigrants often settle, Israel's tense political, economic, and racial divides at least seem familiar.

For these Ramallah teens, rapping is cathartic, funneling the anger of being 17 and powerless into raging lyrics. In a strange way, hip-hop is also a way for them to connect with Palestinian culture, using rhymes to describe the conditions endured by their Arab countrymen. The American-born teens often rap with a sense of guilt about the native Palestinians who risked their lives during the *Intifada*, as if they should have been born earlier so they could have joined the uprising.

Fathi left Cleveland when he was 15, arriving in Ramallah with his six siblings, his mother and his father, a wholesaler of poultry and meat products. "It was like hell," Fathi remembers. "I hated it, I didn't want to be here. I wanted to go back. I look around and think, these are my people and this is how they're living, and I can't change it. The President can't even change it, so how am I gonna change it? It was real hard to see what these people, my people, are living like."

Palestinian-Americans like Fathi, raised in Israel on money brought in from their parents' businesses in cities like Houston or Detroit, are nevertheless better off than their Arab peers. Ramallah

(Arabic for "Heights of the Lord") is one of the more affluent towns on the West Bank. But while these teens can move freely through Israeli checkpoints thanks to their American passports, as Palestinians, they are still part of Israel's underclass. This marginalization is why they relate to hip-hop, a genre born out of social injustice and oppression in urban America, where a rapper can reinvent his surroundings with tall tales of power and money.

"Blacks came up hard," says Fathi. "They went through slavery, civil rights. But Palestinians have had it harder than any other culture in the world. We went through having our country taken from us. Strong men watching their mothers and sisters dragged around by Israeli soldiers with guns, and they couldn't do anything about it. And the worst is, it still isn't recognized as happening. That's just sick."

Such feelings of disenfranchisement fuel the ire of Ramallah rappers. Fathi's cousin, Mighty 'Mad ("'Mad is short for Ahmad, and Mighty 'cause I'm one mighty nigga' "), a loud and wily 16-year-old rapper, is a prime example of what parents worry their kids will turn into in America. By 14, he'd already been in Northern California's juvenile hall system twice, busted on a variety of charges, from aggravated assault to possession of marijuana. He dropped out of high school and now works at a local bakery to make money for his ticket back "home." By far the wildest of the group, Ahmad nevertheless busts raps that are riddled with guilt for being a "bad kid." It's a common sentiment among these teens, who've grown up amid the excess of American culture but also inside the rigid dictates of Islam.

Sitting at an Israeli coffee shop in New Jerusalem, Ahmad puffs out his chest and stretches his arms across the back of a couch, looking like he owns the place. He's already called out to a couple of women outside, causing some in his posse to look around nervously for police. Ahmad takes a sip of coffee and begins rapping, loud enough for people at nearby tables to turn a wary eye. *"No more dope game, no more fame/ no more comin' home late bustin' down doors man,"* recites Ahmad aggressively. *"I've been out for too much, too long/ it's time to kick back, relax, let the pain be gone/ I ain't runnin' with these kids no more, all they do is burn the dough that they work hard for . . . / I got faith that God will forgive me. And if he don't, I'll drink a bottle of Hennessy."*

He stops, abruptly drops the cocky air and says, "Um, I think I could do better."

Calls from the Mosque for the last prayer of the day echo across Ramallah as we drive toward the smoke shop belonging to the uncle of a teen named Ashraf. Inside, old men with craggy faces and dark, worn hands sit loading *nargiles* (water pipes) with fruit-flavored tobacco, then suck the sweet smoke out through a long piece of decorated piping. The older men acknowledge the baggy-clad teens—Ashraf sucking a lollipop and Mohammed in a puffy, white down jacket—as they head for the back and up spiral stairs to the second floor. The boys plop down at a table and begin freestyling, making up silly raps in Arabic and English (*"Ana wahed Arabee/ Meclani not karawi/ I'm a go to America and drink a real Pepsi . . . "*). An ancient man, an employee of Ashraf's uncle, ascends the stairs and hobbles over with a water pipe for them.

Fathi, for one, prefers his Marlboros to smoking the pipe. "Over there [in America], I'm considered Arabic. I come over here, and I'm not Arabic, I'm American," he says. "I was raised in America. I dress different. Wherever I go, I'm not what I'm supposed to be. We're kind of like our own little world, the Americans that are here on the West Bank."

So they've created their own society between two worlds. "We're all the same culture and we understand each other," says Emad, a blue-eyed blond, though a full-blooded Palestinian. "In America, you can't trust your boys as much as here. You know they'll turn on you in one second, and maybe even shoot you for money."

Inevitably, many in this group will end up returning to America. "We always talk about it: 'Hey, when you get to America, you got to call me,'" says Emad. "When they leave, you feel bad. You want to go, too, but then you also don't want to leave your true boys, because you know that in America you won't find anyone like them."

Though the teens tease one another about who knows the most about basketball or rap, they have a gentleness, a naivete that would be seen as a weakness in American boy culture. Perhaps that's why it's Tupac and DMX they love—rappers who, underneath all the ultra-masculine posing, still let sentimentality seep out between muscled-up raps. Like their idols, the Palestinians rap about mom, childhood, and complicated relationships with dad between lines about a life of Hennessy and 'hos.

The next day, inside a Ramallah café, New Jersey's lost son, Ata, looks nervous. In front of him is a school notebook filled with carefully written raps. We walk downstairs to a quiet corner and he reads me a rap about his mom, who died when he was 12. "*I'm asking why I still mourned, court adjourned, Allah wanted to take you early, luckily I was born,*" he begins, his voice deep and his phrasing choppy. "*I'm rememberin' you telling me I'm the cutest kid in the world, I say you the best mom in the world, you my girl/ So if I can sit on your lap, look at pictures, watchin' home videos, go to sleep, wake up and feed me Cheerios/ Gettin' us to look our best and go to school, but I was a fool to not see your life almost through.*" When I ask this half-Polish blond about his Arab father, he says they "don't talk much anymore," not since they moved back to the West Bank and dad remarried to a Palestinian woman.

Ata and his friends have grown up in an entirely different world than their parents, making for strong bonds with forgiving moms and troubled relationships with disappointed dads. "They all lived the old Arab life, 10 families in the same room, straight from school to the house, eatin' bread and humus," explains Ahmad. "We lived in the States—ballin', money, cars, the fast life—so they can't relate to us at all. When I was younger, I wanted Super Nintendo, and [my father] would look at me like 'I never had that, why should you?' It's like a whole different world."

The gap is painfully apparent as Fathi raps about platinum records and Bentleys, a cartoon lifestyle not only galaxies away from that of his father, but also in direct conflict with the tenets of Islam. Though he does rap about his faith ("*Can't you see my doggs, we related by blood, dedicated through love/ use Islam for the ticket to the heavens above/ Jesus is the prophet and not the son/ For all ya'll that's mistaken, Allah is the one"*), a good Muslim is taught to practice clean, modest living, which doesn't exactly fit with Fathi's other raps about *"knocking boots with supermodel ladies."*

"My mom's really into Islam, really religious, so she tells me that wanting to make money [off rap] is just as bad as selling drugs," he says. "At the same time, she loves me and knows that's what I want to do. Do I pray? No. Do I fast at Ramadan? Yes. Do I believe there is only one God and Mohammed is his prophet? Yes. There're a lot of things forbidden in my religion. I can't even date, that's hard."

While Fathi and company may listen to the sexed-up tales of non-stop macking on CDs brought in from the States by the latest influx of teens, the reality is that here, in Ramallah, they are taking chances by simply fraternizing with the opposite sex. Most girls, even those raised in the more open settings of New York or Los Angeles, wear head scarves and spend their free hours at home.

"Over here, people do date, but it's really bad for the girl," explains Fathi. "Even if you're not doing anything sexually, she's considered a whore. It's the way people look at it. Like what the rappers say, they might live like that or they might not. If they don't, it doesn't mean they're lying. That's just how they *want* to live. I don't take it like they're faking it, I think that's what they want. I rap about Bentleys and Jaguars, and I don't even own a car."

Stretching reality through hip-hop combats boredom, which seems to be the main danger for kids. In lower-rent areas, boys hang out in dirt lots, throw rocks at each other, and taunt feral dogs. Fathi and friends regularly loiter near shops in downtown Ramallah, occasionally dropping by an Internet café to check their e-mails under online names such as Arabplaya, SoloPLO, Thugpassion, and Getoboy. The search for excitement has even inspired the strange appearance of Chicago Arab Posse gang graffiti on the walls of Urdoniah school in Al Beireh, which Fathi and half his friends attend—though today, the graffiti outside the open basketball court and aging administration building is fairly benign: "7th Grade Sux and 8th Fulz."

The home of Emad Abdel Jabbar (aka Sunshine) seems worlds away from the shanty-type towns in lower Ramallah or on the outskirts of nearby Shu'fat. It's dinner time, and Emad's mother serves up rack of lamb, roasted chicken, pita bread with melted butter and onions, and, of course, a platter of rice. The family lives on a cul-de-sac outside of Silwad, a rocky, mountainous area 20 minutes from Ramallah. They share the small street with the mother's three sisters and brothers-in-law, who also happen to be the brothers of her husband.

The spacious house, with its numerous gold religious plaques and silk flowers, gradually fills with teenaged boys in baggy jeans who just "happen" to drop by. They move in and out of the house, spinning a flat basketball on their fingers, until Emad's dad comes home, causing them to all assume the universal teenaged-boy posture: the silent slouch on the couch.

This house was the dream of Emad's father, one he saved for by moving back and forth between Palestine and New Orleans, where he ran a supermarket in the projects with his brothers. "Most Palestinians don't have a life like this," he says. "Back in the U.S., I worked from 6 a.m. to 10 p.m. I hardly saw my family. But I can come back here and build my own house. I moved the family back because I want them to know the language, the culture like I do, but all they do here is speak English." He waves his arms towards the boys. "They don't appreciate what we have here. They are spoiled."

The boys slink even lower into the couch, as if they're letting him down by their mere presence. Later, up in Emad's spare yet spacious room, Fathi and Ata play Nintendo while Emad defends his father. "They're just looking out for us," he says in his throaty, Louisiana-meets-the-West-Bank accent. "They're always afraid that if we stay in America, we might become too bad. They're used to working in bad areas, like the projects, where a lot of people are drunk and high. My dad thinks that's how all my friends are in America."

Most of the kids are counting the minutes to their return to the States. Fathi will be gone in a year, when he graduates, and Emad leaves this summer. When asked if they'll ever come back, nearly every one of them says yes, probably—a long time from now, when they're 30 or so, ready to get married and have kids. They even say they'll raise their kids here. "Yo, I'm Palestinian, my parents are Palestinian, my blood flows from Palestinian blood," says Fathi. "Just because I was raised in America does not mean I am American. I may look, talk, act and speak English, but my heart, my blood and roots will always be in Palestine."

But before returning to Palestine, Fathi needs to accomplish one small task: become a famous rapper, one who can afford Armani suits, Bentleys, and a new house for mom. "I have this dream. Even my mother, who's really religious, never holds me back. When I tell her, 'Mama, I want to be famous, rich,' she tells me, *'Insha Allah'*— 'If God's Willing.'"

Northern Light

Thirty-six hours before Jeff Buckley died, I saw him standing on a quiet Memphis street corner. A sheriff's car had pulled over, and the beige-suited *federale* stood towering above him. Jeff was my neighbor and friend, so I turned my car around to see if I could extract him from this tangle.

The incident had ended by the time I got there. It began raining. I pulled up next to Jeff. He didn't like strangers stopping him, and he kept his face forward as I drove beside him. He didn't look up until I spoke, then he stormed into the car, furious that the deputy had stopped to ask who he was: Jeff thought the lawman recognized him from his videos. I tried telling him their paths happened to cross at a corner known for drug activity, but he wouldn't hear it.

At the corner, instead of turning toward our street to go home— he lived a few doors from us in a rental house—I turned away. An anger I didn't know flared up. He demanded to be let out and opened the door while we were moving. The rain was hard and heavy, a dark rain. He did not want to know that I was only going one block out of the way. To calm him I told him I'd take him home directly. F— it, if he wanted to act like a rock star, I'd indulge his fame, don my chauffeur's hat, take his assholiness home, and then do my errand.

If he'd not died, the incident would have meant nothing.

I see my happening onto him right after the cop as proof—if he was seeking proof—that he could not take a walk and be alone. He had owned Manhattan and walked away for a place he could be alone.

He leapt out of my car and was immediately soaked. "I'll walk," he said. "It's nice out." It was not nice out. Is this what he had to say to be alone?

Jeff rang our doorbell at six sharp. "Look at this," I told my wife, leading Mr. Clean into the kitchen. He wore a frilly green three-piece thriftstore suit, two-tone black and white shoes, and a wide-brimmed hat tilted forward over his face. I assumed a matching green Cadillac with a fake fur steering wheel was parked out front. He said, "I like to dress for dinner."

He and I drank red wine outside in the pre-summer heat. My four-month-old daughter cooed at him, he cooed back, and they laughed. After dinner he wanted to retrieve a notebook he'd left at the downtown club where he had a weekly gig. "Sure they're open," he said, "live bands seven nights a week." We walked to his house, where he got the keys to his rental car. Before leaving the house, he put on a Dead Kennedys CD and left it at top volume. On the street I could hear every thudding syllable. An Avon lady lived next door to him. I didn't ask questions.

He drove like his verbal riffs: all over the place. The club was, of course, closed. But his outfit was glowing, we were half-lit, and we hit a Beale Street beer hall that had a pool table. He put down two quarters in line for a game and steadily pumped the jukebox.

In Memphis Jeff could play at anonymity: a dangerous, green-suited pool hustler running Beale. The bartender found his Grifters selection too noisy and pulled the plug. Jeff leapt onto the pool table and demanded not only that the machine be turned back on, but that he be given his money back so he could play the song again. A pretty girl recognized him and between pool shots she handed him a menu and asked for an autograph. He was polite: I think the occasional recognition was enough to sate his ego, but not so much that it interfered with his daily affairs.

My wife and I fed him a couple times, hung out a bit. Usually his
blinds were drawn, and we mostly left him to his work. One evening
I stopped by on my way to the neighborhood bar. He talked about
his dad that night, also a singer with a clarion voice. Tim Buckley
was twenty-eight when he found a packet of powder and, mistaking
the heroin for cocaine, laid out a fat line, inhaled, and died. Jeff was
eight at the time. He lived with his mother, her husband, and his
half brothers, and back then his name was Scott J. Moorhead. Then
he'd entered his old man's business, and though he didn't know him
(he'd only spent a week with his dad), he was feeling the weight of
his father's shadow. Dead at such an early age, Tim Buckley would
be forever young. "The only way I can rebel against him," Jeff told
me, "is to live."

You don't go swimming in your boots without some kind of intent
somewhere. Jeff was thirty when he drowned in the Mississippi
River. I don't imagine that his father's specter ever left him, but I do
believe life must have refracted through the ghost differently during
Jeff's last couple of years. My wife's father died accidentally when
she was a child, and she speaks of the mixed feelings she had when
she passed her father's age. Survivors' guilt tinged with survivors'
triumph: "It didn't happen to me" becomes "it couldn't."

People like me who write about musicians have a relationship
with celebrity that is either symbiotic or parasitic, depending on
the perspective. Jeff and I had met accidentally, laughed a lot at
that first meeting but were never introduced, and I left thinking
he was just some new guy in town. It took an effort by me to sup-
press the opportunism presented by his fame and maintain that
purity in our friendship. We never discussed doing an interview,
though I took notes for one. He had recorded an Alex Chilton
song on his first EP; Chilton plays a significant role in my first
book, *It Came From Memphis*, but we never discussed that either.
He'd never played his fame card before, and offering to drive him
a mile home that day it rained, when I was a block from doing
that anyway, made me painfully aware of the shared natures of fan
and servant.

Fame is a buoy that raises you up and a weight that brings you down. Jeff Buckley was beautiful to behold, a blast to be around, a singular talent. He seemed strong enough for fame. His core bubbled with energy, an excitement that sometimes overpowered him. Talking about his dad in the bar, he bent to his drink and gnawed on the glass with his teeth. Though he could wrangle his power, like when he made music, he seemed most at ease letting it pour forth: A rush of comic routines. Impulsive actions. His wardrobe. Swimming in the river.

The day after the rain, I saw a furniture rental truck unloading beds at his house: Jeff's band was arriving. When a British magazine editor called the next morning asking me to confirm that Jeff had died of a drug overdose, I reamed the guy. "Let him work!" I said. "He wants to be alone." The editor assured me that this news was based in fact, that someone at Microsoft News had—but I cut him off and told him to leave the guy alone. Ten minutes later a friend at Jeff's label called to say reports were that Jeff had drowned, and what did I know about it? Geez, I thought, can't *anyone* let this guy work?

My wife said if I'd been called about another of my neighbors having an accident, I'd have run to their door and knocked, made sure everything was okay. I did walk down to Jeff's house and stood in front of it, dumbly—his house looked like his house—but I wasn't about to disturb him with rumors of himself. An hour later, back home, I glanced out front and an image of his bandmates—their stooped backs, the shade of the magnolia tree, red Converse hightops on asphalt—seared into my brain. Death. I'd never seen them before, but their dyed hair and disheveled look announced them as Jeff's guests, and their dazed walk and stupefied manner instantly confirmed the worst. It rained for four days after that.

The first daylight hours passed as we waited for the phone to ring— for Jeff to tell us that a current had swept him away and deposited him, tired and delirious, in a forsaken corner of a cotton field, and he'd walked for hours between rows to dirt paths to gravel and was finally calling from a gas station near a stupid Tunica casino, could someone please come pick him up right away and bring dry clothes, he was miserable. But that call didn't come. His mother came, his girlfriend, an aunt, a lawyer, and some record company people.

When Jeff Buckley immersed himself in that inlet of the Mississippi River, he swam out on his back, looking at the stars, singing a Led Zeppelin song. A tugboat passed and left a wake. He swallowed water. The shadow was heavy. The refraction was blinding. His boots were full.

It's said about the blues singer Robert Johnson that he lived a compartmentalized life. That to some he was Robert Dusty, to others Robert Spencer, and that his personae were as varied and as independent as the people to whom each was known. Jeff had a life in New York I knew little about, and his family was in California. But his absence broke down those partitions, and we survivors clung to each other in his house, surrounded by his belongings, waiting for him.

The undercurrents in Memphis swelled in Jeff's absence. This city reveres obscurity, is hostile toward success. Beneath the reverence for the celebrated—here or anywhere—is a mean-spirited envy, a rooting for the lions over the gladiator. The tide of gossip rose: He staged his death for publicity. Or for solitude. He was on drugs. Suicide. Black magic.

On the fourth day, before his body floated up, his mother called his friends to his house for a wake. His beautiful photograph was propped on the table, along with a candle and maybe a flower. She wanted to celebrate her son's life and she made a toast, reminding me how little we can each know of even the ones we call friend. She raised her glass, and we raised ours. Her words startled me: "To Scotty."

His singing was magisterial, like a pipe organ, natural like the northern lights. Jeff's voice made me want to build shrines—though now I see Jeff Buckley was the shrine to his voice. His sudden end has seeped into my memories of his passion and vitality, and I can't separate the purity of his tone from the tragedy of his fate.

My child is drifting off to sleep in my arms. She has learned to crawl, is beginning to understand spatial relations. The puzzle that is everything she sees is beginning to have pieces, and the pieces are beginning to fit. Her dreams have become more lifelike, and as she is momentarily disturbed into consciousness, her eyes open. She can't tell the worlds apart, and since the dream feels so much nicer than the coldness of reality, she doesn't fight the return. She drifts off.

ERIC BOEHLERT

Invisible Man: Eminem

Accountants for Interscope Records and rapper Eminem weren't the only ones cheering last week when the star's new album, "The Marshall Mathers LP," debuted at No. 1 in blockbuster style. The aggressively demented album, which features the white rapper weaving rapid-fire tales about rape, faggots, bitches, drug overdoses and throat cuttings, sold 1.7 million copies in just seven days, according to SoundScan, becoming the second-biggest-selling debut week in industry history—and certainly the most successful showing by a rapper ever.

Also applauding the sales tally for the new record were the nation's music critics, who, for the most part, have been wildly enthusiastic about the rapper's work. "Eminem has not only become the legitimate heir to Tupac Shakur and the Notorious B.I.G.," gushed *Newsweek*, "he's arguably the most compelling figure in all of pop music." Fed up with watching boy bands and girl pop posers win over the hearts of consumers, critics welcomed the chance to bond with fans of some tougher sounds.

And with a love as true as theirs, it's doubtful critics will show Eminem any less affection even after he was charged Tuesday with carrying a concealed weapon and assault with a deadly weapon. Michigan prosecutors say Eminem was spying on his wife late Sunday night in a Hot Rocks Cafe parking lot in Warren, Mich., and pulled a gun on a bartender after seeing him kiss his wife. Eminem faces up to nine years in prison if convicted on both charges.

Eminem, 26, is from Detroit; he has short blond hair and an insolent stare. His rap debut came in the little-noticed form of "Infinite," which was void of Eminem's now trademark slurs. It flopped. In '97 a sample of Eminem's new, harder sound landed in the hands of Dr. Dre, a founding member of hardcore rap group NWA and mentor of Snoop Dogg. Dre signed Eminem to his Interscope-distributed label; by the time last year's "The Slim Shady LP" was released, Eminem's single "My Name Is" was already a blockbuster in the burbs. The album went on to sell 3 million copies and remained near the top of the album charts for the better part of a year.

> *Bitch I'ma kill you!*
> *You don't wanna fuck with me*
> *Girls leave—you ain't nuttin' but a slut to me*
> *Bitch I'ma kill you!*
> . . .
> *You better kill me!*
> *I'ma be another rapper dead for poppin' off at*
>   *the mouth with shit I shouldn'ta said*
> *But when they kill me—I'm bringin' the world with me*
> *Bitches too!*
> *You ain't nuttin' but a girl to me*

—"Kill You," a song about Eminem's mother

Of course, Eminem has the right to rap about whatever he wants, and if executives at Interscope are comfortable releasing that sort of CD, then the debate ends right there. But should the nation's tastemakers, the ones supposedly pondering the connection between art and society, align themselves with an artist as blatantly hateful, vengeful and violent as Eminem?

Not only have Eminem's foul lyrics not sparked a debate among serious music observers, they've barely even caused a stir. It'd be as if Bret Easton Ellis wrote the murderous *American Psycho* and no critic questioned his judgment or the book's content—and those who did pause briefly to consider the book's moral or social implications simply dismissed the consequences because: A) the story's only fiction and B) Ellis is a really, really good writer. That's basically what most music journalists have done as they eagerly explain away Eminem's psychopathic subject matter.

So afraid are music's defenders to give an inch in their battle with the Bill Bennett moralists of the world that they're now championing an artist who raps nearly nonstop on his new slanderous CD about sluts, guts, cocaine and getting "more pussy than them dyke bitches total."

Of course, the problem with "Marshall Mathers" isn't simply R-rated lyrics. They're nothing new, although Eminem has taken them to a new and oddly focused level. Other rap records might create a world of clichéd bitches and ho's to lay down party beats for good times or hold up a mirror to their environment. Some of the better ones (Jay-Z, Ice Cube, Ice-T) even took time out occasionally to reflect on the consequences of their gangsta actions. But Eminem's not interested in any of that. Instead, the rapper simply delivers 75 minutes of nearly nonstop hate (that is, when he's not whining about his fame). How hateful? According to GLAAD (the Gay and Lesbian Alliance Against Defamation), the album "contains the most blatantly offensive homophobic lyrics we have ever heard. Ever."

> *New Kids on the Block, sucked a lot of dick*
> *Boy-girl groups make me sick*
> *And I can't wait 'til I catch all you faggots in public*
> *I'ma love it [hahaha]*
> . . .
>
> *Talkin' about I fabricated my past*
> *He's just aggravated I won't ejaculate in his ass*
>
> **—"Marshall Mathers"**

No matter, critics love this record. "It's mean-spirited, profane, shocking—and actually quite entertaining if not taken too seriously," the *Arizona Republic* opined. "Guilty pleasures rarely get as good as this," added *CDNow* in a record review. "A bona fide masterpiece," raved VH1.com, adding that Eminem is "possibly the greatest storyteller in all of hip-hop."

The new record "may be among the most objectionable albums ever to receive mainstream release, but that does not make it a bad album," Alona Wartofsky assured us in the *Washington Post*. "The new album from Eminem is absolutely outrageous. And I mean that in the best possible sense," cheered Neil McCormick in London's *Daily Telegraph*.

> *'Cuz if I ever stuck it to any singer in showbiz*
> *It'd be Jennifer Lopez and Puffy you know this!*
> *I'm sorry Puff, but I don't give a fuck if this*
>   *chick was my own mother*
> *I still fuck her with no rubber and cum inside her*
>   *and have a son and a new brother at the same time*

—"I'm Back"

Time Out New York thought this incestuous, quasi-rape fantasy about Jennifer Lopez was "sidesplitting." The *Times* of London agreed it was "extremely funny." CDNow insisted, "The man is fearless." Why? Because he has the courage to insult, among others, pop stars Puff Daddy, Will Smith, Britney Spears and 'N Sync. Eminem also has things to say about quadriplegic Christopher Reeve. Talk about picking fights you can't possibly lose.

In a recent cover profile of Eminem for the *Los Angeles Times Sunday Calendar* magazine, the paper's longtime music critic, Robert Hilburn, came this close to comparing Eminem with Elvis Presley, a tenuous stretch that won the writer an insightful reply from a reader in Studio City, California: "Let's see . . . self-described white trash who raps about mindless violence, misogyny, murder, child abuse—one who proclaims 'anything is possible as long as you don't back down' and then makes whatever lyrical changes are required to conform to retailers' guidelines of acceptability. Gentlemen, please."

A few days later, in his review of "Marshall Mathers," Hilburn, like so many before him, apologized for the rapper in advance: "Eminem is simply exercising his creative impulses—putting on disc all the forbidden thoughts and scandalous scenarios that accompany adolescence and just watching the fallout." In other words, Eminem's the John Rocker of hip-pop (calling the slurs like he sees 'em), and music journalists are his hometown apologists who can see no wrong in their star.

Elsewhere, *Newsweek* explained away the "Marshall Mathers" hate by noting with approval, "He picks on himself almost as much as he does the people on his enemies list . . . By flipping his razor-sharp lyrics on himself, Eminem subverts the smirking superiority that plagues mainstream rap, a wily underdog move that lets him get away with more than he could otherwise." That's been a popular defense, most often invoked right after '99's occasionally jocular "Slim Shady" album. But the truth is that "Marshall Mathers" is far darker and more disturbed than most critics are willing to admit. Which explains why *Newsweek* didn't include any new subversive lyrics of Eminem picking on himself. They don't exist.

> *Don't you get it bitch, no one can hear you?*
> *Now shut the fuck up and get what's comin' to you*
> *You were supposed to love me [sounds of Kim choking]*
> *NOW BLEED! BITCH BLEED!*
> *BLEED! BITCH BLEED! BLEED!*
>
> **—"Kim," a song about Eminem's wife**

When you get done parsing the critics' language and logic about how it's all just satire, or cartoons, or Eminem's alter ego talking, the bottom line is that they've given Eminem a pass. (Ask the Michigan bartender if that was Eminem's alter ego brandishing a pistol over the weekend.) Regardless of what he raps about, because he's so dynamic and funny on the mike (which he can be) and his beats are so tight (which they are), his lyrics are irrelevant. Makes you wonder what it would take for music journalists to sit up and take offense. A song or two about lynching bothersome blacks, or gassing a few Jews? Even then, it'd probably be a close call.

One thing is for sure, ever since the release of "The Slim Shady LP" last year, critics have been working overtime trying to soften his gruesome lyrics. In analogy after analogy reviewers have tried to convince readers (and perhaps themselves) that Eminem's odious tales are simply the latest in the grand tradition of shocking youthful rebellion as championed by the Rolling Stones (*Sacramento Bee*), Freddy Krueger (*Times* of London), a Quentin Tarantino film (*Los Angeles Times*), the wood-chipper scene from "Fargo" (*Boston Herald*), shock jocks (*Washington Post*), Rodney Dangerfield (*Rolling Stone, Baltimore Sun*), the gallows humor of Alice Cooper (*Los Angeles Times*), "the wink-and-nod allure of horror film violence" (*Detroit Free Press*), comedian Robert Schimmel (*Washington Post*), "Scream" and its sequels (*Times* of London), Redd Foxx and Richard Pryor (MTV's Kurt Loder), "bombastic wrestling telecasts" (*Entertainment Weekly*), "South Park," Jerry Springer, Howard Stern, "Cops" (*SonicNet*), a Robert Johnson blues classic (*Kansas City Star*) and the Beatles' "Run for Your Life" (*Kansas City Star*).

Really? Who does the following verse most remind you of— Richard Pryor, the Beatles, Robert Johnson or Alice Cooper?

> *My little sister's birthday, she'll remember me*
> *For a gift I had ten of my boys take her virginity*
> *("Mmm-mm-mmm!")*
> *And bitches know me as a horny-ass freak*
> *Their mother wasn't raped, I ate her pussy*
>   *while she was 'sleep*
> *Pissy-drunk, throwin' up in the urinal*
> *("You fuckin' homo!")*
> *That's what I said at my dad's funeral*

> **—"Amityville" (featuring rapper Bizarre)**

MTV, which prides itself on running anti-violence public-service announcements, has embraced Eminem like no rap act in its history. The mighty music channel celebrated the new album's release with at least four separate Eminem specials. One was a biopic that gently painted Eminem as a wisecracking free spirit who beat the odds and did it all for his daughter. (No, really.) Another featured a sit-down with Loder, who asked Eminem about his gay-bashing, although not in a confrontational way. Instead Loder merely offered up an opportunity for Eminem to make nice. He declined. Instead, he told Loder that when he uses the word "faggot" it doesn't necessarily mean gay person, it means "sissy" and "asshole." Oh. "Do I really hate gay people or not? That's up for you to decide," said Eminem.

At least his producer and hip-hop guardian Dr. Dre was honest when Loder asked him about the gay-bashing on "The Marshall Mathers LP." Sneered Dre: "I don't really care about those kind of people."

In his *Los Angeles Times* review, Hilburn deducted half a star from his four-star "Marshall Mathers" review "because of the recurring homophobia." A nice gesture, although in the big picture it's rather comical. Why just half a star? And what about the woman hating that drips off the CD? (Eminem seems more interested in killing girls than fucking them.) Doesn't that constitute a deduction from the morals score card?

Entertainment Weekly tried to have it both ways as well. Declaring "Marshall Mathers" to be "the first great pop record of the 21st century," *EW*'s final grade for the album included a D plus for "moral responsibility" and an A minus for "overall artistry," which of course begs the question of what "artistry" is. And if that's not a clear indication that lyrical content is no longer relevant to music criticism, what is?

> *Some bitch asked for my autograph*
> *I called her a whore, spit beer in her face and laughed*
> *I drop bombs like I was in Vietnam*
> *All bitches is ho's, even my stinkin'-ass mom*
>
> **—"Under the Influence"**

A handful of critics have managed to break free of the Eminem groupthink—and they deserve credit. Christopher John Farley at *Time*, Renee Graham at the *Boston Globe*, Chris Vognar at the *Dallas Morning News* and Oliver Wang at *SonicNet* called Eminem on his horrendous, hateful lyrics. Yet none of them seemed willing to really pull the trigger and condemn the project outright.

Perhaps they remember what happened to *Billboard* editor Timothy White last year when he wrote a scathing attack on "The Slim Shady LP," connecting the dots between the rapper's misogynistic rants and the rise of spousal abuse. "If you seek to play a leadership role in making money by exploiting the world's misery, the music industry remains an easy place to start," White wrote. The reaction? The music press looked at him as if he had three heads, with the deep thinkers at *New Times LA* so busy calling him names they forgot to actually read his column. ("Timothy White . . . publicly called for the CD to be banned," the paper wrote. He did no such thing.) Or look at what happened to Christina Aguilera when she questioned the playground bully:

> *Shit, Christina Aguilera better switch chairs with me*
> *So I could sit next to Carson Daly and Fred Durst*
> *And hear 'em argue over who she gave head to first*

> **—"The Real Slim Shady"**

Aguilera, portrayed as a blowup doll in the song's video, is one of today's platinum, girl-next-door teen pop singers, Daly is the host of MTV's hugely popular "Total Request Live" show and Durst is the lead singer of the metal band Limp Bizkit. All agreed the line about her giving them head was untrue. So what set the rapper off? Turns out that last year Aguilera hosted a special on MTV and introduced Eminem's breakout clip from '99, "My Name Is." After the video she told her on-camera friends she'd heard Eminem was married to his longtime girlfriend, Kim (which he was), even though Eminem rapped about murdering her on record (which he did). "Don't let your guy disrespect you," Aguilera urged her young viewers. And for that common-sense message she has been slandered in a Top 40 song that MTV can't stop playing.

Did anybody come to her aid? Hardly. In fact, the *Washington Post* cheered on Eminem's attack: "We're all tired of pop moppets like Spears and Aguilera, and he obliges us by slurring them both."

(And just in case you care, both Durst and Daly assured MTV News they were not offended by the fact that a new hit song suggested they were getting blow jobs from a famous teen pop singer. Oh, good.)

By defending and celebrating the likes of Eminem while willingly turning a blind eye to his catchy message of hate, music critics continue to cheapen their profession. They're also lowering the bar to such depths that artists will soon have to crawl to get under it. Don't think Eminem won't try.

The Tao of Esteban

Esteban is stressed out and exhausted.

The immensely popular Tempe-based flamenco guitarist usually spends about three months recording an album, but, for reasons that have more to do with marketing than art, he's given himself only a week to cut an ambitious double CD, called *At Home With Esteban*.

It's a Friday afternoon, day five of recording, but the days and hours have begun to blur at the Sound Lab, a state-of-the-art studio nestled behind an allergy lab in south Tempe. All week, Esteban has followed the same grueling schedule: get to the studio at 10 A.M., lay down tracks for 16 hours, go home at 2 A.M.

Recording should have been completed by now, but Esteban has decided to cut one final tune, a solo version of an old Russian folk song that, in English form, provided Mary Hopkin with the 1968 hit "Those Were the Days." Normally, he has sheet music to work from, but since this song is a late addition, he's having to rely on a skeletal chord chart—and his own memory.

If one of his many devoted fans walked into the Sound Lab today, they probably wouldn't recognize him. Seeing him in street clothes is a bit like catching KISS' Gene Simmons without his platform boots and makeup. Onstage, Esteban is the personification of the dark, mysterious Latin lover. He dresses in all-black Zorro ensembles, with a bolero hat and impenetrable shades. Whenever he tilts his head down in deep concentration, it's easy to imagine that he's younger than his 52 years. His right hand sports long, acrylic fingernails that dance across his guitar strings with dramatic tremolo flourishes. In the minds of his fans, he's Rudolf Valentino and Antonio Banderas rolled into one, and wrapped in Ricardo Montalban's rich Corinthian leather.

But the guitarist sitting in the recording booth at the Sound Lab with his foot propped on two Yellow Pages books is not Esteban the stage persona. He's Stephen Paul, the blue-collar gringo kid from Pittsburgh with hippie affectations. He wears a gray tee shirt, navy blue shorts and white athletic socks, but no shoes. His long blond hair is bundled in a ponytail. He refers to everyone he meets as "bro." Periodically, he lifts his shades to look at his chart, squinting like an old man trying to decipher a road sign.

He makes a few practice passes at "Those Were the Days," then decides he's ready.

"I'll probably screw it up, but let's try it," he softly grumbles to house engineer B Gerdes.

Sure enough, he struggles through seven or eight takes, botching a few performances by scraping his nails across the strings.

Finally, with a note of exasperation that's rare for this placid man, he blurts out, to no one in particular: "What am I doing?"

The answer is simple. Esteban is punishing himself with this breakneck schedule because, after nearly half a century of devoting himself to the guitar, his career is suddenly accelerating beyond his wildest dreams, and he doesn't dare slam on the brakes.

Last November, Esteban made his first national television appearance on QVC, pitching his musical wares alongside the Miracle Mop, the Marie Osmond fine porcelain doll collections and the gaudy pink pendants that are the lifeblood of the home-shopping industry. He wasn't the first musician to market his product on TV. People like Kenny Rogers and Lionel Richie had already experienced moderate success with it.

But Rogers and Richie were already established names. Esteban was a nobody, a star only to the devoted cult that repeatedly returned to the lobby bar of Scottsdale's Hyatt Regency, where he'd slowly built a worshipful following over the last decade.

To the astonishment of many in the home-shopping biz, Esteban was an immediate sensation at QVC, quickly selling more than 100,000 CDs. He's since moved on to the Home Shopping Network, and two months ago, after a rapturously received debut appearance on the network, he sold 56,000 CDs in one week, simultaneously placing two of his albums in the Top 54 of the *Billboard* 200 album chart.

Incredibly, a middle-aged instrumental artist with no record-label support, minimal radio airplay and negligible press interest had outsold Limp Bizkit and Celine Dion.

The Esteban phenomenon is also a business coup for his self-created local label, Daystar Productions. Only folk-punk troubadour Ani DiFranco, with her Righteous Babe imprint, can rival his success at moving product without relying on the muscle of the record industry.

But DiFranco built her following with the help of stacks of glowing reviews and positive buzz from her peers. When Esteban is not being ignored by other musicians, he's generally being ridiculed, accused of taking classical guitar techniques and dragging them through the mire of cheesy song selections ("Don't Cry for Me Argentina," "Happy Trails") and bland new-age arrangements.

"I'd put him in the category of a John Tesh: easy-listening music without harmonic or rhythmic complexity," says Eric Bart, a local jazz guitarist. "And something that's very, very heavily marketed."

Bart is one of several local musicians who cringe at the mention of Esteban's name, and they're all quick to emphasize that it's neither sour grapes nor their considerable dislike of his music that fuels their animosity. What really gets up their noses is the way Esteban has spent the last decade milking his murky 1970s association with the late, legendary classical-guitar master Andrés Segovia.

Although the only evidence of his studies with Segovia is a photograph and a brief, autographed note that Segovia wrote to him, Esteban has rarely missed an opportunity to invoke the name of his beloved "maestro." He's repeatedly claimed to be one of only 14 guitarists in the world endorsed by Segovia, a number unsupported by

any factual evidence, and even says that he began using the name Esteban (Spanish for "Stephen") because that's what Segovia called him.

Cynics are quick to note that this appropriation of Segovia's reputation didn't begin until after the Spanish classical-guitar virtuoso
died in 1987, and therefore could no longer speak for himself.

"It's disrespectful. It's like pissing on his grave," Bart says.

Frank Koonce, music professor and director of guitar studies at
Arizona State University, agrees with Bart.

"Segovia dedicated his life to elevating the guitar to the stature of
a serious concert instrument, and he had a disdain for popular and
commercial music," Koonce says. "With regard to Esteban, I think
it is fine that he has found a formula for success with his brand of
popular music. However, I think it is inappropriate for him to use
Segovia's name as though it is an endorsement of what he is doing."

If it's hard to imagine Segovia embracing Esteban's Latin-lite
sound, at the very least, Esteban does share his hero's all-consuming
work ethic.

He's scrambling to ready his next album for the holiday season,
because HSN is already preparing a big campaign to coincide with
its release. He must finish mixing the disc on a Monday night,
because on Tuesday morning he's flying to New York for two weeks
to talk business with several major record labels who are awed by his
power to reach the housewives of middle America. As soon as he
gets back to the Valley, he must prepare for another round of HSN
showcases, a performance at the Arizona Biltmore and a concert at
Scottsdale Center for the Arts.

"I don't have any furniture, I don't have a girlfriend, I don't have
time for anything but music," he says, with a mixture of pride and
embarrassment. "I'm a weird guy. I don't have any of the normal
things."

Esteban's contention that he owns no furniture is slightly exagger-
ated, but the interior of his pink stucco, two-story Tempe home
does have a slapdash quality about it. Books are scattered all over
the floor, and his living room has little room for anything but

instruments, amplifiers and a Harley-Davidson pinball machine. His upstairs office is more like a storage room, where CDs, press packets and sheet music are stacked on tables.

It's Saturday, the day after Esteban completed recording his album. Because another band booked the Sound Lab for the day, he'll have to wait until tomorrow to begin mixing the tracks. So he has a rare day off. He tries to unwind.

"Where's my Mozart? I always have Mozart playing," he mumbles as he walks into the study.

The moment you enter the room, it hits you. Up on the wall is a mammoth framed photo of Esteban with Segovia, taken sometime in the mid-'70s. The two men are sitting on a couch. Esteban has long black hair, parted down the middle in a manner that makes him look like '70s teen idol Shaun Cassidy. He's holding a guitar in his left hand, and he's got a giddy smile on his face.

Segovia, well into his 80s, looks old and frail. He's leaning back on the couch like he's about to fall asleep. His face is a blank page.

The picture dwarfs everything in the house, and not just physically. After all, the spirit of Segovia has dwarfed everything in Esteban's life since he was a child.

Esteban was born Stephen Paul, the first of four children, to a Pittsburgh steel-mill worker and his wife.

"It was a blue-collar atmosphere and there wasn't a lot of culture," he recalls. "The only thing that was good was when I went to visit my uncle George. He was always playing music. He was a great clarinet player. He loved Benny Goodman and all the '40s swing stuff.

"He always put on Segovia or flamenco guitarists like Vicente Gomez. I always heard these songs and liked the feeling and the sound of the guitar and the big old stereo he had with a 15-inch speaker. It was the coolest thing and it sounded so great."

It was Esteban's uncle who bought him his first guitar, a nylon-stringed Goya ("the same one they used in *The Sound of Music*"), at the age of eight and a half.

"That cost my uncle a couple hundred bucks, and that was a lot of money back then. A lot of times kids get guitars and they're hard to play, so they give up. But that was a dream to play."

He says that he taught himself to play well enough to win talent shows at his parochial school. By the time he started taking lessons, at the age of 12, he was already teaching other kids how to play, charging $3 for a half-hour.

The only interest that could compete with music was baseball. He says he was a promising pitcher, but at the age of 12 he was blinded in his left eye by a screaming line drive. From then on, all he had was the guitar.

After high school, he enrolled at Carnegie Mellon University, where he double majored in English and music. During the same period, he says, he taught 150 guitar students a week and found time to play in clubs at night.

He'd progressed as a player over the years, but he says no one in Pittsburgh could teach him the authentic classical guitar skills that he craved. He knew that he needed to study with the best in the world: Andrés Segovia.

Born in 1893, Segovia had practically defined the instrument since the 1920s, not only adapting much of the classical repertoire for guitar, but also playing with a virtuosity which had never before been heard from the instrument. He approached the guitar with a near religious sense of commitment, stubbornly refusing to allow concert microphones to be placed near his guitar, for fear that it would spoil the acoustic purity of his sound.

"I had this insatiable drive to study with Segovia," Esteban says. "Everybody tried to study with him and very few got to. The waiting lines were immense. So it was disheartening. I couldn't figure out a way to study with him."

After graduating from college, Esteban moved to Los Angeles, where he began avidly pursuing his idol. For two years, he sent unsigned notes to every hotel at which Segovia was staying. The message was always the same: "My life is meaningless unless I can study under you."

In 1972, he finally met Segovia in L.A. The details of the encounter have varied a bit, depending on whom Esteban is telling the story to. Most often, he says that he impersonated a courier, knocked on Segovia's hotel-room door and was rebuffed by a suspicious road manager. When Segovia came to the door, Esteban repeated the message he'd written on his cards, and Segovia shouted, "It's you, it's you."

However, in a 1998 interview with *Scottsdale Magazine*, Esteban offered a different account of the meeting, saying, "Finally, [Segovia] looks me up in L.A., knocks on my door, and I greet him with the same phrase. He says, 'So you're the one.'"

This discrepancy is only one of the puzzling components of Esteban's relationship with Segovia.

Esteban says that after nervously playing for Segovia, the master gave him a list of music to study. A year later, when Segovia was back in L.A., they hooked up again, and Segovia invited him to Spain.

He says he took part in Segovia's master classes in Santiago and was invited by Segovia for private classes at the guitar legend's home in Madrid.

"He would only teach once in a while, but one class with Segovia could last you three years," he says.

"He would just stop me in the middle of tunes. As soon as he heard an imperfection or an incorrect analysis or a wrong note, he would just stop you, look for a moment, and point out what it was. Then he would play it himself. The next hour or hour and a half would be like that. So I'd study for the next two or three weeks."

Esteban says he studied with Segovia, off and on, for five years, splitting his time between Spain and California. In Spain, he often stayed at youth hostels for four dollars a day, earning money by playing in flamenco clubs or busking on the street.

He says Segovia, the classical purist, objected to his playing flamenco music.

"The only thing that bothered me about Segovia was he didn't like flamenco music, and that's the real essence of the folk and peasant music of his country," Esteban says. "So I asked him about it. Well, he had a little ego, and he talked about it. He was the father of the classical guitar and here's this kid asking him about it. He's ready to hit me over the head with his guitar case. So I learned my place from that."

In 1976, Esteban got married in Los Angeles. Two years later, while Segovia was in California, Esteban obtained a note from the master. Segovia signed a copy of his then-new autobiography, adding the following message: "To Stephen Paul, who loves the guitar and the guitar loves him—an artist."

It was a modest compliment, particularly considering that Segovia was known to be very generous with his fans. But Esteban has used this simple message as proof that he was "endorsed" by Segovia, and has made it a crucial part of his mystique. The implication is that Esteban is the heir to Segovia's legacy, carrying it into the 21st century by delivering music "for the new global awareness," as his Web site proclaims.

The problem is that most musicians don't buy it. Chris McGuire, president of the Fort Worth Classical Guitar Society, studied with Segovia and says he saw him sign autographs for countless people.

"There are literally thousands of autographs like that out there," McGuire says of Esteban's note from Segovia. "There is a very clear distinction between signings on memorabilia and his actual written endorsements."

Local classical guitarist Chris Hnottavange agrees: "No doubt, hundreds of people have received autographs from Segovia or have had pictures taken with him. It's unlikely that that alone carries the weight of a special endorsement."

McGuire says he once saw an attractive young female guitarist approach Segovia for an autograph. Segovia flirted with her and wrote a note that praised her guitar work, although he'd never even heard her play.

Although there is no doubt that Esteban met Segovia, many musicians question whether he was as close to the master as he claims. They point out that Esteban is not mentioned in any of Segovia's biographies and never received the kind of public acknowledgements that Segovia reserved for his true favorites.

For example, Segovia wrote of John Williams, one of his most talented disciples: "A prince of the guitar has arrived in the musical world. . . . God has laid a finger on his brow, and it will not be long before his name becomes a byword in England and abroad, thus contributing to the spiritual domain of his race."

Williams subsequently asked his record company and management not to use the quote, because he didn't want to ride Segovia's coattails.

Another Segovia favorite was Eliot Fisk, whom he described as "one of the most brilliant, intelligent and gifted young musical artists of our time." After Segovia's death, his widow, Emilia, specifically asked Fisk to record some newly discovered compositions by her late husband.

Esteban argues that he doesn't like to make a big deal about his "endorsement" from Segovia. Pointing to the handwritten note, he says, "That's what all the little guitar critics around the world wish they had. But I don't even care. I don't say anything about this unless somebody asks. It's a personal thing."

Such a statement appears disingenuous, to say the least. Every piece of publicity surrounding Esteban, every interview he's given and every appearance on the home-shopping channels has been dominated by references to Segovia. What's most galling to Segovia loyalists like Bart—who says his life was transformed at the age of 12 when his dad took him to see the master in concert—is the way Segovia's name was appropriated for the Hyatt's drink menu, which cited Esteban as "one of 14 guitarists in the world endorsed by the legendary Andrés Segovia."

In an August 7 front-page story in the *Wall Street Journal*, Esteban conceded that he doesn't know how he arrived at that number or who else is on the list.

When asked about his critics, he says he won't utter anything negative about another musician. But he does offer a passive-aggressive jab at Bart, a musician he says he's never met.

"He's so frustrated," Esteban says. "The guy's working for 40 or 50 bucks a night. He's pissed off, so he says, 'Esteban plays elevator music. It's the worst shit in the world.' People can say that if they want, but usually people don't feel that way."

Esteban's musical direction changed drastically, and irrevocably, in 1980.

He says he'd spent the previous two years playing straight classical music, touring colleges, and making between $600 and $700 a night. "I wanted to do other things, but I didn't dare tread off the path that Segovia had laid for me."

In 1978, after suffering through a frightening Southern California earthquake, he sold his house and moved his wife, Jackie, and his young daughter Teresa (the first of his three children) to Phoenix.

Two years later, he was driving north on Third Street at McDowell at 1 A.M. with his mother, whom he had just picked up at the airport. A drunk driver going south at 60 miles an hour smashed into the driver's side of Esteban's car, fracturing his ribs, knocking his teeth out and rendering his one good eye resistant to bright light.

He says he spent a month in the hospital, but even as he slowly recuperated, he couldn't regain his ability to play. Nerve damage had left him with no feeling in his fingertips.

With a wife and two young daughters, and no way of supporting them, he applied for a variety of jobs.

"Nobody would hire me," he says. "I was this long-haired hippie-looking guy, although I never did drugs. So I tried to cut my hair short.

"I went into sales to make money. I sold energy-management systems, I sold solar systems for Reynolds Aluminum, and I was very successful at it. I ended up running a franchise dealership for Reynolds Aluminum. I did pretty well, but I was so unhappy. I felt like I was going to explode inside, so I put everything into business."

He says that in 1988, a combination of acupuncture and Chinese herbs brought back the feeling in his fingers. By the end of 1989, he'd started playing a few gigs. But his approach was different than it had been a decade earlier.

"After that car crash, an enlightening thing happened," he says. "I said, 'I don't give a damn about precedent. I'm going to play music for anybody that I want to and I'll play any kind of music that I love.' And since I love all these kinds of music, that's what I do: I play everything from love songs to bossa nova, jazz, world music, classical music, flamenco, and I mix it all up."

He began playing at the Hyatt Regency at Gainey Ranch. Initially, he'd play Sunday brunches for three people and a bunch of empty chairs. But, even early on, if there was a convention happening, he'd draw a huge crowd, and the reaction was usually enthusiastic.

He started playing five nights a week, five hours a night. In 1991, he released the first of his nine CDs. In 1992, he added keyboardist Robert Brock to the mix. It was his first step in putting together a band, which now also includes drums, bass and trumpet.

Brock, whom Esteban described in a 1995 concert video as "my best friend in the music world," had played in a series of Top 40 bands and gotten burned out on the local bar scene. But playing with Esteban rekindled his enthusiasm for music.

"His gig at the Hyatt was a totally different vibe," the 30-year-old Brock says. "It was awesome. As far as a musician having a steady gig in town, there was absolutely no better gig to have."

As audience response became more boisterous, the Hyatt began to promote him. They sold his CDs in their gift shops and paid for full-color ads in trade magazines.

On the rare occasions when Esteban performed at concert venues, he found that about half of his audience would buy his CDs, an unheard of figure in the music business.

"Locally, he's always had a good following, but you always wondered whether he could take this to a much bigger level," Brock says. "And one thing I've always known about him is that when you see him live it's a very different experience from what you hear on the records.

"It's very difficult to capture that whole vibe and persona that he has. I've always known that when people see him, they immediately fall in love with him."

Last year, Esteban's name came to the attention of Joy Mangano, a popular QVC fixture who'd invented household accessories like the Miracle Mop and the Rolykit closet organizers. A fan of Esteban's kept telling her that the guitarist was ripe for stardom and would be an ideal addition to her company, Ingenious Designs LLC. Mangano wasn't interested in working with a musician, but after she heard one of his CDs, she was intrigued enough to fly from New York to Atlanta to see Esteban play at the Hyatt.

"Everybody I watched, everybody who came into the hotel stopped and sat down," says the 44-year-old Mangano. "He was just so captivating. It was really mind-boggling to think that 10 fingers could do that. I instantly knew that if you could get it across on TV, he'd be hugely successful."

Convincing the executives at QVC was a bigger hurdle. No one at the network believed that an unknown musician could be successful with home shoppers.

So Mangano organized an Esteban concert in one of the network's West Chester, Pennsylvania studios. She invited QVC execs, but didn't tell them what they were going to be hearing. She says they immediately sensed the same power that had captivated her in Atlanta.

"His appeal is what made Elvis Elvis," she says. "There's a star quality, a charisma. Included with the talent, there's a picture that goes with it. It's the ability to take an audience and truly mesmerize them."

Weeks after his history-making November appearance on QVC, Home Shopping Network bought Mangano's company, including Esteban. So, after the six-month non-compete period that was in his QVC contract, he made his debut at HSN on June 29. The network packaged together his two most recent albums, *Heart of Gold* and *All My Love*, as a $24.50 special discount deal.

The prospect of playing with cameras whirring and TV hosts bopping to the wrong beat would be unsettling for many musicians, but Esteban's years of experience at the Hyatt pay off mightily on HSN. He comes across as relaxed yet enthused, and his band—which recently added former Tower of Power trumpet player Jesse McGuire—is a solid, efficient unit.

On June 29, the group romped through slightly shortened versions of Esteban staples like "Malagueña" and "Don't Cry for Me Argentina," sat for interviews with a chirpy female host and took gushing calls from devoted fans. In two sets of appearances on the network, Esteban sold an estimated 132,000 CDs.

He says he sells his CDs to Mangano's company for "a couple of dollars each," she sells them to HSN for about two dollars' profit, and they sell them to home shoppers for $10-$12 a pop. It's not a perfect setup, but it's still a better percentage deal than most artists have with major labels, and it's provided Esteban with several hundred thousand dollars in the last year alone.

"It's not that I haven't sold a lot of CDs before this, because I have," he says, adding that his record label has moved a million units domestically over the last nine years. "But I've never been on TV. This is the thing I've always dreamed about, to find a way to sell my product, to get my music out there so people can buy it easily."

Esteban likes to say that there's no precedent for the kind of music he's making, that it's a revolutionary ethnic fusion of styles.

But if Esteban's musical approach owes a debt to anyone, it's not Segovia, or some modern world-beat artist. It's Liberace, the patron saint of Vegas kitsch.

Liberace, like Esteban, was a classically trained musician who realized there was more money to be made doing frilly, pseudo-classical versions of lightweight pop songs than attempting to compete with serious concert pianists.

While Esteban convincingly argues that he started playing pop music because he genuinely liked it, some of his detractors suggest that practicality played a part in the move. They doubt that he would have ever been able to make a mark on the classical world.

"One has to realize the playing field," Bart says. "There are 12-year-old kids who are virtuosos compared to Esteban. At best, he's a remedial classical guitarist."

Liberace's bejeweled costumes and trademark candelabras may have made him a joke to serious music aficionados, but his power was with the silent majority, which didn't care about musical authenticity, but simply wanted to be entertained.

This same crowd gasps at Esteban's every glissando.

"I can't tell you how many times people have come up and said, 'I've never even listened to music, but I really find that I can listen to this all the time,'" Brock says.

One of those fans, a woman from Pennsylvania, called into QVC last November during Esteban's showcase. She asked the host: "Is that the most exciting and sexy music you've ever heard?" The woman said she'd seen him for the first time in Scottsdale, and was so impressed that the following year she rerouted a vacation so she could see him perform again.

The Esteban experience was a bit less exhilarating for Devon Bridgewater, a jazz musician who played violin and trumpet for Esteban for four and a half years, until he was fired by the guitarist.

"It was one of the most embarrassing situations I was ever in as a musician," Bridgewater says. "Because other musicians would walk into the lobby after working in different parts of the hotel, and they'd just look at me and shake their heads, like, 'How can you be doing that, man?'"

He says when Esteban went through a 1996 divorce, he asked Bridgewater a few questions about his own divorce, but aside from that, Esteban never opened up to him.

"I never went to his house, I never knew where he lived," Bridgewater says. "And we never rehearsed. When we went in for a recording session, I never got to hear any of the playbacks, and I was never invited to any of the mixdown sessions. When I heard it, it was already packaged, and there were a lot of things I thought I could have done better."

As for Esteban's musicianship, Bridgewater acknowledges that the guitarist "has got a good right hand," but says he's limited in his ability to improvise with his previously injured left hand, and as a result, the musical arrangements tend to be mind-numbingly repetitive.

Bridgewater also found Esteban's song introductions to be rife with questionable anecdotes.

"He'd say, 'This song was found in an archaeological dig in Egypt in the '20s and we found it and have written it out.' And it was just some kind of minor scale. I mean, there's no notation from Egypt. He'd tell people some song was found on a piece of papyrus in the temple of the gods. I don't know how people bought into it."

Bridgewater says in 1998, Esteban contacted him on his pager and fired him, with no warning. He offered the standard "creative differences" rationale, but Bridgewater had a hard time believing it.

"He said, 'I'm taking the band in a different direction,'" Bridgewater says. "But, after that, it was just the same old 30-minute versions of 'Don't Cry for Me Argentina.'"

Esteban is a major record label's dream. He's a hard-working artist with a built-in following that isn't dependent on radio airplay or positive reviews.

He says he's currently being courted by Warner Bros., Sony, Atlantic and Universal, among others. He can't decide whether he wants to sign with a major label, but he knows one thing for sure: He's tired of dealing with business issues.

"I want to play, bro," he says. "I just want to play and write. I don't want to have anything else going on. Because life is so complicated, if you take on other things, it gets hard to focus."

For someone so comfortable with the hard-sell hustle of home-shopping television, he gets remarkably cosmic when he talks about his music.

"This is really a quiet voice in a world of noise and confusion," he says of his sound. "So it's something that's appropriate for the times. We're so bombarded by outside influences and by nonpeaceful entities, that it's really nice to have peace. And that's what it brings people. And that's what's gratifying.

"The world is kind of like a penal colony at times. And one of the things that helps is beautiful music that people can relate to and think of good times in their lives."

He talks about keeping up with musical tastes—he says he's even written a hip-hop tune—but one of his most endearing traits is actually his lack of understanding of contemporary music. When he talks about how he's started to get into "New Wave," you wonder if he's aware that the term hasn't been in vogue for two decades.

As he reclines in his study and soaks in his Mozart, Esteban ponders for a moment, and recalls the last time he played for Segovia.

He says Segovia listened, then pointed at him and said, "You will play for countless millions of people."

Thinking about the recent splash he made in *Billboard*, Esteban says, "We were beating Def Leppard and all these rock bands. And I'm just a classical guitar player, turned eclectic. So Segovia's prophecy is turning out right."

CHARLES C. MANN

The Heavenly Jukebox

Part 3: They're Paying Our Song

Every year Austin, Texas, hosts South by Southwest, the nation's biggest showcase for independent rock-and-roll. Hundreds of bands play in the city's scores of enjoyably scruffy bars, which are thronged by young people with the slightly dazed expression that is a side effect of shouting over noisy amplifiers. When I attended the festival this spring, I was overwhelmed by the list of bands—almost a thousand in all, most of them little-known hopefuls. I had no idea how to sort through the list for what I would like. Luckily for me, I ran into some professional music critics who allowed me to accompany them, which is how I ended up listening to the Ass Ponys late one night.

Led by a husky singer and guitarist named Chuck Cleaver, the Ponys crunched through a set of songs with whimsical lyrics about robots, astronauts, and rural suicide. At the back of the room, beneath an atmospheric shroud of cigarette smoke, was a card table stacked with copies of their most recent CD, *Some Stupid With a Flare Gun*. By the bar stood a tight clump of people in sleek black clothing with cell phones the size of credit cards. With their Palm hand-helds they were attempting to beam contact information at one another through the occluded air. They didn't look like local students, so I asked the bartender if he knew who they were. "Dot-commers," he said, setting down my beer with unnecessary force.

Silicon Valley had overwhelmed South by Southwest. In a festival usually devoted to small, colorfully named record labels with two-digit bank balances and crudely printed brochures, the slick ranks of the venture-capitalized were a distinct oddity. It was like a visitation from a distant, richer planet.

Music, especially popular music, has been a cultural bellwether since the end of World War II. Swing, bebop, blues, rock, minimalism, funk, rap: each in its own way has shaped cinema, literature, fashion, television, advertising, and, it sometimes seems, everything else one encounters. But the cultural predominance of the music trade is not matched by its financial import. Last year the worldwide sales of all 600 or so members of the Recording Industry Association of America totaled $14.5 billion—a bit less than, say, the annual revenues of Northwestern Mutual Life Insurance. As for the tiny labels at South by Southwest, many of the dot-coms in attendance could have bought them outright for petty cash.

After the show I asked Cleaver if he was concerned about the fate of the music industry in the Internet age. "You must be kidding," he said. With some resignation he recounted the sneaky methods by which three record labels had ripped off the band or consigned its music to oblivion, a subject to which he has devoted several chapters of an unpublished autobiography he offered to send me. (He had nicer things to say about his current label, Checkered Past.) Later I asked one of the music critics if Cleaver's tales of corporate malfeasance were true. More than true, I was told—they were typical. Not only is the total income from music copyright small, but individual musicians receive even less of the total than one would imagine. "It's relatively mild," Cleaver said later, "the screwing by Napster compared with the regular screwing."

Although many musicians resent it when people download their music free, most of them don't lose much money from the practice, because they earn so litt le from copyright. "Clearly, copyright can generate a huge amount of money for those people who write songs that become mass sellers," says Simon Frith, a rock scholar in the film-and-media department at the University of Stirling, in Scotland, and the editor of *Music and Copyright* (1993). But most musicians don't write multimillion-sellers. Last year, according to the survey firm Soundscan, just eighty-eight recordings—only .03 percent of the compact discs on the market—accounted for a quarter of all record sales. For the remaining 99.97 percent, Frith says, "copyright is really just a way of earning less than they would if they received a fee from the record company." Losing copyright would thus have surprisingly little direct financial impact on musicians. Instead, Frith says, the big loser would be the music industry, because today it "is entirely structured around contracts that control intellectual-property rights—control them rather ruthlessly, in fact."

Like book publishers, record labels give artists advances on their sales. And like book publishers, record labels officially lose money on their releases; they make up for the failures with the occasional huge hit and the steady stream of income from back-catalogue recordings. But there the similarity ends. The music industry is strikingly unlike book publishing or, for that matter, any other culture industry. *Some Stupid With a Flare Gun*, for example, contains twelve songs, all written and performed by the Ass Ponys. From this compact disc the band receives, in theory, royalties from three different sources: sales of the disc as a whole, "performance rights" for performances of each of the twelve songs (on radio or MTV, for instance), and "mechanical rights" for copies of each song made on CD, sheet music, and the like. No real equivalent of this system exists in the print world, but it's almost as if the author of a book of short stories received royalties from sales in bookstores, from reading the stories to audiences, and from printing each story in the book itself. The triple-royalty scheme is "extraordinarily, ridiculously complex," says David Nimmer, the author of the standard textbook *Nimmer on Copyright*. Attempts to apply the scheme to the digital realm have only further complicated matters.

As a rule, the royalty on the CD itself—typically about $1.30 per disc before various deductions—goes to performers rather than composers. After paying performers an advance against royalties, as book publishers pay writers, record labels, unlike publishers, routinely deduct the costs of production, marketing, and promotion from the performers' royalties. For important releases these costs may amount to a million dollars or more. Performers rarely see a penny of CD royalties. Unheralded session musicians and orchestra members, who are paid flat fees, often do better in the end.

Paying back the record label is even more difficult than it sounds, because contracts are rife with idiosyncratic legal details that effectively reduce royalty rates. As a result, many, perhaps most, musicians on big record labels accumulate a debt that the labels—unlike book publishers—routinely charge against their next projects, should they prove to be successful. According to Whitney Broussard, the music lawyer, musicians who make a major-label pop-music compact disc typically must sell a million copies to receive a royalty check. "A million units is a platinum record," he says. "A platinum record means you've broken even—maybe." Meanwhile, he adds, "the label would have grossed almost eleven million dollars at this point, netting perhaps four million."

As a standard practice labels demand that musicians surrender the copyright on the compact disc itself. "When you look at the legal line on a CD, it says 'Copyright 1976 Atlantic Records' or 'Copyright 1996 RCA Records,'" the singer Courtney Love explained in a speech to a music convention in May. "When you look at a book, though, it'll say something like 'Copyright 1999 Susan Faludi' or 'David Foster Wallace.' Authors own their books and license them to publishers. When the contract runs out, writers get their books back. But record companies own our copyrights forever."

Strikingly, the companies own the recordings even if the artists have fully compensated the label for production and sales costs. "It's like you pay off the mortgage and the bank still owns the house," says Timothy White, the editor-in-chief of *Billboard*. "Everything is charged against the musician—recording expenses, marketing and promotional costs—and then when it's all paid off, they still own the record." Until last November artists could take back their recordings after thirty-five years. But then, without any hearings, Congress passed a bill with an industry-backed amendment that apparently strips away this right. "It's unconscionable," White says. "It's big companies making a naked grab of intellectual property from small companies and individuals."

The other two kinds of royalties—performance and mechanical rights—go to songwriters and composers. (The Ass Ponys receive these because they write their own songs; Frank Sinatra did not, because he sang mostly jazz standards.) Songwriters receive performance-rights payments when their compositions are played in public—executed in concert, beamed over the radio, sprayed over supermarket shoppers from speakers in the ceiling. Individual payments are calculated through a complex formula that weighs audience size, time of day, and length of the composition. In the United States the money is collected primarily by Broadcast Music Incorporated and the American Society for Composers, Authors, and Publishers, known respectively as BMI and ASCAP. Mechanical rights derive in this country from the Copyright Act of 1909, which reversed earlier court rulings that piano rolls and phonograph recordings were not copies of music. Today the recording industry pays composers 7.55 cents for every track on every copy of every CD, pre-recorded cassette, and vinyl record stamped out by the manufacturing plants. The fee is collected by the Harry Fox Agency, a division of the National Music Publishers' Association, which represents about 23,000 music publishers. In 1998 performance and mechanical rights totaled about $2.5 billion.

Because U.S. labels, publishers, and collecting societies do not break down their cash flow, it is difficult to establish how much of the $2.5 billion American songwriters actually receive. But in an impressively thorough study Ruth Towse, an economist at Erasmus University, in Rotterdam, ascertained that in Britain from 1989 to 1995 the average annual payment to musicians was $112.50. Musicians in Sweden and Denmark made even less. Although the system in the United States is different, the figures, as Towse drily observed, "do not suggest that performers' right considerably improves performers' earnings."

A few composers—the members of Metallica, for instance, who perform their own songs—do extremely well by copyright. But even some of the country's most noted performers and composers are not in this elect group. Among them was Charles Mingus, who wrote and played such now-classic jazz pieces as "Goodbye Pork Pie Hat" and "Better Git It in Your Soul." According to Sue Mingus, his widow and legatee, "Charles used to joke that he wouldn't have recognized a royalty check if it walked in the door." She meant royalties on record sales; Mingus did receive checks for performance and mechanical rights. But when I asked what Mingus's life would have been like without copyright, she said, "It would have been harder. He took copyright very seriously. But what kept him going financially was that he toured constantly." Few rock performers have this alternative: their equipment is so bulky and expensive that their shows can lose money even if every seat is sold.

Musicians, who are owed many small checks from diverse sources, cannot readily collect their royalty payments themselves. Similarly, it would be difficult for radio stations to seek out and pay every label and publisher whose music they broadcast. In consequence, there are powerful incentives to concentrate the task into a small number of hands. Further driving consolidation is the cost of marketing and advertising. Promotion is expensive for book publishers and movie studios, too, but they aren't trying to place their wares on the shrinking playlists of radio-station chains and MTV. Because singles effectively no longer exist, playlists are not based on their sales; songs on the radio function chiefly as promotional samples for CDs. Instead playlists are based on criteria that people in the trade find difficult to explain to outsiders, but that include the expenditure of large sums for what is carefully called "independent promotion"—a system, as Courtney Love explained, "where the record companies use middlemen so they can pretend not to know that radio stations . . . are getting paid to play their records." Although Love didn't use the word, the technical term for paying people to play music is *payola*.

Payola wasn't always illegal, and similar schemes still aren't in many industries: consumer-products firms, for example, pay super-markets "slotting allowances" to stock their wares. According to the author and historian Kerry Segrave, one early payola enthusiast was Sir Arthur Sullivan, who in 1875 paid a prominent singer to per-form one of his compositions before music-hall audiences. Until his death Sullivan sent a share of his sheet-music royalties to the singer.

Although the payola market thrived in the vaudeville era, it did not become truly rapacious until the birth of rock-and-roll. Chuck Berry divided the royalties from his hit "Maybelline" with two DJs. Dick Clark, the host of *American Bandstand*, had links to a record company and several music publishers. After a chest-thumping con-gressional investigation, highlighted by appalled evocations of the evils of rock-and-roll, anti-payola legislation was passed in 1960. The labels outsourced the practice to "independent promoters," a loose network of volatile individuals with big bodyguards and spe-cial relationships with radio stations. Millions of dollars went for payola—much of it recouped from artists' royalties. A second wave of investigations, in the 1980s, did not end the practice.

At present the music industry is dominated by what are called the five majors: Warner, Sony, EMI, BMG, and Universal. (Warner and EMI have announced plans to combine; the joint label will become part of the merged America Online and Time Warner.) The majors control about 85 percent of the market for recorded music in this country. They do this by routinely performing the paradoxical task of discovering and marketing musicians with whom a worldwide body of consumers can form relationships that feel individual and genuine. "You want to fill up stadiums with people who think that Bruce Springsteen, the voice of working-class America, is speaking only to them," says David Sanjek, the archives director at BMI and a co-author, with his late father, of *American Popular Music Business in the 20th Century* (1991). "The labels are often incredibly good at doing this."

Music critics frequently sneer at the practice of manufacturing pop concoctions like Britney Spears and the Backstreet Boys. But in this way the labels helped to create Elvis, the Beatles, and the

Supremes—musicians who embodied entire eras in three-minute tunes. As Moshe Adler, an economist at Columbia University, has argued, even listeners who grumble about the major-label music forced on them are probably better off than if they had to sort through the world's thousands of aspiring musicians on their own. But this benefit to consumers comes at a cost to musicians. Records that are hits around the world inevitably draw listeners' attention from music by local artists that might be equally pleasing. "The money is made by reducing diversity," Adler says.

For better or worse, the star-maker machinery behind the popular song, as Joni Mitchell called it, is the aspect of the music industry that would be most imperiled by the effective loss of copyright to the Net. If the majors can't reap the benefits of their marketing muscle, says Hal Varian, an economist and the dean of the School of Information Management and Systems, at Berkeley, "their current business model won't survive." The impact on their profits could be devastating. Musicians have much less to lose, and much less to fear.

CARLY CARIOLI

Napster Nation

One crisp afternoon last spring, armed with a copy of the *Billboard* charts, I walked a few blocks from work to visit my little sister at Boston University so she could teach me how to use something called Napster, about which I knew very little except that it was supposed to be a tool, in the words of a friend of a friend, to "steal all the music you want for free." At first I dismissed the idea out of hand as being too ludicrously good to be true—all the music in the world, whenever you wanted it, flowing like tap water. There had to be a catch somewhere. But when universities began blocking access to Napster—so many students were using it, and were downloading so much, that they were causing the cyberspace equivalent of a traffic jam—it seemed worth a gander, and so I set out with piracy in my heart.

My sister Tia, as it turns out, is one of the vast numbers of college students who are uniquely equipped to exploit Napster's resources. She has a sturdy late-model PC with a built-in writable CD burner and high-quality outboard speakers, the whole of which set her back just a little over $1000. Her connection to the Web, by virtue of the high-speed lines with which dorm rooms are now equipped, is extremely fast. Like many other college students, she has relatively exotic tastes (faves: Blonde Redhead, Godspeed You Black Emperor, Miles, Eno's weird side, Nick Drake) and plenty of time on her hands. She doesn't have much in the way of disposable income—but with Napster, lack of cash is suddenly no obstacle to accumulating a weighty music library.

By the time I visited Tia, she and her roommate already had about 700 songs stored on her hard drive (the result of a couple of months' worth of late-night Napstering) in the form of MP3s: condensed, bite-sized morsels that provide a reasonable facsimile of CD-quality sound in the form of files small enough to travel quickly over the Web. More than a dozen MP3 players can be found to download from the Web, many of them free—Tia's pops up on her PC screen looking like a digitized car stereo. Or, with a few keystrokes, you can use your MP3 player to decode the MP3 files and burn them onto blank CDs, in which case you have essentially set up your own miniature CD-pressing plant. Tia played me a couple of songs from her hard drive: something new by Yo La Tengo and a Dirty Three song. Then she played me the same two songs, which she'd burned onto a CD, this time through her shelftop stereo: the difference in sound quality was to my ears minimal. There's also software to reverse the process: she can stick the new Belle & Sebastian disc in her computer's CD drive and, using a program called Adaptec, have it converted, or "ripped," into MP3 form—at which point there's nothing to stop her from sharing it with the rest of the planet.

The Napster software, available for download free of charge at www.napster.com, is a fairly simple program that allows you to trade MP3 files with anyone else who is logged on to one of the company's servers. The servers compile a continuously updated database of all the MP3 files on the computers of everyone logged on at any given moment and then provide you myriad ways to navigate that database—you can search by artist or song title or album, as in an on-line record store, or you can browse the libraries of individual users. At any given time, my sister explained, you're connected to between 5000 and 8000 other users, who have a combined library of between a half-million songs (on off-peak hours) and a cool million (during prime time, which for Napster is usually around 1 A.M.).

That day, when we joined the party, there were 5872 different people with combined holdings of 726,823 songs. I took a look through the hip-hop singles chart in *Billboard* and decided to search for "Whistle While You Twurk" by a group called the Yin Yang Twins. The Napster console—which looks and operates not unlike your Web browser—told me that four people had the song, that all four song files had the same "bit rate" (an indication of sound quality, with higher rates meaning better sound), and that each file would take up 4.2 megabytes of disc space. Three of the four versions were four minutes and 35 seconds long, but the last version was a few seconds shorter; of the three full-length versions, one resided on the computer that had a very slow connection to the Web. Of the remaining two versions, I picked the one with the lowest score in a column marked "Ping," a kind of Internet radar that bounces a signal off the user's computer to measure response time.

So I clicked on the low-ping version of "Whistle" and—voilà!—in less than a minute it was ensconced on Tia's hard drive. (On a good day, with the right connection, she can download a five-minute song in 40 seconds.) The means by which this transfer occurs has become the focus of much litigation recently. The song never actually resides on the Napster server: my computer contacts this other person's computer and the song goes straight from him or her to me—or from me to him or her. While we were downloading "Whistle While You Twurk," other users had begun to download songs from my sister's computer—as soon as you connect to one of Napster's servers, the list of MP3s on your hard drive (or at least in a file you set aside for people to copy from) is added to the master list of available songs, and in this way, as people log on and off, the available library shifts and heaves and breathes. Soon, Tia's console showed eight users copying tunes from her hard drive—rare Nick Drake, live Radiohead, Red House Painters, Pizzicato 5. Someone with a slow connection was trying to download an obscure Brian Eno track—with your standard 56k phone-line connection, it can take up to half an hour to download a single song—and with a click of the mouse, we booted him out of our library. Even in Napster's free world, hierarchies are unavoidable.

By now I could smell blood. I wanted to hit the ol' record industry right in the gonads—if you're gonna steal big, steal the family jewels—so I headed straight for the *Billboard* Hot 100 singles chart: Britney, Christina, Destiny's Child, the Backstreet Boys, 'N Sync. The Top 40 was available almost in its entirety—in fact, if a song's on the radio (say, Sisqó's "Thong Song"), chances are there'll be a dozen or more copies of it available at any hour, day or night, along with remixes, edits, answer songs (Strings' "Tongue Song") and parodies ("Bong Song"). *Billboard*'s country, rap, and R&B specialty charts fare slightly less well than mainstream pop and modern rock—most of the Top 40 rap and country singles can be found in abundance, but you also tend to encounter fewer high-speed DSL and T1 connections. I grabbed tunes by George Strait and DMX, Cledus T. Judd and Juvenile and the Bloodhound Gang. My sister's roommate told me about a song one of their floormates had discovered called "Fuck You in the Ass" by the Outthere Brothers, a low-budget Miami club-pop duo, and in under two minutes we'd located and downloaded it and were guffawing along with its bootacular whimsy. The sheer mass of three-quarters of a million songs sprawled in front of me, the echo of a great howling congregation swept up in an orgy of acquisition, and in the swirl of digital commotion—uploads/downloads, matches made, connections brokered—I had the sudden image of the floor of the New York Stock Exchange, its harried and panicked roar, as if everyone could suddenly own everything without spending a dime.

Metallica's Lars Ulrich has likened Napster users to shoplifters, and that's exactly what it felt like—it was akin to breaking into a record store. Or like eBay without money changing hands. There was an illicit thrill about it, as if a gate had been unlocked, as if an iron curtain had fallen. I giggled: "Elvis and Cartman singing 'In the Ghetto'!" I sniggered: "They've got Mr. Bungle covering Britney Spears!" I cackled: "When did Nick Cave do 'I Put a Spell on You'?" I gasped: "Look look look—Danzig singing Misfits songs with Metallica!" The next thing I knew it was five hours later and my sister's hard drive had expanded its library by about 50 songs. I could've continued all night—I hadn't even scratched the surface, and I still haven't.

For casual fans or hardcore record fetishists (who savor such things as packaging and serial numbers and first pressings), Napster might—as has been suggested by the company's lawyers—serve as a consumer resource, a way to sample before buying. But for music junkies like me, it's is nothing short of compulsion-inducing, at least at first. My sister recalled her first encounter with Napster in much the same way that several other friends subsequently described their own introductions: a period ranging from several days to several weeks spent obsessively grabbing as much as they could, hour after hour late into the night and early morning, following tangents from artist to artist, song to song.

A brief and subjective glimpse: Black Flag's "Six Pack." Kate Smith's "God Bless America" (the version generally credited with winning the Philadelphia Flyers several Stanley Cups). G.G. Allin. Django Reinhardt. The Descendents' entire *Milo Goes to College* album. Art Pepper & Chet Baker. Seventies Canadian punk obscurities the Monks ("Drugs in My Pocket," "Nice Face, Shame About the Legs"); Thelonious Monk; plainchanting monks. Songs called "Night Train" by Wes Montgomery & Jimmy Smith, the Ventures, Oscar Peterson, James Brown, Guns N' Roses, the Bill Black Combo, Boots Randolph, and Bruce Cockburn. Vivaldi compositions performed by Yo-Yo Ma (with Bobby McFerrin), Wynton Marsalis, Mike Oldfield, and an anonymous techno producer. A Rolling Stones unreleased Decca live album from 1972. Freestyles from the Wu-Tang Clan. Forty or 50 Anal Cunt songs. Eighties thrash kings Nuclear Assault covering Venom. A bootleg of the Beatles practicing "Maxwell's Silver Hammer." Bob Dylan's "Talkin' Bear Mountain Picnic Massacre Blues." Elvis stoned out of his gourd and forgetting the words to "Are You Lonesome Tonight?" Prince and Miles Davis doing "Let's Go Crazy" at Paisley Park.

Everyone, it seems, has two favorite Napster stories. The first is about that initial, mad rush of discovery, like homesteaders staking out their 160 acres. The second story is about some unbelievable obscurity he or she has downloaded—a white-label Slint live album, or Lowell George on the radio with Linda Ronstadt in 1975. And the overall lure of Napster is something between these two, between the overarching, all-encompassing nature of its enterprise (it's got everything), and the personal specificity of singular buried artifacts (it's got *my* thing). I know I have at my fingertips access to today's Top 40 (and tomorrow's: as Madonna and Metallica have found out, upcoming singles have a way of making their way onto Napster's lists before their official release). But I also have a mental checklist I run through every time I log on of bands who *might* show up (and occasionally do!) against the prevailing odds of their making an appearance on a platform as mass-culture-friendly as Napster: Teengenerate, Son House, Backyard Babies, John Zorn.

If pop culture is fragmenting into ever-smaller sub-audiences, Napster seems to be an agent for navigating pop music in an age where consensus is but a memory. You could read Napster as a direct result of that fragmentation: if its runaway popularity says anything about consumer desire, it's that the traditional means that fans rely on to evaluate and keep in touch with the pop market— radio, MTV, magazines, record stores—are failing them. It seems obvious to me that the transactions made using Napster constitute a violation of at least the spirit of the copyright laws—if they didn't, we wouldn't be here. But the major record labels have done such an exquisite job of squeezing profits out of consumers and artists alike that it's hard not to think of this as payback time.

Although Napster is unlikely to displace the industry, it does offer a tantalizing glimpse of what ordinary people might choose to listen to if the industry and its conventions didn't exist. It begins to smooth out the differences in accessibility between such market-imposed distinctions as rare and abundant—Captain Beefheart out-takes and import B-sides are as accessible as the new 'N Sync album, regardless of how many people want to hear them. The prohibitive costs of manufacture, distribution, and promotion no longer apply, since the only requirement for distributing music via Napster is that a single person own a recording and be willing to share it.

Last Thursday it appeared that the RIAA had finally rung Nap-ster's bell, and a court injunction was in place to take the service off-line. With a mere 27 hours to go, Napster's servers were packed, and it took me a half-dozen attempts to log on. There were 7000 users, 800,000 songs. I typed in searches, frantic: Hellacopters, Gluecifer, Backyard Babies. Results, bingo: the Backyard Babies

covering Social Distortion's "Mommy's Little Monster"—go, get it.
More: John Williams conducting the Boston Pops in the *Battlestar
Galactica* theme. Metallica's "Jump in the Fire" live from 1983, with
Dave Mustaine on lead vocals; Rob Zombie interviewing Glenn
Danzig. I did a search for Sonic Youth and found them backing
David Bowie on a version of his "I'm Afraid of Americans"; SY's col-
laboration with William Burroughs; Pavement doing "Expressway
to Yr Skull"; versions of "The Diamond Sea" ranging in length
from 3:52 to 11:01; SY's cover of the obscure Nirvana B-side "Moist
Vagina"; a live version of "Schizophrenia" recorded in July of 1995.

When I logged off, there was a message on my telephone-answer-
ing machine from a friend of mine. She'd recognized my screen
name on her upload console. "You're totally downloading Backyard
Babies songs from me!" she gushed. It's easy to dismiss the notion
that a real community is emerging on the byways of Napster amid
the hustle, but this chance encounter, like bumping into an old
acquaintance in a crowded subway, seemed to confirm that a community is being built, perhaps even in spite of the software's original
purpose. For cheap thrills, you can comb through lists of users and
rummage through their libraries, looking for their guilty pleasures,
reminding yourself that people's tastes bloom irrespective of the
confines of genre and focus groups. The gospel fanatic with Rev-
erend James Cleveland songs out the wazoo who also has Beck's
"Sexx Laws." The jazzhead teeming with Ornette Coleman, Arto
Lindsay, Dexter Gordon—and Juliana Hatfield. The black-metal
fiend with the Christina Aguilera house remix. Voyeurism reigns:
you can listen to Courtney Love ranting on a journalist's answering
machine, or Fred Durst chewing out the band Taproot for signing
with another label after he'd courted them.

In just a few months, Napster has even begun to foster its own
idioms. A genre has emerged on its byways in which two different
artists' hits are spliced against each other—for instance, Metallica's
Anti-Nowhere League cover "So What?" answering Britney
Spears's "Crazy"—in a manner that, however frivolous, makes Neg-
ativland's infamous U2-sampling culture-jamming stunt appear
tame by comparison. Scads of novelty numbers and song parodies

are being produced on low budgets by artists who suddenly have a huge audience just a few keystrokes away. There are some two dozen parodies in which Bill Clinton impersonators are heard to sing pop hits—"Gettin' Sticky with It," "Mo' Booty, Mo' Problems." And that's not the only politics to be found—there's Winston Churchill's "finest hour" speech, Martin Luther King's "I have a dream" speech, Marilyn Monroe singing happy birthday to JFK, Jello Biafra lecturing on the subject of Mumia Abu Jamal. That, to this particular pirate, is the most astonishing revelation to be found in Napster's cyberspace: the spectacle of free music evolving into a new paradigm of free speech.

LORI ROBERTSON

Golden Oldies

The hip and trendy Joe's Pub at the Public Theater is a pricey bar in New York's East Village that glows a soft red—a candlelit, cabaret-style space that hosts artsy bands and martini-drinking patrons. Robert Christgau, pop music critic for the *Village Voice*, glances around the tables, wondering aloud how many people there aren't critics or friends of the band.

He had told me he wasn't that keen on the night's act, The Lullaby Baxter Trio, before we walked a few blocks from his Village apartment to the "tony"—as he aptly puts it—Joe's Pub. But he wanted to check it out. The relatively new band, named for its female singer, takes the stage and proceeds to wander from jazzy to folksy to bossa nova, in between chatty introductions from Lullaby. Christgau taps me on the shoulder.

"Is that a green star on her forehead?" he asks, sounding struck by the peculiarity of the shiny gem above the singer's eyebrows.

"I'm not sure if it's green or blue," I answer.

Christgau scribbles notes on a piece of paper, possibly for something he'll write, possibly not. I'm sure he's seen more oddly placed body jewelry than most people his age. The 58-year-old first wrote about pop music for *Esquire* in 1967, penned his first *Voice* music column two years later, spent two-and-a-half years at *Newsday* and has been with the *Voice* since '74, as music editor for two years and then as a critic and editor.

There are a handful of writers, like Christgau, who started writing about music near the birth of rock criticism in the mid 1960s—and are still going strong. (Influential pioneer *Rolling Stone* broke onto the scene in 1967, and rock criticism has flourished ever since.) More writers who are in their 40s started their gigs in the '70s. And they've stuck with the odd task of covering an inherently young subject matter as they become more and more removed from the target generation. As the *New York Times'* Jon Pareles puts it: "Rock criticism is the only job where people would question . . . if you learned to do your job better as you did it longer."

Sure, music critics get thousands of free CDs each year, free passes to just about any show they'd like to see and interviews with cool rock stars. But it's also the world of late nights, smoke-filled clubs, loud music and periodic waves of teen pop, à la 'N Sync and Britney Spears—and the sex, drugs and rebellion attitude every post-'60s generation has in its teens and twenties, but usually leaves behind to "those kids" growing up behind it. And it's "those kids" whom record companies and music artists often target.

The fact that most pop music critics, particularly those who write for newspapers, are baby boomers and up does prompt speculation. How do they do it? And why? Can aging critics continue to understand and relate to music meant for people decades younger? And, conversely, are there young critics out there who are able to bring the needed perspective to their writing that living through history lends? Does age matter?

In the case of the *Washington Post's* Richard Harrington, the courts may give an answer. The 53-year-old was taken off the full-time music beat after 20 years in the position. He's now suing the paper for age discrimination, though the *Post* has said that wasn't the reason it switched critics. Harrington's suit asks for the return of his job—one he wasn't ready to leave. The reason he and other critics are often the oldest people they know listening to rapper Kid Rock, they say, is a love of music.

"This is what I know, and I can write about it well," Christgau says. "I still have a lot of fun doing my job."

Chuck Eddy, the *Voice*'s 39-year-old music editor, also present for the Lullaby Baxter show, adds some admiration later that night. "One of the cool things about somebody like Bob [Christgau is that] he totally keeps up on what people half his age, a third his age maybe, listen to," he says. "It's great."

Los Angeles Times pop music critic Robert Hilburn, 60, started writing about the subject for the paper as a freelancer in 1968 and came on full time in 1970. "Every 10 years I probably say, 'I'm not going to be doing this another 10 years,'" he says. But it's the freedom and range of music he can write about that keeps him around, and the excitement of hearing a terrific new act. "Every time that greatness happens, you say, 'Wow, I can't wait to write about that person.'"

Jane Scott, at Cleveland's *Plain Dealer*, first wrote about rock 'n' roll when the Beatles came to town in '64. At 81, she's still a rock writer with the paper. "I just feel that it's exciting, and it's fun, and I love to go to concerts, and I love to talk to people. . . . And besides, I don't have to pay for my ticket," she says.

"Some journalists write about stuff they're not interested in," says Pareles, 46, who first got paid for his music criticism in 1975 and has been writing for the *Times* since '82. "I don't think rock critics do that. . . . It's not like we do it for the status. . . . We do it because we love the music."

He continues, "Rock 'n' roll is an endless extension of high school, but at this point of my career, I'm not that susceptible to peer pressure."

Of course the pressure is coming from a different generation, one that's singing and listening to music that speaks of its needs and desires, depression and angst—in its own language. Music is often meant for the young. "Popular culture is created to annoy your parents," says *Rolling Stone* contributing editor Touré, 29.

There's supposed to be a generation gap.

That gap, the sheer chronological chasm between older critics and new music, creates difficulties in coverage, some say—difficulties that can't easily be overcome.

Robert B. Ray, director of film studies at the University of Florida and a singer and guitarist in the rock band The Vulgar Boatmen, talks of "overcomprehension" among older critics. It's a tendency to go overboard in praising acts that the critic doesn't understand and fears may be the next big thing. Young acts "that critics think are hip" get the hype treatment, Ray says, along with older artists, such as Lou Reed, who are eternally glorified. As in other types of criticism, the acts that have made it into greatness generally don't fall too far from the pedestal when any of their subsequent works are evaluated.

Ray, 57, has devoted a chapter of an upcoming book on rock and the press to the idea of overcomprehension, a term he borrows from the surrealist painter Max Ernst. He pegs its beginnings to the Impressionist movement. Art and culture critics of that time, he says, didn't like Impressionist paintings because they just didn't get the concept. They couldn't understand art not of their generation, Ray says, and they admitted as much. Critics who vilified one of Impressionism's greatest painters, Edouard Manet, realized shortly before his death that they were wrong. "Critics will live in fear of that from now on," Ray says.

He writes in an essay: "In many ways, 'overcomprehension' has become the ruling mode of rock criticism, as critics eager not to repeat the mistake of those who denounced Elvis and Little Richard (with his nonsense like 'Tutti Frutti'), praise everything, because anything—2 Live Crew, Bikini Kill, Mudhoney, Fiona Apple— might be the next Elvis or the Sex Pistols."

Some critics interviewed for this story agree there is too much praise in criticism today. But, they add, it's not as if there aren't any negative reviews—the scathing pans that readers love. Nevertheless, Pareles says Ray has a point. "Sometimes if you're not sure of something, you have to hit a deadline, it's possible you'll overpraise it," he says. Pareles may listen to an album 10 times, laud it, then listen to it a year later and wonder, " 'What was I thinking?' " he says.

"Making really stupid mistakes in public and not being able to take them back" is part of the job. But he doesn't see people biting their tongues and then saying they like something they don't.

Personally, Pareles says he's confident enough "to think when I don't like something it's not because I don't understand it."

But Ray would argue Pareles isn't even supposed to get it. Many bands, he stresses, are for youth only. "Bands like Rage Against the Machine are not meant for people in their 40s," he says. And, he adds, aging critics find it increasingly difficult to relate to new music, a condition Ray calls critical senility.

But isn't it possible that some 40-year-olds can enjoy music 20-year-olds do? Can't some comprehend what Korn's heavy rock-rap means, as well as Bob Dylan's poetics? No, says Ray. "If they're doing it, they're faking it."

Those who say aging adds real struggle to a rock critic's job are often those who felt they had to bail out on the beat. James Miller quit as *Newsweek*'s rock critic in 1990, "in part because I no longer felt able to feign enthusiasm," he says in his 1999 book, *Flowers in the Dustbin*. Now a professor of political science and director of liberal studies at New York City's New School, he began covering music in the '60s. Two decades later, he no longer had an interest in much of the music of the time. Part of his dissatisfaction was a feeling that music had become more about marketing. But also, Miller says, he and his wife started having children, and "I no longer felt like hanging out in clubs. . . . Frankly, I didn't feel young at heart." And he grew "tired" of bands like the Rolling Stones that would pretend to be young at heart.

A more harsh criticism: Growing old with the beat, says Miller, 53, can be intellectually stifling. He says he finds it "extraordinary" that Christgau, "a guy of great intelligence in his mid-50s . . . sits around once a month and grades records. . . . I find it just a deep puzzle."

Christgau calls that comment "a function of [Miller's] spiritual limitations." He adds of the music beat: "I don't think it's beneath me. Jim thinks it's beneath him."

Many critics take issue with Miller's book, equating his ideas with those of a baby boomer who thinks nothing great has happened in music since 1969. Jim DeRogatis, pop music critic at the *Chicago Sun-Times*, ends a review of the book with, "Geez, gramps: Didya ever once consider that you got too old and the music got too loud?"

DeRogatis, 35, is certainly not short of words on rock critics who just don't get it. In an August 1999 column for Ironminds.com, a college-oriented site that hosts writings and essays, he wrote that "the number of no-longer-give-a-shit critics nearly matches the number of geezer rockers riding the nostalgia train on the summershed circuit."

But in an interview, DeRogatis says it's not as much a product of chronological age. "It's a, 'Do you still care about the beat?' . . . and, 'Have you been seduced by the industry?'" he says. He sees plenty of young critics "who are already too old," because they're into the hanging-out-with-the-stars aspect of the business.

The critics who don't care anymore don't give the music the coverage it warrants, says DeRogatis, a music critic for 10 years, six of them with the *Sun-Times*. He tells the story of Woodstock '94, the 25th anniversary of the first peace-love-and-musicfest: A group of aging critics spent the majority of the time in the press tent, watching the concert on television, he says. Outside in the mud and overflowing port-a-potties, "it was Calcutta." The *Village Voice*'s Christgau, DeRogatis says, "slept on the ground in a poncho . . . at the ripe old age of 55."

Christgau says he considered staying at a relative's house nearby, but it quickly became apparent that wouldn't work. He shared a tent with a reporter from Florida. "It was great," he says, "obviously the best way to cover it." But he didn't get much sleep.

Being a part of what's happening in young music, a part of the hot and sweaty crowds, the fevered clubs, can add an intimate aspect to writing. It's writing from the experience. But that kind of youthful stamina often takes a hit as the years go by. While twentysomethings may dance til 5 A.M. at a rave, you won't find the likes of

Anthony DeCurtis there. DeCurtis, contributing editor at *Rolling Stone* and a music critic since 1978, says that type of participation isn't necessary. You write from what you know.

DeCurtis recalls a panel discussion featuring older critics at the South by Southwest Music Conference, a huge annual showcase of music acts held in Austin. At the March 1993 event, a young woman in the audience questioned the critics' authority, asking if they weren't too old to cover rock 'n' roll. The panelists reacted defensively to the notion that they needed to listen to music through the ears of a teenager to get it.

DeCurtis says the idea is ridiculous. "My response would have been, 'When's the last time you saw Jimi Hendrix?'" he says. "You have your experience. . . . Write out of that perspective."

The music each person listened to from about age 14 to 25 has the most staying power. It's the time most of us were listening to and buying a lot of music and, for some, watching MTV. The Violent Femmes are going to mean something different to a 30-year-old than they will to a 45-year-old. As will Hendrix, the Rolling Stones, the Sex Pistols, Nirvana. The different perspectives inform the writing.

But many say that with a good writer's work, you can't tell the author's age. Plus, as DeCurtis says, some young critics can write with a maturity and rigor you'd associate with age, while some older critics may be "just as quick to shoot from the hip as when they were 19."

Most others dismiss Ray's notion that you have to be 19 to understand what the latest hip-hop or alternative rock artist is about. It's a matter of maintaining openmindedness, says the *L.A. Times'* Hilburn. The really good music doesn't just speak to youth, he says, it speaks to all. The best music "transcends" generations, he says.

The *Plain Dealer's* Scott says she likes covering older acts, but prefers checking out new bands—she mentions Scottish alt-rock band Travis, for one. "I love going to something new that people don't know about," says Scott, who also attended Woodstock '94 and "slept in the mud once."

Rolling Stone music editor Joe Levy says the too-old-to-rock idea is ridiculous. "The theory that rock 'n' roll should only be made, listened to and written about by young people is a specious one," says Levy, who adds that older critics such as Christgau and Hilburn are doing "excellent, excellent work."

Those who get out of the field do it more because they're just plain tired, he adds. "It's the grind that wears you down," Levy says, "not the fact that the music is hard to be in touch with, or it's meant for someone younger."

Richard Harrington began writing music criticism in 1969 for the *Washington Free Press*, an alternative journal in Washington, D.C. He became the *Post's* first and only pop critic in 1980 and, up until January, he covered the beat full time. That's when Arts Editor John Pancake replaced Harrington with a 36-year-old *Post* legal writer, David Segal, who once played in a rock band. Harrington was demoted to a part-time job writing reviews, mostly for the Weekend section, and took a pay cut.

The move is not popular with many music critics, who praise Harrington's work and/or question how a reporter who has never covered music could be a better choice. The anyone-can-be-a-rock-critic attitude doesn't sit well with seasoned critics. (Segal declined a request for an interview.)

When Harrington's easing out was announced in March 1999, *Post* staffers and area musicians responded with petitions calling for his reinstatement. Harrington said at the time he was told that he "didn't do enough trend stories and wasn't doing enough coverage of the hot new young bands." He wouldn't comment on the idea he was deemed too old then, but, in March of this year, he filed a suit charging that the *Post* demoted him simply because of age.

His attorney, Michael Kane, says the idea that papers need a young person to cover young music is prevalent. "I think Richard was just a victim of that," he adds. He says the demotion was made "not for quality, but for appearance."

Pancake disputes that notion. "The issue was the coverage and not his age," Pancake said in an interview in February, before Harrington filed his suit. He declined to elaborate. Segal was chosen because he is a skillful writer with a breadth of knowledge, important characteristics, Pancake says, for newspaper writers who have to address both the general public and the aficionado. "I must've read the clips of 50 to 60 people, a lot of them bad," says Pancake. "The people we came up with for finalists . . . most of them had some expertise outside of pop music."

In a recent conversation with *AJR*, Harrington said it hasn't been difficult to grow older and write about music, particularly because his coverage runs the gamut, from blues to folk to hip-hop. "It's a perpetually fascinating field," he says. "And I love doing it. . . . That's the thing that makes it easy."

Pareles calls Harrington "one of the best." As for the lawsuit, he adds, "I hope I get called as an expert witness." He, like many other critics, finds little evidence of washed-up, way-too-old music writers hanging on to the beat.

Many say the problem of writers who tarry too long at the bandstand takes care of itself: Anyone who doesn't care and isn't into the music doesn't want to stick around. But others question the authenticity of some critics, particularly those who are older. Even critics who have passed the 50 mark and say their enthusiasm for the beat hasn't waned see out-of-touch older writers out there.

"It does get harder," says Dave Tianen, 53, pop music critic for the *Milwaukee Journal Sentinel*. "It becomes more of a stretch because you're more and more distant from that generation." The Milwaukee paper, where Tianen's been on the beat for 12 years, uses two general assignment reporters in their 30s to cover some of the more youthful acts.

"Sometimes when I see middle-age people just raving over, say, Nine Inch Nails," says Tianen, "there's part of me that arches an eyebrow and wonders how genuine that is."

Newsweek's Lorraine Ali, 35, can detect the generational gyrations of an older critic in pieces that show an aloofness. Age, she says, "either manifests itself in A., becoming bitter and discounting anything that came after [older critics'] time. . . . Or B., trying to be down with the kids and sounding really silly."

The most striking example? Older white critics covering hip-hop and electronic music, she says. They often don't understand it, she says, which is fine, "if they just cop to it."

"Hip-hop," says Christgau, "is the great generational divide." Pareles uses the exact same words with me. The comments affirm there are new categories of music that build up a wall between older and younger generations, stuff the parents just don't understand. And both critics say it's a line they've crossed.

Hip-hop is the wave of music that separates older—mostly white—critics who can't relate from those who can. Its roots date back to the '70s, with funk bands like Parliament Funkadelic, and even earlier to the likes of James Brown. Christgau admits it took him years in the late '70s to understand P-Funk. "I just played the fuckers and played them and eventually, I got it," he says. When hip-hop came along, he says, he was ready. "But a lot of critics didn't get it, or got it very late."

Certainly, it's hard to envision a white, 60-year-old newspaper guy grooving to rapper Eminem's album. But Hilburn recently interviewed the artist, whose often violent lyrics have spawned criticism, and gave his record three-and-a-half stars. He does see evidence of some older critics not "adjusting to [hip-hop] fast enough," he says. "They don't respect Eminem as much as they should."

The people who can most respect and understand acts like Eminem are members of the young generation. Consequently, it's easy to assume that they're the ones who should write about the music, and that they're being hired at papers that want to increase coverage of youth-oriented subjects for youthful readers.

Well, no, they're not. In fact, with such a vital older generation of critics, there aren't many desirable spots at newspapers and established magazines for up-and-comers. "The profession is somewhat limited," says *New York Times* pop music critic Ann Powers, 36. The younger generation, the one below Powers, "must feel very daunted," she says. There are more magazines, fanzines, Web sites at which to write; however, "that just makes it harder to distinguish yourself."

Powers started writing music criticism when she was 17, and considers herself lucky to have landed at the *Times*. Other critics point to the fact that it's not easy to break onto the scene, particularly at newspapers, where you just don't find writers in their 20s with a desirable beat like music.

The young perspective, says Ali, is found mostly in fanzines or Webzines and is largely lacking in the mainstream press. "I don't think that voice is really out there enough . . . that younger voice," she says.

The absence has some critics concluding there are fewer aspiring critics and less interest in criticism. "I wish there were young critics I was afraid of. . . . There are damn few," says the *Baltimore Sun*'s J.D. Considine, 43, who joined the paper as music critic in 1986, having first published a music piece in '77. "I've talked to magazine editors, and they've kind of said the same thing. It seems to be on a certain level, there aren't as many people who are interested in the criticism aspect of music." It's more about celebrity, he adds.

Jann S. Wenner, editor, publisher and founder of *Rolling Stone*, wouldn't say there's been a decline in interest in criticism from readers. The record review section, he says, remains one of the most popular sections of the 1.25 million-circulation magazine. And Levy says he's still deluged with clips from young writers.

Rolling Stone is 33 years old and still covering the artists who were around at its founding—as well as the new music of each successive generation. The challenge in staying fresh and youthful, Wenner says, isn't much of one. "Just keep your eyes and ears open," he says. "Stay young at heart."

Wenner, 54, certainly seems to have done just that. A scruffy start of a beard on his face, he talks glowingly of his creation and gives off a what-a-way-to-have-made-it smugness as he twists in his chair in an office that overlooks New York's Avenue of the Americas. Almost every critic interviewed for this article and many of the rest have written for *Rolling Stone*.

Criticism that *Rolling Stone* is sometimes out of touch with new waves of music doesn't make sense to Wenner, who says the magazine's average reader is 27. The audience is spread among young and old alike. The issue of whether older critics can still relate has only become an issue as rock has aged, he says. Back when *Rolling Stone* launched in '67, says Wenner, "the only reason it was being done by younger people then . . . was because the older people didn't know anything about it."

Now, the 40-and-over critics in the country, for the most part, do know what's going on and are encountering an extremely broad range of styles on as many of the 30,000 or so records released each year as they can listen to.

That historical perspective they have is sometimes lacking in younger critics, but most say you write from your own experience. "I think a lot of times younger critics feel they have to use the same reference points as their . . . forefathers," says Ali. It's not that they shouldn't know history, she adds, but "they have different reference points." And, she emphasizes, it's OK to use them.

Rolling Stone's Touré says there are times when youth is an advantage—such as in feature writing. "When I'm the same age or similar age as the artist, then it helps in terms of the language and the vibe you create with somebody . . . to establish trust."

Touré has given some thought to what will happen to that connection as the years pass. "What am I going to do when I'm 34, going to interview some 24-year-old kid about his hot record?" he asks.

While Ali wouldn't say 34 is getting up there in music criticism—she's 35—the recent *Newsweek* hire does say she'll reach a point where she'll outgrow it. She's "trying to build the bridges now into other areas of writing. . . . So when it gets to that point, I don't have to be sad . . . and bitter."

Many pop music critics have questioned whether the beat is respectable enough, grown-up enough, for an intelligent, creative person to pursue for an entire career. Those who are still around have decided, yes. DeCurtis says it's something with which he came to terms when he abandoned his career as an English professor to write about that silly little thing called rock. He recalls some friends from grade school initially getting a kick out of his writing for *Rolling Stone*. But one friend asked if he'd thought about working for a "real" magazine.

Powers talks enthusiastically in a Brooklyn coffee shop near her home about her beat and its significance, about why music is so important to our culture, politics, personal relationships. I barely have to ask a question in the interview. She's given the "is this good enough for a career" issue a lot of thought.

"I always fought against it," she says. "I didn't think it was legitimate." Powers thought she should be a poet. It took her some time to believe pop criticism "could be an art form"—a realization that came after reading Greil Marcus' *Mystery Train*, a book on rock 'n' roll and its contribution to American culture. Unlike Ali and Touré, Powers is confident she's in it for the long haul. It's almost a mission.

It all comes back to a love of the music. That's the reason old dudes really can cover rock—and rap and techno—and add something to our cultural discussion. For critics like Christgau and Hilburn, it's unlikely they'll switch careers. And why should they? What would they know more about than music? But the perspective of youth shouldn't be left out. The one advantage, at least, is that a few more grown-ups are on its side.

"Pop music is at its most intergenerational," says Powers, glad her beat is something that touches our society so broadly and deeply. Music "is the public conversation we share," she says. "We speak to each other through music."

JIM DeROGATIS

Singer Gets an
Eye for Eye

I am not a fan of Third Eye Blind.

"Even by the standards of the decaying grunge genre, the San Francisco quartet is forgettable," I wrote the first time I saw the group perform at the Riviera Theatre in 1998.

"Early on, singer Stephan [CQ] Jenkins made great show of taking off his shoes and socks. From time to time, he sat down in a big red leather chair near the drum riser. As unexciting as these acts were, they offered welcome respite from his non-stop prancing, preening, and posing. Rarely has such a mediocre singer, uninspired songwriter, and uninvolving stage presence been lucky enough to be deigned a rock star."

I saw the quartet again a few months later when it was still riding high on its self-titled multi-platinum debut. The hit "Semi-Charmed Life" had won the band a prime spot on Q101's Twisted Christmas concert at the Allstate Arena, but my conclusion that night was that its set was the evening's nadir.

"There is simply no bigger bozo in rock today than singer Jenkins," I wrote. "He snapped a bullwhip on stage, hammed his way through the Who's 'Baba O'Reilly,' did an embarrassing rap that desperately tried to offend someone (anyone), and of course led his prefab corporate-approved band through its brainless hits."

My opinion hadn't changed when I caught the group for a third time last month at the Q101 jamboree, touring in support of its second album "Blue," and performing at the New World Music Theatre. This time, Jenkins decided he'd had enough. He called and asked if I'd let him have his say in the newspaper, allowing him to rebut my criticisms.

As a firm believer in the importance of discourse in the rock 'n' roll community, I happily agreed, and promised to print a transcript of our conversation (edited only for length) before the band's next Chicago show. Third Eye Blind returns on Saturday to perform as part of the Hard Rock Rockfest—and here is my conversation with Jenkins.

J.D. *So you think I've done you wrong? Give it to me.*

S.J. Indeed you have. I have a copy of your review from the Q101 Jamboree, and what you said was, "On the other side were the unrepentant boneheads, chief among them the Bloodhound Gang and Third Eye Blind." Both of my records—what we write about and the way that we play—we're not boneheaded.

J.D. *What you write about is not necessarily boneheaded, but the way you put it across on stage is, with this sort of generic, lusty hard-rock persona.*

S.J. What you wrote was, "Third Eye Blind's thoroughly generic and ham-fisted music was distinguished only by the degree of frat-boy misogyny inherent in the lyrics and stage antics."

J.D. *I maintain that that's true.*

S.J. Ham-fisted? If you listen to "Motorcycle Drive By," you can't say that I can't play. We can play! We're really good musicians. To say that we're not tight, to say that the band doesn't move as one, that we don't have dynamics . . .

J.D. *You're ham-fisted in the sense that you lack subtlety, not that you can't play.*

S.J. But if you take a song like "Narcolepsy," where we shut it down to where we're playing at like 2 dBs, or a song like "Motorcycle Drive By"—there are subtleties inherent in that. There are bands that are ham-fisted that make a career out of that, like, "We're gonna democratize guitar by just playing barre chords." That's not what we're about. We have really intricate voicings. The

Village Voice wrote about this and said that, quite the opposite of ham-fisted, this band works with the intricacy and subtlety of a finely-tuned chamber-music outfit.

J.D. *Ham-fisted isn't necessarily bad. You could have said the same about Led Zeppelin or Queen; they could also be ham-fisted in the sense that they could be as subtle as a block of ice to the head. The problem with you guys—and I've seen you play three times now—is that you not only lack subtlety, but soul.*

S.J. You're saying that about the performance, not the actual songs?

J.D. *Yes; the songs are just generic. You asked me to go back and listen to "Blue" again, and I did. I listened to it three or four times before I saw you at the World, and three or four times again afterward. And my opinion is still that your music is generic and lacking anything at all that makes it distinctive.*

S.J. You are the worst example of how the media distorts things, in that what you've said about me is not really related to what I do. Generic means you can't tell one song from the other. But what does "Never Let You Go" have to do with "Jumper"? What about "Wounded"—what genre is this repeating the formula for?

J.D. *Watered-down mainstream modern rock. It's a lowest-common-denominator radio sound that's not that far off from Matchbox 20.*

S.J. That's just absurd! They're not the same chord changes or lyrics . . .

J.D. *Sure they are. You both write romantic pop trifles—manufactured music from the corporate-pop songwriting mill.*

S.J. If you go see Matchbox 20's concerts, they are coming from a very heartland-rock pose. That's their thing; that's what they do. And that has nothing to do with the chord progressions we do, the voicings that we do, the allusions that we make lyrically. And for you not to notice that, it's malicious.

J.D. *It's not malicious; I just find your music incredibly boring and ordinary and average. I admire the fact that you want to convince critics otherwise—and I've talked to a couple of peers who've gotten the same sort of phone calls from you—but I don't think you're gonna do it.*

S.J. This is what I'm talking about with the American press and why American critics are in large part a bummer, more so compared to even English critics, where there's a requirement that people have context and know what they're talking about. Next you're gonna make a comparison between us and Hootie and the Blowfish.

J.D. *That fits! Sure, you guys have a harder edge, and that's where my sexism comment comes in: You have this hard-rock edge that you flaunt that elevates your pop trifles from Hootie's pop trifles. But it's essentially the same kind of radio-friendly pap.*

S.J. Do you really think I'm a misogynist—that I hate women?

J.D. *That you are threatening to women? Yes. You walk around on stage with this strutting, cocksure persona that is the oldest rock cliché in the book. It was old when Robert Plant asked us to squeeze the lemon 'til the juice ran down his leg. Your mike stand as phallic symbol is the hoariest act in show business. There are other ways of asserting a strong male sexuality, you know.*

S.J. You have a completely warped idea about what sexuality is. I say this to people: "Walk like kings, all of you." I go strutting around on stage like a king and invite everyone to come along with me. I say in the song "Red Summer Sun," "This is my time to walk with the mighty." If I see a guy fighting, that guy gets singled out. If a girl's getting her tits grabbed when she's crowd-surfing, the guy who does it gets tossed. Our show is not a violent place; you do not see anyone being called a "bitch" or a "faggot"; there's no sense of exclusion. Do I have a cock? I sure do. It's a totally extroverted male kind of thing, but women, who make up about 41 percent of our audience, do not feel threatened or that they're somehow being seconded.

The issues that we talk about—for example "Ten Days Late" or the song "Wounded" that talks about sexual assault—are not looking at this in some sort of P.C. way. The song "Jumper"—which is about a friend who killed himself who is gay—is not anti-gay. Our message is one of inclusion and people who are wounded becoming whole. Our atmosphere is joyous, positive, and healthy.

J.D. *Joyous, positive, and healthy? What about cracking the whip onstage at the Allstate Arena?*

S.J. What's wrong with the whip?

J.D. *It's symbolic of a sado-masochistic relationship. You're a man cracking a whip and singing about women, signifying that you are putting*

a woman under your control or threatening a woman. A whip is a threat-
ening symbol.

S.J. You know what else I do sometimes? I'll take a cowboy hat
and swing it around like I'm riding a bronco. Is that subverting animals? This is what's sad: You see a guy cracking a whip as a misogynistic act and a guy who struts around with a mike stand as a
misogynist. What it really is is a sort of outward sexuality. I have a
cock. Am I violent? Yes I am. Do I have violent urges? Yes I do.
Have I turned those into protective urges? Yes I have. And that's
what we talk about in the song "Wounded"—I sing, "Back down the
bully to the back of the bus/'Cause it's time for them to be afraid of
us." It's about a friend of mine who got date-raped.

J.D. *So you're onstage singing lyrics like that but adopting the persona*
of the strutting guy with the whip—the persona of the rapist?

S.J. Why is that the persona of the rapist? We have a lot of queer
fans and a lot of female fans and they come to our shows and they
don't feel threatened, but you do. That's what this is about, me
holding you accountable.

J.D. *I'm not threatened, and that's not what this is about. This is about*
me respecting you wanting to have your say. There's not enough meaning-
ful dialogue in rock today; it's all about hype. I don't like your music, but I
respect your desire to talk.

S.J. Hype is something that our band has certainly eschewed. Our
band has been, if not the most D.I.Y. next to Fugazi, then number
two or three.

J.D. *How can you say that? Third Eye Blind is a creation of MTV and*
modern-rock radio and a major label. And you're taking money from the
Hard Rock Cafe to play a festival that has corporate sponsorship up the
wazoo.

S.J. All of the things that go on with the making of our music
come from us; we are a homegrown entity and make our own decisions. If there is a corporation out there, and we can take AOL's
money or a radio or TV show and leave people with our music, then
we will. You work for a newspaper that's corporate-owned; does that
change anything you write?

J.D. *Nope. Anything else you wanna say before we wrap this up?*

S.J. I just want to say thank you for this, Jim, and that your take on misogyny is a comedy. I hope that comes across. That, and long live Led Zeppelin.

J.D. *Hey, I love Led Zeppelin. John Bonham was a ham-fisted drummer, and he was a god.*

S.J. The only thing ham-fisted here is your writing.

J.D. *Thanks. Subtlety is overrated anyway; I like people who say what they mean.*

BILL BUFORD

Delta Nights

A Singer's Love Affair with Loss

It's a damp Delta night in January, and we've pulled into Lambert, in Quitman County, Mississippi, at one time a modestly prosperous cotton town, now reduced to a rather curious thing. The railway station—stripped down and operated in an only-one-man-needs-to-run-it kind of way—is still functioning as an agricultural freight stop, more or less as it always has, but it seems to be the exception. The town center consists of two rows of Main Street–like buildings, vaguely Victorian in design, relics of nineteenth-century antebellum cotton commerce, almost all of them abandoned. One of these would have housed the barbershop, or the bank, or the post office. Now they're home to whomever, whatever, anybody, nobody. One was the Rexall drugstore. (The "x" in Rexall has broken off.) The feeling of the place is of impoverished improvisation, variations on a squatter's theme, and Lambert's empty buildings have been taken up by anyone who has the know-how to crack open a padlocked door and get the electricity turned on. As we pull in, flames leap out from a corner, the only light on a street without street lights: it's a barbecue, the pit constructed from fallen loose bricks, right out on the sidewalk. The town seems to be deadly desolate, and yet, weirdly, it is also busy with people.

It's Saturday night, and we're in the heart of the heart of the Delta, the homeland of the blues. Our drive began in Clarksdale, near the birthplace of Muddy Waters, and continued through the very crossroads where Robert Johnson, seventy-two years ago, was supposed to have done his legendary transaction with the Devil, exchanging his soul for a satanic facility on guitar. And for half an hour we've been on county highways, all straight lines and right angles, cutting through plowed fields of cotton and soybean, seeing no other vehicles, no people, no lights except the distant dull blue of a farmhouse television, and then this explosion of busyness, in this place near no place, an embellished dot on a road map. We park, get out. Main Street is thrumming—a heavy, amplified bass coming from behind a number of boarded-up storefronts. We pick a solid, thickly painted door, which gives after I push against it, and it opens up to the sweet, acrid smell of a woodstove, a smoky array of blue and green lights dangling from an overhead pipe, and, atop a stage in the corner, a sixty-year-old man in a two-piece suit and brown patent-leather shoes—Johnnie Billington playing electric guitar.

This is the first stop on a visit to Delta juke joints, and it's impossible not to be impressed by that profoundly unmodern, unreconstructed feeling that you still find in the South. I'm here because of an interest in Lucinda Williams, the Louisiana-born singer and writer, and although she isn't with me tonight (she's in Nashville, singing with the North Mississippi All Stars—as it happens, a Delta blues band), the Delta has served Williams as a highly personal, emotional reference library, something she keeps coming back to in her music, for images or metaphors or, sometimes, for its famous twelve-bar arrangements and its flattened blue notes. Williams is forty-seven, and, obsessively working and reworking a small collection of tunes, has created a concentrated repertoire of around three dozen exceptionally powerful songs. For a thirty-five-year effort (Williams began playing when she was twelve), that works out to about a song a year, and it's still possible to see a live show in which she gets a little carried away—and she always seems to be on the verge of getting a little carried away—

and hear almost the entire oeuvre, as was the case about eighteen
months ago at New York's Irving Plaza, when Williams's encores
went on longer than the act, and the audience emerged, after
nearly two and a half hours, thoroughly spent, not only by the
duration of the program but also by the unforgiving rawness of the
songs. They're unforgiving because they are so relentlessly about
pain or longing or can't-get-it-out-of-your-head sexual desire, but
most often they're about loss, and usually about losing some
impossible fuckup of a man, who has got more charm and charisma
than a civilized society should allow, and who never lives up to any
of the promises he made when he was drunk, on drugs, in lust, in
love, incarcerated, in pain, insane, in rehab, or, in some other
essential but frustratingly appealing romantic way, unaccountable.
He's usually from Baton Rouge, Louisiana (and a bass player), or
from Lafayette, Louisiana (and a bass player), or from Lake
Charles, Louisiana (and a bass player), or maybe from Greenville,
Mississippi (and a bass player), and the songs come across as both
very Southern and also painfully autobiographical. Ouch! you
think after you've heard Lucinda Williams for the first time, this
girl has gone through some shit. Her songs are not traditional rock
and roll, if only because they are more written, more preoccupied
with the concerns of language and image, than most rock tunes.
They're not country, although there is an occasional twangy country element. They're not folk, even though "Car Wheels on a
Gravel Road," her 1998 album (and her first commercial success),
got a Grammy award for the best contemporary-folk record of the
year. And they're not blues, even though they are informed by
something that might be described as a blues attitude.

This quality of being both one thing and another (and yet
another) is at the heart of Williams's achievement—thus the knotty,
contradictory labels she gets stuck with, like the blackest white girl
in Louisiana (or the white woman with a black man's soul), or Raymond Carver with a guitar (because of her stark narratives), or a
female Hank Williams. At some point, I started asking her colleagues to characterize her music and was met with a kind of stuttering bafflement (gruff-speaking Gurf Morlix, for instance, who

worked with Williams for eleven years and wrote most of the guitar hooks on her songs, paused for a long Marlboro Man, spit-out-your-tobacco minute and said, "Shit, I never thought about it as anything except the music of a genius, but I don't know what it is") until I was rebuked for even trying by Hobart Taylor, a champion of Williams going back almost to the days when she wore a granny dress and sang on street corners: "Don't even go there," he said. "It's a trap."

Whatever this music gumbo might be, the blues remains one of its spicier ingredients—thus this visit to the Delta, where, after Johnnie Billington surrenders the stage to younger colleagues, including a teenager on bass who is hunched over in pain from what people are saying is a degenerative spinal disease, and a keyboard player so diminutive that his head disappears behind the piano, we wander out, get back into the car, and eventually find ourselves on a long dirt road, a shortcut to some place where, if we're lucky, we might catch the last set of Robert Walker, another aging giant of the blues. The woman in the back seat with me is telling me that I need to be careful, that Saturday nights in the Delta are wild. There have been gang killings, and trouble between whites and blacks, and it might be advisable for me to stick close, because, she says, whispering in a tone that is meant to be reassuring, she's got a loaded pistol in her handbag, and, you know, hey, shit happens.

After miles of empty fields, a church appears on our right, a white clapboard shoebox, resting atop brick stilts, nothing else in view, and then, a few minutes later, we turn, and, just before the town of Bobo, we come upon the Holmes Grocery & Diner, a square building with white bulbs draped across its awning like Christmas lights, a gravel parking lot, and a big barn of a room in the back.

When Lucinda Williams was starting out, she sang "country blues" (unlike the urban Chicago variety), the kind that would have originated in places like this Bobo juke joint, and her first album, recorded in a single afternoon in 1978, consisted only of classics by the country-blues masters—Robert Johnson and Memphis Minnie, of course, but also an ancient shuffling geezer called Blind Pearly Brown, who used to play wizardly guitar sitting on a stool on a street corner in Macon, Georgia, on Saturday afternoons, when six-year-old Lucinda was a mesmerized member of the audience. And although the blues are no longer a feature of her concerts—with the exception of a slow rendering of Howlin' Wolf's "Come to Me, Baby," which she performs as an encore, with a slippery sibilant last line ("Slide a little love in me") that transforms a simple tune, sung originally by a man, into a womanly erotic declaration—they seem always to be present in some way. This Holmes Grocery & Diner in Bobo, for instance, is remarkably similar to the juke joint pictured on the cover of Williams's "Car Wheels" CD, another shoebox in the country, with Christmas lights, looking utterly ordinary, pushed back into the corner of the photograph, behind a dirt road (in that inimitable Southern way, which finds its aesthetic not in what is pleasing or symmetrical or obvious but in the miserable thing that— indirect, off center, out of focus—is distinguished by its overwhelming authenticity).

The Holmes Grocery & Diner also calls to mind a song from that last CD, "2 Kool 2 Be 4-Gotten," a hymn to the Magic City juke joint, in Rosedale, Mississippi. (The title is written just as it appears on one of the juke joint's walls.) Again, the tune is not actually a blues number but something inspired by the blues, and while it seems to be musically evoking the place it describes—starting off with a slow percussion, the stress in the back, in a syncopated funk style, the drum just behind the beat (in a way that musicians often describe as a Southern sound), laid back, very cool, very juke—what Williams had in mind was the way Beat poets performed their work, with someone on drums and someone playing a bass, and a guy in front reading a poem, singsongy but still spoken. The tune is a recitation, a series of images: the signs mounted around the place ("House Rules, no exceptions. No bad language, no gambling, no fighting. Sorry, no credit. Don't ask"), the graffiti in the bathrooms, the gang rivalries ("June bug vs. hurricane"), and the essential amorality of a joint that's an escape, beyond accountability, and where shit happens.

The next morning, the birthday of Martin Luther King, Jr., I drive out to Rosedale, wanting to see the place that informed the song. Rosedale is built against the levee, the houses of the whites, west of the interstate, with driveways and lawns, and the homes of

the blacks, on the other side, crowded, higgledy-piggledy, ram-
shackle, the timber of the porches and doorways disintegrating in
the Mississippi air, an unchanged, unchanging picture that could
have been taken any time in the last hundred years. This part of
town is full of churches—the Gospel Temple, the Riverside United
Baptist, the God's People in Unity, the Assembly of God—and I
stop at one, a garish thing with turquoise walls and pink window
frames and a white steeple, a great cotton candy of a place. I decide
to join the well-dressed families, rushing across the parking lot, late
for the eleven o'clock service, and as I step inside everyone at the
back turns to stare. I feel I've transgressed, and leave, but as I walk
back to the car it occurs to me that I've been composing a selective,
romanticized picture in my head. I made notes the night before,
describing the highly sexual bump-and-grind dancing at the juke
joint in Bobo, but I wrote nothing of the fact that half the people
were fat, no-neck whites—croupiers and kitchen staff from the
riverboat casinos. I note that, when we walked in, the band was
playing "Mustang Sally" but not that it got bored and suddenly quit
midtune, in seeming disgust at its audience. I describe Robert
Walker, sitting against a wall, tired, possibly ill, a tall man in a drap-
ing white suit, white spats, with a Little Richard bouffant hairdo, a
shiny white guitar, and a long melancholy face, but not the two
white people who were sliding around the joint, "inconspicuously"
trying to get the good angle in order to take his picture—this Delta
postcard shot—including the man whose camera had an elaborate
fashion-photo attachment, with a hooded white canopy above his
flash, plus all sorts of high-tech gizmos spread across his table. And
even in Lambert I noted the cheap-and-cheerful assortment of
chairs, the cracked floors, the New Year's decorations that still hadn't
been taken down, but not the banner stretched across the back of the
stage: "Sponsored by the National Endowment for the Arts."

Daddy-Girl

I am in Lucinda Williams's bedroom, and have been struck by a
number of things. Above the headboard, and nailed to the wall, is a

shiny, glitter-sprinkled, heart-shaped pink valentine from Jesus, who is depicted inside a diminishing succession of crucifixes, like so many Russian dolls, as pretty and effeminate, with a golden halo and dreamy blond hair. I don't think I've ever seen Jesus as a blond. Even so, it makes you wonder: Do you want God above your bed? There is a matching valentine alongside; in this one, Jesus is a brunet. Hanging on the wall by the bathroom is a similar arrangement, this one devoted to the Virgin Mary, a shrine of sorts, including an image that changes shape as you walk past: one moment it's the Virgin, and then—what do you know?—it's the Son of God! This house seems perfectly normal, almost suburban, from the outside—a two-story brick-and-wood affair, set back from the street, in a birch forest, in a semirural district of Nashville (Emmylou Harris lives two doors down)—but inside it's a floor-to-ceiling museum of Southern religious kitsch. There is a wall mounting of Jesus in a conch shell and another of Jesus inside a scallop; as you come up the stairs, you are met by a painting of exceptional ugliness, featuring an eye and a clock (the second hand pivots from a point in the pupil) and a piece of text, written in silver glitter, declaring that we love thee, O Lord, "at all times!" High on a kitchen wall is a cross that says "Bless Our Home," and if you look closely you can see a tiny amplifier, which, when triggered by the vibration of the screen door closing, plays a blast of a choir singing "Hallelujah!" On the refrigerator are magnetized bottle caps with a minuscule likeness of Jesus painted inside, decorated delicately with tiny gold stars and red glitter.

There are snakes. One has such oily-looking scales that I can't resist touching it. Several are rather abstract: stretched across the wall is a particularly crude thing that, in keeping with the governing aesthetic, is painted turquoise. (Many things in the house—including a Jesus night-light—are turquoise.) These are not actually snakes; they are serpents. Raving reverends, preaching the Gospel between bouts of gargling strychnine, walk barefoot atop serpents, not snakes. A joke, I assume. Or is it? Upstairs, in Lucinda's study, I discover that serpent handlers are a special interest, and she has photographs and books about people whom I can only regard—forgive me, O Lord—as insane weirdos.

What is her attitude toward all this? I can't tell; I'm not sure she knows. She owns photo collections of juke joints, hillbillies, cross-eyed Appalachian sharecroppers, rural pig guttings, preachers in a trance, the faithful showing off their fang scars, dumbass farmers displaying their guns, and Shelby Lee Adams portraits of sprawling families crowded onto buckling porches in places like Hooterville and Happy. At one moment, I wonder if she collects a certain kind of friend. During a five-day stay in Nashville, I meet a man named Dub Cornett, and then later both Lucinda and Richard Price, her boyfriend of nearly five years (and her bass player), whisper into my ear that Dub is from a family of backwoods hillbillies—"the real thing." On another evening, I'm introduced to a young songwriter named Hayseed, who stays with Williams when he has business in town but still lives with his Pentecostal family. He, too, I'm told, is "the real thing." I wouldn't think twice about them except that later, going over a press file of pieces about Williams, I notice that Dub and Hayseed were trotted out to meet journalists on some of those occasions, too. Is a point being made? The eccentric friends, whose authenticity is in their extreme Baptist intensity; the serpent handlers; the poison drinkers; the turquoise Jesus; the glittery Marys. Is this another illustration of that odd, indirect Southern aesthetic of miserable originality? (It might be white trash, but it's ours.)

Williams is of modest height (five feet four), and slim, almost preternaturally so—"It's the thing I share with my dad. I've always been a rake." Dad is the Arkansas poet Miller Williams, the bean-pole figure you might have spotted reading at Bill Clinton's second Inauguration; his poems are hanging on the walls, including one written for Lucinda's boyfriend when he turned fifty:

> *Year in, year out, most of us do our best*
> *To make a hundred, perfect on the test.*
> *The problems get harder, the teachers don't grade fair,*
> *But hell, the bell ain't rung and you're halfway there.*

There's a room given over to exercise equipment—a weight machine, a stair-climbing machine, a dual-motion cycle machine, a rowing machine, a Nordic-Track, an "abs-workout station"—but Williams seems not to use it. It's both new and noticeably untouched. So much kit, however, betrays a certain unease. The unease is evident in Williams's hair. It's streaked. It was dark brown (almost black) when I first met her, before she performed on "Saturday Night Live" last year. I've also seen it blond. When I eventually leave Nashville, and am reminded that I've foregone Williams's invitation to stay at her house ("You'd have been the first journalist to see me without makeup"), I suddenly appreciate how much time she puts into her looks. This is "the appearance thing," having to come across as attractive and sexy, to be, as she puts it, "someone you look at and say, 'Whoa, what a babe! I wouldn't mind . . .'" It is a preoccupation of a forty-seven-year-old only now breaking into a business that, committed to discovering the next Christina Aguilera, considers twenty-seven to be getting on. "I know I shouldn't be so bothered about this stuff," Williams says. "Politically, I know I shouldn't—what do I want to be, every guy's sex fantasy? But when you're in it, as I am, it's hard to ignore."

For all that, Williams's politics seem a bit sixties-ish ragbaggy. A characteristic Williams statement was her reply to a question put to her by *Rolling Stone* last December about her hopes for the next millennium: Lucinda, expressing a loathing for the boom economy, called for a stock-market crash and longed for a Depression, a peculiar dream for a woman who only now—that is, in the past eighteen months, say—has money in a bank account. In 1998, when the film-maker Paul Schrader agreed to make a video for Lucinda's last album and flew down to Nashville to discuss possible ideas, he was struck by how badly this woman needed a break: here was someone in her mid-forties who was having trouble meeting the essential needs of food and shelter. (In the event, no video was made; no video has ever been made—another Williams tenet, MTV culture is a bad thing, although it's unclear if this arises out of a loathing for television or a paralyzing anxiety about appearing on it.) And last year, when I joined Lucinda in New Orleans, it was evident that the money troubles weren't quite over. We spent an afternoon shopping for old music posters—Fats Domino, for her brother, and Clifton

Chenier, "King of Zydeco," for her friend Margaret Moser, a
Louisiana-born music journalist—only to have Williams's credit
card rejected.

In many of these things—the ethic of dissent, the antiestablishment
stance, the ease of doing without—her father's influence is unmistakable. Miller Williams, a man of indefatigable productivity, has
twenty-nine books to his name, including twelve volumes of poetry.
Lucinda has memories of his writing a poem every night after dinner, and he appears in the family photo albums very much playing
the part, with an untrimmed beard and a black beret, flopped over a
chair, writing verse on a yellow legal pad. Does a poet father make
for a poetic, songwriting daughter? The answer must be yes, but it's
not so obvious. Miller Williams sometimes performs with his
daughter—he reads a poem, she sings, then he reads another
poem—but you would be hard-pressed to hear a genetic link in
their diction. And while Lucinda submits the text of her songs to
him before she records them—there will be nothing for years, and
suddenly the songs start arriving in the mail—his editorial interven-
tions seem to be modest at most: she cites his objection, for
instance, to the phrase "faded blue dress" in the song "He Never
Got Enough Love." (She changed it to "sad blue dress.") You get
the sense that what she wants is not Dad's advice but his approval,
almost like a report card. Lucinda's friend Margaret Moser finds the
whole thing peculiar—"this Daddy-girl thing," she calls it, this need
to be patted on the back by a man who has nothing to do with the
kind of rough-hewn, laconic cigarette ads for masculinity whom
Lucinda has been consistently attracted to, although the disjunction
that Moser describes is revealing in itself (and might well explain
why so many of the Marlboro Men don't work out).
    In any case, the idea of Daddy as a benign patriarchal pedagogue
isn't a new thing; for much of Lucinda's life, that was his role. In
1969, when Lucinda was in the tenth grade, she was suspended from
high school more than once—the first time for refusing to pledge
allegiance to the flag—and her father eventually assumed the responsibility of completing her education. (He had already assumed the

responsibility of her upbringing, having got custody of her and her
two siblings after he divorced Lucinda's mother.) His solution to her
education was to give her a reading list of a hundred great books,
from the Iliad to "One Hundred Years of Solitude."

When I met Miller Williams, on a visit to Fayetteville, Arkansas,
where he teaches at the university, I was interested in his account of
Lucinda's suspension, an episode that must have been distressing in
the extreme. I was wrong. Dad had been delighted—"just tickled
pink!"—and he pointed out how the showdown involving Lucinda's
refusal to pledge allegiance was similar to one of his own, twenty
years before, when he was fired from McNeese State University for
refusing to take the Louisiana loyalty oath required of state employees. But the parallels didn't stop there. Just after Lucinda was kicked
out for being a dissident, he quit his job at Loyola University in an
act of protest. The university, unhappy about a piece he had published as the editor of a new college literary magazine (a review of
Anne Sexton's "Ballad of the Lonely Masturbator," which included
too many graphic quotes), had insisted that it approve the contents
of future issues before they were printed. This was censorship and
not something Miller Williams could tolerate. An out-of-work
father, an out-of-school daughter—what a peculiar family it must
have been, I found myself thinking, but Miller, also the child of a
dissident (a socialist Methodist minister so committed to challeng-
ing the status quo that he eventually questioned the Resurrection,
discovered that he could no longer conduct the Easter service, and
quit), wanted me to understand that this was the Williams way. On
the drive from the airport, he bubbled over with more happy show-
downs involving his daughter, including her recent confrontation
with the producers of "Good Morning America" after they asked
her to cut a verse from the song she was about to sing, "Right in
Time," her paean to autoeroticism. The lines, Williams added, were
not cut, and you could see him making a connection— her song
about masturbation, his review about masturbation; like father, like
daughter—and he chuckled merrily.

Lucinda never got a high-school diploma; for that matter, she
never learned to read music, and although she later passed a college-

entrance examination and was admitted to the University of
Arkansas, she was bored by the rigors of formal education and was
at a loss in harmony class. After one semester, she took her guitar
and left Fayetteville, heading first for New Orleans, then for Austin,
before settling in Houston—the folk scene of the early seventies.

When she returned, in 1977, four years later, it was under a doctor's orders. She had been singing so punishingly, in smoky clubs, on
street corners, busking for rent, straining the rough, husky,
untrained, almost Janis Joplin–like voice that characterized her early
singing—a sound so sandpapery that Emmylou Harris described it
as capable of peeling the chrome off a trailer hitch—that she was in
danger of losing it altogether. Nodules had formed on her vocal
cords. She was twenty-four. She had a notebook of songs, but no
demos, no deals. And that was when she met Frank Stanford, the
first of the men who would end up informing so much of the music
she'd write for the next two decades.

Beautiful as the Sun

Stanford, whose story still deserves a book (or a movie), was a pre-
cocious, original, highly accomplished poet, a huge personality, with
an engine of charm and devastating good looks. "He was like Charl-
ton Heston when he was a young man," Miller Williams tells me,
recalling that, years before, Stanford had been admitted to a graduate writing workshop at the University of Arkansas while he was still
a teenage undergraduate, an unprecedented thing.

"He was as beautiful as the sun," the poet Carolyn (C. D.) Wright
recalls when we meet to talk about Stanford. She ran a small press
with him, the Lost Roads Publishers, and they were lovers, although
Stanford was married to a painter, Ginny Stanford. "He had girlie
curly hair and hazel eyes and big white teeth and a wide jaw and a
wide mouth, which women loved. And men did, too. Everyone
loved Frank. They couldn't help it." The writer Ellen Gilchrist
knew him, she tells me, when I reach her in Mississippi, "very, very,
very, very well," and representations of him are scattered throughout her short stories. "To know Frank then," she says, "was to see
how Jesus got his followers. Everybody worshipped him."

Stanford was a Mississippi-born illegitimate child, abandoned at the Emory Home for Unwed Mothers, near Hattiesburg, a "convenience" run by one Sister White for politicians and businessmen. He was adopted by Dorothy Gilbert, who subsequently married Albert Franklin Stanford, an older man, a gentlemanly, worldly embodiment of the Old South. Albert Franklin Stanford built the levees along tributaries of the Mississippi, and this was where the boy passed his summers, alongside his much older "father," spending nights in tents on the levee, sitting in on the campfires the black laborers made, listening to their stories. The experience had a practical consequence. Stanford was working as a surveyor when Lucinda met him, in the spring of 1978, a quiet, enchanting figure who avoided cities and cultivated a manner of strangeness, appearing suddenly, unannounced, from out of the woods, smelling of earth, in suspenders and leather work boots. The experience also informed his poetry, and by then he had published nine volumes, and had just completed the four-hundred-and-fifty-page narrative poem "The Battlefield Where the Moon Says I Love You," a surreal account of a clairvoyant eleven-year-old's crusade for racial justice, with cameo appearances by movie stars and boxers ("I saw Sonny Liston crying in a short-order café"). Stanford's poems are distinguished by their easy, appealing voice—an intimate, companionable, please-stay-and-have-another-drink kind of voice—and a language that is local and highly vernacular, and that often features the speech of Mississippi blacks. "He evoked the Delta in his poems," Ellen Gilchrist recalls. "His poems were the Delta." There are images of women by campfires, of peas being shelled, of fingers smelling of backwater, of escaped convicts and people called Ray Baby and Born-in-the-Camp-with-Six-Toes. And there is Stanford's own half love affair with easeful Death, who appears in various guises—as a cool hipster in shiny loafers and a Cadillac, as a man in a bow tie running a hotel. Stanford was irresistible to the young singer, and she fell heavily in love.

Or so Lucinda concedes, more than twenty years after the event, embarrassed, awkward, in the company of her boyfriend, Richard Price, who has been, on every occasion I've seen them together, a paradigm of understanding, but who is unnerved by the Stanford story. "I just can't believe you fell for it," he says, the "it" being the easy charm, the good looks, the dark Byronic act. "I mean, you're so smart. How could you be so stupid?"

"It was just a fling," C. D. Wright tells me of Lucinda's relationship with Stanford. "And," she adds, sounding a little testy, "only because I was out of town at the time." But Stanford was having a lot of flings—more, it seems, than will ever be known, a frenzy of philandering. He was living with C. D. Wright while promising his wife that they'd get back together. ("He'd stop by every week," Ginny Stanford recalls in a piece published in the *New Orleans Review*, "to tell another lie.") And, by Wright's own count, he was making the same promise to six other women (a writer, a potter, a poet, a sculptor)—actually, maybe there were seven, if you include "that intense thing he was having in New Orleans." Well, who knows how many? "In that last month," Ginny Stanford recalls, "he was seeing lots of people." Frank Stanford, Wright says, was one of the greatest liars she has ever known.

He had spent two weeks in Louisiana. This was in June. On the day he returned to Fayetteville, he sent flowers to Lucinda, who was out, and her father accepted them. Stanford went home and discovered there was a problem: for ten days, the woman he was living with and the wife he said he was returning to had been together, dismantling his lies. "There was a scene," C. D. Wright recalls, "and I'm not sure Frank had been rejected before. Suddenly he wanted to go to his office. I didn't know why. We were all upset." The two women accompanied him and waited in the car. They learned later that he'd gone to pick up a pistol. They drove home. Then he went into the bedroom and shot himself three times. "That deadly duet," his wife recalls of the gun and the moan: "Pop. *Oh!* Pop. *Oh!* Pop. *Oh!*"

Miller Williams got a call, asking him to help. "There was blood all over the bed and on the telephone," he says. "When you've had that much to do with someone's career, and someone so promising, and then to be asked to clean up after him—well, it was pretty tough." When he returned, exhausted, unspeakably sad, he found Lucinda waiting—she'd put the flowers in a vase. She hadn't heard the news.

At the funeral, she and her father stood back, out of the way. "And then after everyone had left," Miller Williams recalls, "and the coffin was lowered, and we were all by ourselves, we walked up to the grave, and Lucinda picked up a handful of dirt and sprinkled it across the coffin." (The act echoes a line in one of Stanford's last poems.) "And I remember thinking, Oh, Lucinda, God bless her, and I felt she was just going to disappear from the pain of it all. And, as we walked off, we turned, and there was a girl of about eighteen, very pretty, who had stood even further back—we hadn't seen her. And she then walked up and picked up a handful of dirt and threw it over the grave."

Lucinda Williams wrote several songs about Stanford's death. "Pineola," an example of what her friend Hobart Taylor calls her documentary songs, is a heartfelt, angry rendition of the thing, more or less as it happened. There isn't much that was changed— Pineola for Fayetteville, Sonny for Frank, and a Pentecostal burial instead of a Catholic one. The song describes how Lucinda got the news ("When Daddy told me what happened"); her own flattened response ("I could not speak a single word. No tears streamed down my face. I just sat there on the living-room couch, staring off into space"); and the funeral, where Stanford's mother stood baffled by the hundreds of strangers who had shown up to mourn her adopted child's death. The song ends with a refrain about the handful of earth thrown onto the casket. Like several other Lucinda tunes of this time, "Pineola" is in what might be called a country style, reminiscent, say, of Bobbie Gentry's old AM radio favorite "Ode to Billie Joe." It's the song that hooked the novelist Annie Proulx, who heard it for the first time on the CD compilation accompanying the *Oxford American* Southern-music issue, and who described it as "the best alternative country song I'd heard in years."

"Sweet Old World" is a different kind of song—more ballad than short story—and its qualities are at the heart of the difficulty involved in articulating the value of any piece of music, which exists first as something in time, as sound and not as text. The difficulty is compounded with lyrical-seeming songs, if only because one part

of their achievement is in language, a language that, once separated
from the melody, can look banal. "Sweet Old World," written in
the second person, is addressed to a suicide. Musically, it is characteristic of Williams's later songs. The more obvious, "pretty" harmonic elements are in the background (those sad, mournful Gurf
Morlix licks, echoing the melody, played on guitar and violin),
which allows Williams's voice to stand out up front, full of rough
feelings and an abrasive sadness. The lyrics are a list of what the
dead man is missing ("See what you lost when you left this world"),
and consist of simple images arising out of the things we feel, see,
smell: dancing with no shoes, the sensation of being touched by
another's fingertips, the sound of your name called by a beloved, a
train at night, the feeling of slipping a ring on your finger, the tin-
gling of being kissed, the act of breathing. But because the song's
images are of the senses it has an intimacy, even a seductive eroti-
cism. This is perfectly understandable, given that it's being sung to
a former lover, but was not something I appreciated until I saw it
performed at an outdoor evening concert in Oxford, Mississippi,
last year, when the air was swollen from a day of heavy thunder-
storms. As a result, the music was rounder-sounding, cushioned,
and the notes seemed to linger. There was a crowd of about five
thousand crushed into the square. They weren't restless, exactly,
but, having spent a day inside, amid reports that the concert might
be cancelled, they had a pent-up attentiveness. The stars were coming out, but there was no breeze, just this heavy stillness, and then
this tune, with its hip-rolling beat, which was about a suicide, after
all. Slowly, people began dancing, everyone swaying, and hands
were holding hips, and hands were slipping down trousers, and
boys were kissing girls, and girls were kissing girls, slow, wet, slow-
dance kisses, and, over to my left, just above Square Books, a couple were undoing their jeans, and, over on another balcony, just
above the bar Proud Larry's, two women were holding each other
so melodically that their embrace was virtually a sexual act. ("The
shit we see people doing when we are onstage," Richard Price tells
me later.) That night was the second night with the band for Greg
Atticus Finch, a keyboard player who has since been dropped; he

still remembers the tune that evening. "'Sweet Old World,'" he said—in a burst of generosity remarkable for a person who has been banished from a band—"that song is simply the best ballad ever written. No one could write a better ballad than it. No one has written a better ballad. It just doesn't get any better."

Williams began writing both "Sweet Old World" and "Pineola" in 1979, the year after Stanford died. She had to wait thirteen years before they were released.

Why so long? "Because," Williams says, "my career has been distinguished by other people, who have always been men, telling me what I should sound like." (To be fair, her first album consisted of all those blues numbers, and none of her own compositions, because that's what *she* thought the male producer wanted.) "Happy Woman Blues," her next album, was produced in 1980, and features "Sharp Cutting Wings," a mournful love tune (inspired by yet another poet) that has a characteristic Williams line: a series of love fantasies—of flying off with her poet lover, of being with him in a foreign country, of wanting no one to know them—that ends abruptly with her need for a small loan of "about a hundred dollars" (and there's something very exacting about that "about," as though it's just enough to pay last month's phone bill, score a Diet Coke and a turkey sandwich, and buy a Greyhound bus ticket). On the last day in the studio, the producer took it upon himself to introduce drums to Williams's string-band mix—not a bad sound, she felt, but it wasn't what she would have done, and wasn't something she was asked about. It was immaterial; the album made so little money that it's legitimate to ask if it was ever sold.

But no record made her any money, despite the fanatical efforts of so many people, including Hobart Taylor, who came upon Lucinda's playing at Anderson Fair or the Full Moon Café, and then embarked on a mission to make her known to the rest of the world. Taylor, a Houston journalist before he abandoned his career to promote Lucinda, helped her with the rent, paid for meals, and spent a modest inheritance on putting Lucinda up in the Chelsea Hotel in New York and producing a demo of ten songs, "Pineola" among

them. Taylor failed to get a record company to take it. So, too, did
David Hirshland, another dreamy disciple, who, like Taylor, abandoned his career (as a booking agent) so that he could throw himself
into the cause. The result was another demo, this one paid for by
CBS, whose executives then dithered, before confessing that they
didn't know what it was and had no idea how to sell it: it was too
much like country, according to the rock-and-roll executives; too
much like rock and roll, according to the country executives.
Williams, meanwhile, was working at a B. Dalton bookstore in a
shopping mall near Glendale, driving a beat-up Saab that had a
party trick of breaking down on the Harbor Freeway. When, four
years later, she was finally taken up by a major record label, RCA,
which was then run by Bob Buziak (who understood that Williams's
music was neither one thing nor another and needed to be left
alone), Buziak got fired, putting her into the hands of a producer
who secretly believed she was a disco babe, a secret he didn't share
with Williams herself until he had taken her already recorded songs
and remixed them, adding a big bass here, a heavy drumbeat there,
which, again, was not necessarily a bad sound, but it wasn't hers,
and, this time, wasn't something she was going to put up with. She
walked out on the deal, even though she was broke. She turned forty
and was still broke when Mary Chapin Carpenter covered one of
her tunes, "Passionate Kisses," and made it into a Grammy-winning
hit. In many ways, it's the Lucinda Williams theme song, asking that
essential question: I've waited so long, why can't I have everything
now, dammit! Why can't I have a comfortable bed that won't hurt
my back, and food for when I'm hungry, and clothes for when I'm
cold, plus some pens that don't run out of ink (a poet's daughter,
after all), and some quiet thinking time, and a big house full of
friends, and a rock band, and a regular supply of passionate kisses?

Weeping Fits

I've been studying Lucinda Williams's face—a youthful face, soft
skin, few wrinkles, a face so much younger-looking than her age
that waspish peers whisper that she must have submitted it to the

surgeon's nip and tuck. (She hasn't.) Its dominant quality is its changeableness. This is a face full of weather—or, maybe, more accurately, it's akin to a weather report, a forecast of the personality you're going to see next. Now, the two of us in her living room, in the evening (Williams is an early-afternoon riser), her face is relaxed and expressive, and yields easily to a teasing, cackling laugh—a laugh that makes you feel appreciated and enjoyed. In concert, she has another face, and one that rarely gives up so much as a smile. It firms up, reveals little, and is at odds with the expressive songs she sings. It's a matter of control. Upheaval makes for these songs, and upheaval goes into the writing of them; she often works herself into such a state, reliving some awfulness, that she'll end up in a dark depression (Williams's depressions are legendary; "Am I too blue for you?" is the refrain of one song devoted to them; "When I cry like the sky like the sky sometimes, am I too blue?"), and these moments can be marked by weeping fits that go on for days. Williams now believes that the songs she writes when she has reached this therapeutic, unprotected rawness are her best, and that she has to go through this kind of trauma in order to write. But then these songs, once made, are performed with a fanatical sense of self-government; and that's what her face conveys then: discipline, containment, control.

She cried for days while writing the ballad "Little Angel, Little Brother," about her younger brother, an exceptional talent on the keyboard ("I see you now at the piano, your back a slow curve, playin' Ray Charles and Fats Domino while I sang all the words"), who has never realized his promise, owing to unhappiness or drink or that old Louisiana gift for self-destruction: "I see you sleeping in the car, curled up on the back seat, parked outside of a bar, an empty bottle at your feet, Little Angel, Little Brother." The song evokes some of the anguish of Lucinda's upbringing, among family members who were distinguished by their artistic ambitions but were held back or frustrated in some profound, soul-destroying way. Her brother also had the makings of a poet. (At fourteen, he'd voraciously read and reread all of Shakespeare.) Then, more disturbing, there was her mother, Lucy, who still had dreams of being a concert pianist when she met Miller Williams, but abandoned them after she quickly had three children, and struggled to bring them up, until, owing to mental illness or depression or something the family is uncomfortable talking about, she yielded her place to a nineteen-year-old undergraduate/housekeeper/caretaker/savior, whom her husband brought in to look after his confused offspring and whom he would eventually marry. (In a domestic ceasefire, the two women lived in the same house for five years.) And there was Miller Williams himself, who, for all his robust confidence, had spent years in an intellectual wilderness. By training and education, he was a biologist, but he had no aptitude for the sciences and kept moving from job to job, unable to secure tenure, until he abandoned both the university and his family and went to New York to work as a junior editor, sending home paltry sums set aside from his paltry salary.

Backstage, at the end of a concert last year at the House of Blues in New Orleans, I witnessed a Louisiana family reunion, which included Lucinda's mother, who had just moved back to the Crescent City ("Come see me," she told me, in a whisper. "I'm so lonely"); her brother Robert, who was also now living in New Orleans, driving a long-distance truck (and who was apprehensive about speaking to a journalist—his having been made the drunken self-destructive subject of "Little Angel, Little Brother" was plenty of attention, thank you very much); plus the much-loved Uncle Cecil, from Sulphur, Louisiana. As a child, Lucinda had seen so much of Uncle Cecil that she asked her mother if they'd lived in Sulphur, too, along with Lake Charles and Macon and a half-dozen other small college towns in the South. "No, no," her mother said, tellingly. "You're thinking of Iowa"—another town in Louisiana—"your grandmother's, where we went so often because we had no money for food and used to go there to eat." Lucinda's childhood was one of testing difficulty, and it is, she admits, an element in why she writes her particular songs of loss and neediness, some of which is touched on in "Car Wheels on a Gravel Road," her account of being a five-year-old in the South, with lyrics that evoke a time of tense domestic hush-hushness: of neighbors watching ("Pull the

curtains back and look outside. Somebody somewhere don't know");
of parents' squabbling ("There goes the screen door slamming shut.
You better do what you're told. When I get back the room better be
picked up"); of a family's having a secret that others don't know
("Low hum of voices in the front seat. Stories nobody knows. Got
folks in Jackson we're going to meet. Car wheels on a gravel road").
When Lucinda's father first heard the song, he sought out his
daughter and apologized.

At one point, backstage, I felt I was seeing a comparably real-life
illustration of the Williams first-person principle—the notion that
her more serious fans engage with her music on a deeper, weirder
level than they might with other songwriters' songs, because
Lucinda's are believed to be so autobiographical. I'd seen the principle expressed in her fan mail, which I'd spent an evening reading in
her company ("Miss Williams, did you ever get your heart stomped
on by a guy named Alex? I figure you must have—or by an evil twin
of his—since about every damn song in your incredible new album
nails me straight in the heart"), and which featured confessions of
exceptional pain that was either relieved, or relived, by a Williams
song. (As the night wore on, and Lucinda kept failing to find a specific letter, one written by a d.j. who was committed to playing
something by her every night, because "Sweet Old World" had
stopped him from killing himself, you could see her face grow pro-
gressively darker—Weather alert!—as she skimmed confession after
heartfelt confession, knowing that she got this kind of mail because
of the kind of song she wrote, and she wrote that kind of song
because she went through Hell living a hurt or humiliation, and
then went through Hell reliving it when she wrote about it, and she
hadn't written a thing now in three years, and she was dreading what
she was going to have to go through again—Hell was beckoning.)
There at the House of Blues, a fan, the cheerfully named Trish
Blossom, had slipped past the tight security, with a husband in tow,
and had fixed on Lucinda. Trish Blossom was blond and tall and
pretty, and came from the backwoods somewhere in Louisiana—she
told this to me, adding that she didn't leave the woods ever, not for
nobody, and she had come to New Orleans to see Lucinda, and here

she was, and did Lucinda know that Trish Blossom never comes out for nobody, which all seemed a little nutty, but not threatening, I thought, until I glanced over at the husband and saw a face that had an unmistakable look of panic. ("Do you realize," he whispered, "how serious this is?") "She just needs love," Trish Blossom was saying, in a kind of trance. "Can't you see that she needs love? Nobody has loved her, and she has so much love to give, and I have so much love, and I will give her the love she needs." She eventually reached Williams, who handled the encounter expertly—this was a regular exchange. (The most recent involved a man who rushed the stage with a dozen roses, screaming "I love you, Lucinda!" before he was tackled and carried off, shouting, "I am not John Hinckley!") Lucinda gave Trish a hug, which became an embrace, but she came back for more ("I just can't let go") until Lucinda let herself be kissed on the lips, and reassured Trish that, yes, she was right, she just needed some love, and she was pleased that Trish had some to give her.

I'm not sure why first-person narratives—in songs, like Williams's, or even in fiction—invade the sentimental nervous system so effectively, but they provided me with a strategy for understanding Lucinda's music. It yields insights into a number of songs—the ones involving Frank Stanford, say, or something like "Drunken Angel," which was inspired by the death of Blaze Foley ("Blood spilled out from the hole in your heart, over the strings of your guitar, the worn-down places in the wood, that once made you feel so good"), a fellow Austin musician. (Foley was a two-hundred-and-fifty-pound subversive, antic, ferociously anticommercial poet of folk rock—he celebrated the self-righteousness of his poverty by decorating his jeans, jacket, cowboy hat, and guitar with the same duct tape that held his boots together—who threatened a youth for stealing his own father's welfare checks until the boy shot Foley in the ribs, an act so enragingly pusillanimous that Foley chased the youth and eventually bled to death. You can see why Blaze Foley would appeal to Lucinda's accept-no-compromises world view. But it makes you wonder: Doesn't she know anyone besides bass players and dead men?)

The strategy is even more interesting in relation to Clyde Wood-ward, probably the most important love interest in Lucinda's life. Clyde, another bass player, who almost came from Louisiana, seems to have informed a dozen songs. But this is where the autobiograph-ical approach gets complicated.

I'm sitting in Lucinda's house in Nashville, going through three meticulously organized volumes of photographs. Clyde appears reg-ularly, a big fleshy man with a flap of dark hair and round cheeks and a barrel chest. Lucinda points out Clyde's characteristic pose—arms thrown out wide, a come-join-the-party look. There are pic-tures of the two of them in Austin. "That," Lucinda says, "is when Clyde persuaded me to pawn a rare twelve-string guitar so we could get food and beer" (whereupon the pawnshop burned down, a typi-cal Clyde touch of fortune). There are pictures of them in New York; Clyde had come along ostensibly to be her manager, although he was jealous of her talent and was always getting in the way. (Clyde, in Lucinda's descriptions, comes across as a passionate, pos-sessive, pigheaded, pugnacious sensualist—jealous and head-butting, but high entertainment.) There is another of Clyde helping her father build a porch in Fayetteville. "That was when we really had no money and nothing left to pawn." And another of Clyde in a kitchen, making gumbo, throwing a party, knocking back a beer, and suddenly Lucinda cries out, "Oh, my God! Oh, my God! Clyde is dead. And Frank is dead. What a thing. All my old boyfriends were in love with the idea of Louisiana, and they're dead!"

Like Stanford, Clyde was fascinated by death, but for Clyde death was an opponent in an elaborate game of combat, the only thing getting in the way of his kamikaze, nothing-can-stop-us approach to life. But Lucinda wasn't interested in dying; she had a career in mind, and so they broke up after four years. And then Clyde did die, more or less just like that, forty years old, jaundiced, anemic, skele-tal beyond recognition, in a hospital in East Texas, trying to get back to Louisiana before his liver packed in—from excesses of all kinds. Clyde's last hours were spent with Lucinda's friend Margaret Moser (Lucinda was on a plane trying to reach him), as Moser read to him from a journal about Louisiana, which she had started com-

piling when she was living far away and feeling homesick. The journal had been Clyde's idea. Moser is from Louisiana. Clyde wasn't,
although he was obsessed with the place and used to preach where
to find its values: not in its open-air rock concerts, for instance,
which you'd find anywhere, but in its parish dances, which you find
nowhere else. Or in the dance halls along the road between Eunice
and Opelousas. ("Inside, you'd be the only whites, and it would be
packed shoulder to butt.") Or in its out-of-the-way crawfish farms,
and its cockfights, and its gnarly French Catholicism. Or in odd
things, like zydeco, which Clyde played. Or in its gumbo—for
Clyde as much a metaphor as a food ("He saw God in a bowl of
gumbo"): the spicy Delta hot pot that said, with its cayenne and its
crawfish and its other crustaceans, this place and no other.

When Lucinda was growing up, Louisiana meant "backward." It
was "country," and people made fun of her father's accent (even
though, technically, his was not Louisiana but northeastern
Arkansas), and he sometimes tried to disguise it. (My Louisiana
father buried his accent deep, and told me once that much of his life
was lived to prove that he could be more than a "hick" from a north-
woods Louisiana papermill town, and I was struck by how the word
"hick," very much his word, like "boondocks" and "sticks," was
already dated and without force.) Clyde appeared in Lucinda's life
when the perception of the place was shifting—in the way of these
things, its hick, redneck ways are now the half-rebel expression of
an inexplicably charismatic, bad-boy code of excess—and he helped
her to recognize the shift. And she repaid him by writing a song
about Lake Charles, her birthplace and his fantasy home, and where
his ashes are now scattered. The song is the only one in her repertoire that affects her in unpredictable ways, and when she performs
it she sometimes breaks down.

Good Liars

The South has a history of mythmakers, and at the heart of the
Southern myth is a love affair with loss. It's what underlies the myth
of the good Southern family; or the notion of the Southern gentle-

man, of honor and Old World grace and hospitality; or the filthy
romance of the Confederate flag; or the sugary fables of "Gone with
the Wind." These myths—still current, even if anachronistic, even
if (like débutante balls and the languid luxury of a south-Georgia
accent) *always* anachronistic—are among those cited by Edmund
Wilson in "Patriotic Gore," in the pages of this magazine forty years
ago, and offered up as examples of how the South is seen to have
retained something that modernizing America no longer has. These
were also illustrations of the way people from the North liked to
think about the South then, units in the elaborate calculation to
compensate for a place that was, when Wilson was writing, still synonymous with defeat and self-righteous pride and a kind of nation-
alized nationalistic bad judgment. In forty years, the South has
changed, but mythmaking remains a habit of mind. I'm not sure
that the myths Southerners fashion today are even necessarily that
different—less obvious, sometimes subtle to the point of obscurity,
but fundamentally founded on the principle that the South has got
something that the rest of America doesn't have anymore. Some of
this is in Lucinda Williams's songs ("I'm going back to the Crescent
City, where everything's still the same"), although the myths she
makes are more sophisticated and of her own private order—it's a
vision in which Jack Kerouac meets Robert Johnson and General
Robert E. Lee, and they form a blues band, singing lyrics dashed off
by Eudora Welty, and after a blowout, never-to-be-repeated concert
they disappear at dawn on their Harleys, where they all die, driving
far too fast, in a terrible accident. Like her Southern accent and her
sense of "country," it's a vision built on her possession of unique-
ness. And it was, I now realize, what drew me to the Delta on my
own, and to Rosedale, looking for a juke joint that may no longer
exist, and then, afterward, heading down Mississippi State Highway
No. 1, the river always on my right, the railroad tracks running parallel somewhere on my left, and the sky big and endless, and nothing else in view, except, every few miles, a white church, an
adornment on the flood-flattened Delta horizon, surrounded by
cars, having mysteriously drawn a crowd from a land that seemed to
have no one on it.

What was I looking for? Something else, something personal, some remembered connection to a place, now lost, farther down the Delta, in Louisiana, in an oppressive, sulfur-stinking Civil War papermill town that, when I got there, later that day, would be proudly flying the Confederate flag on the birthday of M.L.K. It was where my family came from, and not all that far from where I was born, and in this I recognize now that, like Trish Blossom and the obsessive letter-writing fans, and like Lucinda's father, I'd personalized this woman's music—I had been tempted by its complex first-person, identify-with-me inducements—because in fact the songs that arise out of this landscape are not necessarily autobiographical at all; they merely seem to be so; they invite us to think them so. Good mythmakers are good liars. When Miller Williams sought out his daughter backstage, after listening to "Car Wheels on a Gravel Road," and apologized for her upbringing, he surprised Lucinda. ("Why, Daddy—that song's not about you!") And while "2 Kool 2 Be 4-Gotten," her tribute to the Magic City juke joint in Rosedale, is a recitation of juke-joint images, it is also a jumbly catalogue of all kinds of things you'd never see in such a place, including a man writhing around outside, claiming that he has decided to take up serpents and strychnine. What's he doing there? This is one of Williams's Pentecostal weirdos—an unlikely visitor to the wrong side of the tracks, even if the crowds inside now include no-neck white fatsos. In the same song, Robert Johnson (dead long before Lucinda Williams was born) is playing guitar in the corner, when, suddenly, an odd sing-songy digressive poem pops up right in the middle, a nonsequitur remembrance of a self-destructive lover:

> *Leaning against the railing of a Lake Charles bridge*
> *Overlooking the river, leaning over the edge*
> *He asked me: Would you jump into the water with me?*
> *I told him: No way, baby, that's your own death, you see?*

Who is this person in love with death and what does he have to do with the Magic City juke joint? This is Clyde, the Lake Charles obsessive, and he has nothing to do with Magic City (both the key and the tempo change to accommodate his visit), but he enjoys a rightful role in a work that, I now understand, is more poem than song, a surrealistic invocation of Southernness not unlike the kitschy religious shrines and turquoise serpents and bottlecap Christs in Lucinda's own house. It's a bit of mythmaking, by a poet of loss, about a place that's receding from experience, and that might never have been there in the first place. And Williams knows this. She has never been to Rosedale, Mississippi. She's never seen the Magic City juke joint, except in a picture book. For that matter, she's never been to a juke joint.

In a Mood

Lucinda is in a mood. Margaret Moser warned me about these moods. ("She gets all hinky and starts honking like a mule, and then folds up her arms and presses her lips together, and won't look at anyone, and you can stare at her for the longest time and won't have any idea of what the fuck is going through her mind.") Her road manager, Paul Monahan, warned me about them, too, pointing out that he had been her manager for only the last part of her tour, seven months, and in that short time half a dozen people had been fired (including two bus drivers), until the final week, when the remaining band members were let go, too. ("She is the sweetest, most thoughtful, kindest person you'll ever meet. And then, suddenly, the pressure will freak her out, and she doesn't know why it's freaking her out, and she can see she's freaking out but can't do a thing about it.") I once saw the early warning signs of a tempest in the making, after a concert, as everyone was piling into the bus, preparing for the all-night journey ahead, an early-evening show at a festival in Dallas the next day, when Lucinda said she was unhappy with the mix that night, very, very unhappy—something wasn't right, the guitarists were too showoffy, the drummer was too much on top of the beat, something, whatever it was ("What the fuck is it?"), it wasn't working—and was short-tempered and unapproachable, a sudden change in personality that Richard, her boyfriend, recognized and adapted to, not getting too close, finding things to do in another part of the bus, avoiding eye contact, saying nothing, knowing that her questions didn't need answers, until he felt he could make his excuses, and, with relief expressing itself across his face, slipped out for a drink before the bus left.

Tonight, I'm not sure what it is. It's late and Lucinda hasn't eaten ("God damn it, I let my blood sugar fall"), and she's unhappy with Nashville—not to mention Austin, Houston, Los Angeles, and, especially, New York ("I fucking hate fucking New York," she says, eyeballing me provocatively, knowing that I live in the city, and when I don't reply she repeats it, "I fucking hate New York," and when I still don't respond she says it once more)—but it doesn't matter what subject we happen to settle on as we drive into town for a late dinner. Whatever it is, Lucinda is going to attack it.

We've reached the Sunset Grill, an upmarket Nashville music-business hangout, and have been joined by two friends, Vicky, a neighbor, who sits beside Lucinda, and Dub ("the real thing"), who "does something with Steve Earle," and there is talk of other musicians appearing later, and, nearby, the tables are filling up with sidemen arriving from a session with Merle Haggard. Lucinda's state of mind—the blood-sugar level modestly fortified by a bread roll—might now be described as more attitude than mood. She was in a similar way the last time she was here—again, that exhilarating capacity of hers, this tightrope shuffle, of always being on the verge of losing it—when she started ranting about the spinelessness of Nashville music, and, getting more and more worked up, and oblivious of the shushing noises her friends were making, flapping their hands, trying to make her shut up, went on to denounce the overproduced formulaic country sound of Faith Hill in an outburst that culminated in the cry "Oh, fuck Faith Hill"—the allure of those alliterating "f "s proving irresistible—only to realize that an unfazed Faith Hill was sitting at a table right behind her.

Tonight, though, it's anything, everything, the cost of living, the high price of rented accommodation, the yuppies who are driving out the artists, the Southern obsession with guns, the racks of them in the backs of pickup trucks, the nutcases who collect them (including the stepfather of her boyfriend), leading to a repellent horror of the things ("I wish they were all outlawed"), and sliding, somehow, into a denunciation of the Second World War, in which, Lucinda says, the United States should never have got involved, a sentiment that enrages Richard, and, before I realize it, the two of them are in an argument of considerable passion—with Lucinda insisting that she is not an existentialist but a nihilist and doesn't care about the future of unborn children. I'm feeling awkward and not quite wanting to listen too carefully when Richard, having worked himself into a seeming rage, tells her to fuck off. Just like that. "Lu," he says, and takes a breath for effect, "fuck off."

Vicky, the neighbor, sitting opposite, freezes with her mouth open, her fork of food suspended over her plate, staring at Richard with incredulity, and you can see she's about to ask him if he has just said what she thinks she's heard, when her question is rendered redundant because Richard repeats the imperative, with a second-person variation for stress, "Fuck you, Lucinda." Vicky takes a breath. "Richard Price," she says, using his full name in that scolding-mother way, "how dare you—" but she's shut down once more when Richard tells Lucinda that she'd do him and the whole room a great favor if she simply fucked off. And then he adds, "Fuck you, fuck you, fuck you." What are any of us to do? Vicky's hands are fluttering. You can see that she wants to walk out, but she can't do that because she's upset on behalf of her friend—she can't leave her here with someone who is telling her to fuck off, even if he's the man she lives with. In fact, Vicky's indignation has mounted in this way because, in the distress of the moment, she is looking at Richard and not to her side, where Lucinda is sitting. Lucinda, I am surprised to observe, is not upset. All night long, she's been oppressive company— relentlessly whiny and confrontational and negative—until finally she has provoked her boyfriend into being a badass ("You can't fucking mess with the Hombre," he is saying now, punctuating his declaration with the inevitable refrain, "so fuck off, Lucinda"), and Lucinda is loving it. She is beaming. Vicky is telling Richard that he can't get away with this, when, against my better judgment, I interrupt her and say, "No, no, you don't understand, they're liking this, this is actually the way they are together, didn't you know?" and I look over to

Lucinda and her eyes are glistening—they're shiny with pleasure—
and she's looking at Richard with an unnerving intensity. Then she
starts cackling, that rhythmic Lucinda laugh, easy and warm and
deeply sexual.

What I find myself doing—inappropriately, of course—is rooting
for them. The two of them have been seeing each other for nearly
five years—the longest steady relationship in Lucinda's life—and, as
a member of the audience witnessing the theatre of their being
together, I've learned something of the trickiness of being Lucinda's
guy. (It seems to work by inverting the conventional roles, so that
Richard, for all his badass Hombre attitude, is the patient one, the
don't-worry-I'll-run-out-and-get-it one, the beck-and-call guy; in
this household, there's no doubt who is wearing the trousers.) I saw
them openly fighting once before, a tiff of a different order. This
was in New Orleans, late, in a voodoo bar on Decatur Street. After a
night of drinking and reminiscing by the river, Lucinda was suddenly in a mood. She was anxious, at two-thirty in the morning, that
she hadn't written a song in three years. It was a curious time to be
anxious, if only because, with concert dates booked for the next six
months, there wasn't a lot she was going to be able to do to relieve
her distress. The problem, it seemed, was that she was too happy.
Richard didn't believe that this was a problem—happiness, he
thought, was not a bad thing. But Lucinda wasn't listening. She was
speaking longingly of her melancholy "Silver Lake period"—the
time when, fourteen years before, living in a downtown apartment
in Los Angeles and, having just broken up with Clyde, alone, emotionally wounded, with little money and few distractions, she was
focussed and wrote some of her best songs, one after the other:
"Crescent City," "Passionate Kisses," "Changed the Locks," and
"Side of the Road," a song that, describing a lover's need to be apart
from her beloved ("I want to be alone . . . I want to see what it feels
like to be without you, I want to know the touch of my own skin"),
was starting to seem uncomfortably apposite. Richard persisted. You
didn't need to be unhappy to write, he was saying: it's possible to be
both creative *and* personally fulfilled—to have good food *and* good
wine *and* money *and* good sex *and* write good songs. But Lucinda

wasn't buying it (and was impatient with him and thinking something like, Oh, shut up, Richard, what do you know? You're just a bass player), and, again, I found myself wanting both of them to be happy, *please*.

I'm wanting her to be normal. But Lucinda isn't "normal." On some level, the person and the persona in her songs are related, as though her volatile character—this capacity for not knowing how to stop—is a manifestation of the same unguarded personality who can't stop herself from falling wholly in love, over and over again. Or, perhaps, another way of thinking of it: this woman, who has never held a job for any time, doesn't get up in the mornings, is routinely three or four hours late to appointments, who walks out of studios because she doesn't feel like singing that day, and has a knack for both tantrum and wonder, achieves a childlike intensity of emotion in her songs because on some level she isn't, even at the age of forty-seven, quite an adult. And I am probably not the only one who isn't in a hurry to see her grow up.

And then, wholly in character, persona and person still intertwined, last month Lucinda and her boyfriend decided to live apart, and Lucinda made plans to move into an airy loftlike apartment in downtown Nashville, not all that different from the airy apartment she once had in Silver Lake, and, alone now, with lots of space, and few distractions, she has started writing again. That happiness thing, who needs it?

Hipsters and Hoodlums

It was a time, all right . . .

So, anyway, this character, this punk of a disc jockey from Chicago, ends up working here in New York. We had this record, nice little record, "Just One More Tear," by a girl named Laurie Ann Mathews. She was good. She was white, but she sounded black.

We need to break out the record. This is back in 1962 or so. It was pay for play. That's what promotion was all about. A hundred, a few hundred bucks. Five hundred, a thousand copies of the record that they could take down to the store to sell.

So this D.J.—he's like a midget, this guy, about four and a half feet high—I guess he figures he's a big shot. He takes the money, but he don't play the record. What he does, he goes on the air, says "I'm about to break this new record." And then he breaks it—I mean, breaks it, cracks it into pieces—says, "I wouldn't play this record if my mother gave it to me." Like I say, I guess this little prick thinks he's something. Maybe all that candy-ass Chicago tough-guy shit went to his head. Anyway, he wasn't in Chicago no more. This was New York.

It was said that Hymie Weiss, the Romanian-born Jew who had founded Old Town Records in the cloakroom of the Triboro Theatre in Harlem in 1954, chose to call his label by that name because his brother and partner, Sam Weiss, had been working for a Brooklyn paper company called Old Town and had a lot of stationery bearing that name. Hymie remembers his first act as "a guy named

Cherokee," remembers that he sold the guy "a car that wouldn't start unless you pushed it downhill."

Old Town survived through black doo-wop groups, such as the Solitaires, who achieved local success in the northeastern golden triangle of New York–Newark–Philadelphia. The label would later prosper with national hit records by Arthur Prysock—Hy's favorite—and the Earls, a white doo-wop group from the Bronx. Within a year of Old Town's inception, Hy moved into a real office, down on Seventh Avenue, and by 1958 he was operating out of 1697 Broadway, just up the road from the cathedral of the music business, the Brill Building, 1619 Broadway, at 49th Street.

After the Chicago disc jockey's act of insolence, Hy Weiss arranged a meeting with him at the Old Town office, which was on the ninth floor. The record wasn't Hy's; he was only acting as an intermediary for the aggrieved parties. Also present was Carmine De Noia, a Broadway bookmaker who was a friend of those in the music business. Carmine was an imposing man. His friends called him Wassel, a nickname derived from his boyhood mispronunciation of the word "rascal."

"I used to help them," Wassel says, not much less imposing today, at 75, than he was in the old days. "See, I was the only Italian guy on Broadway, and I didn't take no crap from nobody. I respected everybody, but nobody would fool with me because I would never rob anybody."

Wassel laughs, his memory wandering back over 40 years, his voice deep, sonorous, and disarmingly blithe. "Hy goes into the other room. So here's this disc jockey. And I'm looking at him, and he's, like, this little midget. I throw open the window, pick him up, flip him, shake him out by the ankles. Ninth floor. All the change fell out of his pockets. Some friends of mine picked it up."

The disc jockey played the record during his very next broadcast, and he kept playing it. Soon, however, he was back in Chicago.

"He denied it ever happened," Wassel says. "Some guys asked him. He denied it. I said, 'Let him deny it. That's all right. Let him deny it.'"

"See," says another old-timer, "it wasn't that this guy didn't want to play the record. It was that he took the money, then didn't play the record. He wasn't a stand-up guy."

"Same thing as today, a lot of fakers."

We are sitting around a big table in the back room of a restaurant—much talk of recent surgeries and current medical conditions; much ordering of eggs and sausages to be prepared in exacting and arcane Italianate manners; and then the stories.

"Yeah," says Wassel. "I remember, there was this song I liked—and Sid Weiss"—a songwriter, no relation to Hy—"gave the publishing on it to me. So what am I gonna do with it now? Am I gonna put it on the wall? I don't know anything about publishing."

Wassel got a telephone call from a song publisher whose name is lost to the years, as is the name of the song in question.

"Your name Wassel?"

"Yeah."

"You got a song we want."

"I don't want no trouble."

"We want the song."

Wassel wrapped a length of pipe in a rolled-up newspaper. "I went up there, and the guy was a nasty guy. If he would've talked nice to me, I would've gave it to him. I didn't care; I didn't know anything about publishing. So, anyway, I went up there. This guy's sitting at his desk with his feet on the desk."

"Listen," Wassel told the guy, "what do you want?"

"You know what I want. Just put the song over there."

Wassel looked at him. "I says, 'Here.' I came down with the pipe. I broke everything. The desk, everything."

Had the would-be wiseguy asked, he would have received. But, as Wassel says, "he was trying to shake me down."

Everybody was trying to take down everybody. Among the Jews who ran the music business, it was treachery without end within the temple. "Every time guys came up to Hy Weiss's office," Wassel remembers, "they were trying to shake him down. 'Hey, man, you got any bread?' I'd be there. I'd say, 'Look, this ain't no grocery store. I mean, this is a grocery store? It's not a grocery store.' One guy pulled a knife. I didn't care. I was wild then. But we were trying to make a living; that's all we wanted to do."

There was the day he was called up to the Brill Building office of a music-publishing company, which was run by a couple of brothers who were generally regarded as pricks. A kid, a young song-writer who wrote for the Fiestas, a group that recorded for Hy Weiss, was trying to get a long-overdue royalty statement from the brothers. The kid had one of them against the wall and was holding a broken Coca-Cola bottle to his throat when Wassel arrived.

"I took the broken Coke bottle from the kid and told the guys, 'Send him his statement.'"

Money, money, money—"Money Honey," as the Drifters sang in 1953—all the time, money.

But not always money. Men such as Wassel in those days were paid as promotion men; and, as recalcitrant disc jockeys discovered the hard way, they were quite effective as such. But promotion also en-compassed a wider and gentler, albeit often subrosa, range of duties, not restricted to the milieu of the small, mongrel record companies. There was the time when one of the biggest and most established of the major companies called in an outside "promotion man" to tail one of its most successful singers, a household name. Tailing this young performer was a sort of undercover form of public-relations insurance.

"You know," one of the old-timers tells me, "make sure he steered clear of the wrong people, wrong places."

I don't quite understand.

"You know."

I don't know. Was this young golden throat consorting with the Mob?

I get a look that seems to say: I'm talking about *wrong* people, *wrong* places.

"They wanted to make sure nobody caught him with a dick in his mouth."

Hy Weiss had been a bouncer at a White Rose bar in his early years and was himself occasionally called upon to aid a friend in promotion-related undertakings. There was a call one morning from a man who, with his wife, ran one of the premier R&B companies. They were having problems with a distributor with whom they had contracted to share space in their building on 10th Avenue, and they could not get him out.

"You gotta meet me at seven in the morning," the label owner says to Hy. It was a Saturday morning.

"O.K. What for?"

"When you get here."

"You sure it's important?"

"Absolutely."

Hy arrives early Saturday morning. There's the guy, and he's holding a big metal can.

"I got gas."

Hy wants to know "What are you gonna do with this gas?"

"I'm gonna burn down the building."

"Hey, I don't cook on Saturday." The Sabbath.

Wassel's elusive career in the undergrowth of the music business dated to the early 50s, during the golden age of rock 'n' roll. He was, as he says, a bookmaker, taking action on horses among the Broadway crowd, of which the growing cast of characters in the burgeoning world of rock 'n' roll were fast replacing the Tin Pan Alley veterans who had occupied the Brill Building since 1931.

"It didn't last very long," he says of his Broadway bookmaking days, which began in 1949. "I used to go to Jack Dempsey's to get a little action. I used to go to Lindy's, to Gallagher's."

These were the mythic places of old Broadway: Gallagher's, on West 52nd Street, which had begun as a speakeasy in 1927; Lindy's, on Broadway, just north of the Brill Building, a restaurant and hangout that operated around the clock and which had been the "Mindy's" of Damon Runyon's tale-telling; Jack Dempsey's, which was located on the ground floor of the Brill Building. The Jewish entrepreneurs of the music business were inveterate gamblers: their success was built upon daring to venture into an untamed new territory—rock 'n' roll—where the established, major companies feared to enter. But the

gains of their business gambles were all too often lost to gambling of a
more common kind, and it was through their betting that Wassel,
during his short-lived career as a bookie, came to know them.

"He knew them because they were all booking through him," one
of his friends says.

"That was how they all got in trouble. They gambled and they
lost and they couldn't pay off. They shook each other down. But the
Mob never shook them down. The Mob never came to them. They
came to the Mob, because their gambling debts drove them to the
Mob."

Aside from the partnerships of collateral interest pursuant to its
role as rock 'n' roll's lender of last resort, the Mob's primary involvement with rock 'n' roll, as it had been for many years with the music
business in general, was through the jukebox racket. Since 1946,
exclusive licenses to sell Wurlitzer jukeboxes had been held by the
Emby Distributing Company. Located on West 43rd Street, Emby
was controlled by Frank Costello and Meyer Lansky, the two biggest
gangsters in New York. Until recently, in certain quarters, one might
still be urged to pump change into the jukebox with the wry words
"Play another record; their daughters need new Cadillacs."

Coins clinking into the big, incandescent Bakelite jukebox. Coins
showering to the street from a ninth-story window. Yes, it was a
time.

It was the time of rock 'n' roll's innocence—that is to say, its incarnation of innocence. The golden age of rock 'n' roll can be said to
have begun in 1945, when hip black urban music diverged into two
distinct revolutionary currents: the more cerebral and Apollonian
freshet of bebop, and the more febrile and Dionysian torrent of
rhythm and blues, as pioneered by blues shouters of the day such as
Wynonie Harris. That age would last for little more than a decade.
Elvis Presley marked its end, and it was as if the golden age of real
rock 'n' roll had never been: the all-powerful consumer mainstream
of white America, in its belated discovery of rock 'n' roll, knew only
the banal Wonder Bread of its usurpation by the forces of market-
friendly mediocrity.

This is not to say that the inchoate beast of rock 'n' roll had raged in sovereignty from World War II until the ascendancy of Elvis. In 1951—the year that saw the release of Jackie Brenston and His Delta Cats' "Rocket '88'" become perhaps the first truly devastating rock 'n' roll wrecking ball to hit No. 1 in its demolition of the rhythm-and-blues charts—there were also far less feral manifestations of rock 'n' roll that enjoyed even greater success: Amos Milburn's soft and fatalistic "Bad, Bad Whiskey," Charles Brown's haunting classic, "Black Night." And while two of the raunchiest, rockingest vocal-group records, "Work with Me, Annie" and "Sexy Ways," both by Hank Ballard and the Midnighters, dated to the months before Elvis's first recordings, in 1954, the much more innocuous fare of doo-wop had by then come to define the New York vocal-group sound of the Brill Building's ever increasing dominion.

As chronicled in detail in the introduction to my book *Unsung Heroes of Rock 'n' Roll*, the music had begun to change in the middle of a war, when the world was mad and big-band swing was still the rage. Benny Goodman, Harry James, Glenn Miller, and the Dorsey brothers were the men whose music dominated the early 1940s. Columbia, which had Goodman and James; Victor, which had Miller and Tommy Dorsey; and Decca, which had Jimmy Dorsey, were the three companies that dominated the industry. But as the new music spread, and as it became obvious that the prospering major companies were for the most part unaware of and uninterested in the sea change, numerous little labels were founded by men and women who smelled money in what was happening. In 1942, Herman Lubinsky started Savoy Records in downtown Newark. In Los Angeles, in 1944, the songwriter Otis René started Excelsior ("The All Colored Recording Company"). In Harlem, Ike and Bess Berman formed Apollo. The mongrel labels were a book of begats, a Fourth Book of Moses unto themselves—Exclusive and DeLuxe, National and King, Modern and Aladdin, Mercury and Specialty, Atlantic and Chess, Duke and Sun, Vee-Jay and Old Town, and hundreds more. They were the true breeding ground and glory ground of rock 'n' roll.

The industry establishment did not quite know what to make of the new music, and by 1954 the major companies were paying for their sins. Looking askance for too long at rock 'n' roll, regarding it as a fad that soon would pass, they began to see how much money they had been missing out on since the late 40s. All the best-selling rock 'n' roll hits, all the biggest artists, had belonged to those mongrel labels, some of which, such as Atlantic and Chess, were on their way to becoming major labels.

As 1955 began, the big old-line companies were trying desperately to cash in. Since they did not understand what rock 'n' roll was, the maladroit rushing of their greed was marvelous to behold. Columbia decided that Tony Bennett would be its rock 'n' roll star. DIG THE CRAZIEST!! HE SWINGS!! HE ROCKS!! HE GOES!! Bennett's "Close Your Eyes" was advertised as an ASTOUNDING RHYTHM AND BLUES RENDITION. Needless to say, Tony didn't make it as a rock 'n' roll star. But by the end of the year no one was laughing at RCA-Victor. If the label couldn't make it, the label would buy it: in late November, RCA-Victor bought Elvis Presley from Sam Phillips's little Sun Records of Memphis, and in 1956, with Elvis, RCA-Victor marked the beginning of the end not only of the golden age of untamed rock 'n' roll but of that age's mongrel labels as well. Those few that survived became major labels, or lingered on for a while, then were consumed or vanished, and a whole new wave of small labels, such as Paris and Roulette, came into being as the maverick masters of rock 'n' roll's incarnation of innocence.

The ascendancy of the pose of innocence can be traced to 1954, the year of Elvis's first records and of "Gee" by the Crows. Indeed, the Crows' record, which some consider, oddly, to be the first rock 'n' roll hit—a misguided assertion based solely on the fact that, while other records had crossed over from the R&B to the pop chart, "Gee," in the spring of 1954, broke simultaneously on both charts—was about as sweet and innocent as it got. If anything, "Gee," like Elvis, was the sunset of one age and the dawning of another: the first hit not of rock 'n' roll but of rock 'n' roll's silver age, the age of its rebirth, like a virgin, to sing its songs of moneymaking innocence beneath the windows of a new and innocent generation. From rotgut to milk shakes, do-rags to ponytails. In 1950, Wynonie Harris had pulled off a joyous Top 10 R&B hit, "Good Morning Judge," about running wild with a 15-year-old girl. In 1957—the year the Everly Brothers hit No. 1 on both the R&B and pop charts with "Wake Up Little Susie," a song about the anticipation of parental reprimand when curfew is violated by dozing off chastely during a date—Andre Williams, hanging tough and true to the spirit, could not find a breach even at the bottom of the R&B charts with his "Jail Bait." The following year, however, embracing the new, antithetical ethos of innocence, Chuck Berry—who would later do time for violating the Mann Act—captured the R&B and pop charts, and the hearts of young America, with "Sweet Little Sixteen," a saccharine ditty that might have brought a gleam of inspiration to Norman Rockwell's eye.

There would be a lot of good records during the age of innocence, but they would be anomalies. It would not be until the warm days of 1965—the Stones' "Satisfaction," Dylan's *Highway 61 Revisited*—that resurrection would come, in a sudden exundant wave.

George Goldner was in his early 30s, married to a Latin-American woman, and an aficionado of the recent mambo craze when he started his Tico recording company in 1948. Tico became the dominant label in Latin music, and less than two years after its founding, Goldner began a subsidiary label, Rama, to take advantage of the new black doo-wop music. With the immense success of Rama's recording of the Crows' "Gee," Goldner then started Gee Records in 1954. It was Goldner who subsequently "discovered" Frankie Lymon and the Teenagers, whose first and biggest hit, "Why Do Fools Fall in Love?," was released by Gee in early 1956.

"George Goldner," as one old-timer tells me, "was the genius of the business."

We are still sitting around the big table at the back of the restaurant, and as tribute to Goldner is paid, and while others concur, Hy Weiss, frail and gentle in his old age, scowls benignly, nonchalantly shakes his head, and points silently, almost privately, to himself.

"Don't mention George Goldner," says Weiss (just some coffee, plain eggs, no sausage). "He was a figment of my imagination." This dismissal is Hy's way of saying that it was he, not Goldner, who found Frankie Lymon: "I gave him the Teenagers."

Whether or not Goldner was the genius maximus of the business, one thing was certain: by the fall of 1955, Goldner had cut in a curious new partner, Joe Kolsky, the brother of a man named Phil Kahl, who was in partnership in music publishing with one Moishe Levy.

It is difficult to state with certainty the roles played by the brothers Kahl and Kolsky in what became Goldner's dance in the dark with Moishe Levy. Kahl had entered into open alliance with Levy in early 1953, with the formation of Patricia Music, a publishing operation that also handled several performers, including the brilliant but doomed and demon-beset jazz pianist Bud Powell. Whatever his experience in the music business, Kahl was known as Fingers—a reference, not so much sinister as cynical, to his primary career as a hairdresser at the Concord Hotel in the Catskills. Kolsky, George Goldner's new partner who was presented in the course of business as a produce tycoon, was in fact the proprietor of a fruit stand in the Bronx.

The Bronx. It was where Hy Weiss lived. It was where Phil Spector was born. It was where Dion, the greatest of the white doo-wop masters, came from. Dion had a group called the Timberlanes, then he had the Belmonts. "A friend of mine sent them to me," remembers Wassel.

"Who was your friend?"

"Some guy."

"Just some guy?"

"A wiseguy."

Wassel says the guy is still alive, says he'll call to ask if it's all right for me to use his name.

And the Bronx was where Moishe Levy grew up. He went by the name of Morris, but those who knew him called him Moe when they didn't call him Moishe. He was in his early 20s when he took over Birdland, the celebrated jazz nightclub, named for Charlie

"Bird" Parker, that opened in 1949 on 52nd Street at Broadway. Even then there was a mythology about the man who called himself Morris Levy. He had won control of the joint in a card game, it was said—drawing three 7s, playing one-on-one against the owner—though many swear that Levy never gambled except for an occasional game of craps. Wassel remembers him as a kid flipping hamburgers at the Turf, which, like Jack Dempsey's, faced Broadway from the street level of the Brill Building. He had then become a photo developer of pictures taken of patrons by nightclub camera girls and also operated coat-check concessions in clubs throughout town. Then, mysteriously, he owned clubs: not only Birdland and its sister club, Birdland of Miami, but the Royal Roost, the Downbeat, the Embers, and the Round Table—all, at one time or another, were said or known to have been Levy's joints.

Then there was this business with George Goldner, who was on a roll in 1955 and just about to come forth with Frankie Lymon and the Teenagers. George may have been the genius of the business, but he was not without the Achilles' heel that had brought down a multitude of his lessers. He was a degenerate gambler. By 1957, Goldner's record companies, already given over to Levy's forces, were subsumed by a new company, Roulette, whose partners were Goldner and Kolsky—the fruit vendor—and whose president was Levy. Within three months, Goldner was out of the picture altogether, his interest in Roulette, as well as all participation in the right to his Tico, Rama, and Gee catalogues, ceded wholly to what *Billboard* referred to as "the Morris Levy combine."

Roulette under Levy prospered well into the 60s. "Peppermint Twist," by Joey Dee—Joey DiNicola of Passaic, New Jersey—and the Starliters, was released by Roulette in late 1961 and became nearly as big a hit as Chubby Checker's version of "The Twist," making the Peppermint Lounge the most celebrated nightclub in America. It was on Roulette, too, that Arkansas-born Ronnie Hawkins had his first Top 40 hit, "Mary Lou," in 1959. Hawkins remained with Levy and Roulette through 1963, two years before members of his band, the Hawks, began working with Bob Dylan and eventually became the Band.

For all the wealth it brought him, Morris Levy never much cared for rock 'n' roll, a friend of his told me. "Morris loved jazz. He didn't like rock 'n' roll."

George Goldner went on to have some success with two new companies, End and Gone, but these labels, too, ended up in Levy's hands. With the songwriting team of Leiber and Stoller, he went on in 1965 to form yet another company, Red Bird, which had its share of hits, by the Shangri-Las and others; but both the partnership and the label soon dissolved, and Goldner died a few years later, in 1970, at the age of 52.

Not only was he a genius, says one who knew him, by way of epitaph, but "he was one hell of a sharp dresser too."

But what of Morris Levy's genius? In a group, as at that big round back-room table, the old-timers are wary, evasive in answering.

"He could spot a winner," says one.

"The 'essence of his genius'?" says another, smiling and wryly using the phrase I had offered. "Robbing everybody."

"He never gambled."

"He took over underdogs."

"Morris hated to give up money. Money was his god, and he was devout in his religion."

"What was that saying? 'This is my grocery store. I do all the robbin' here.'"

"If you sold a million records, he'd say you sold a hundred thousand. Moe was pretty sharp with that. That was his thing."

"But he wasn't doing anything that everybody else wasn't doing."

"They weren't thieves. They just did business their own way. It was a way of business."

"People say how they got robbed," says Hy Weiss. "They didn't get robbed. I didn't rob anybody, and neither did a lot of other people that are accused. Why? Because at that particular time everybody was offering what they had for sale. In fact, I had a song called 'So Fine'"—a minor Old Town hit by the Fiestas, a Newark group, in 1959—"and I gave it up. Somebody said they owned it, I says good-bye like an idiot. That wouldn't happen again in a million years, you know what I'm saying?"

The most important figure in the introduction of rock 'n' roll—
real rock 'n' roll—to white America was the legendary Alan Freed
(1922–65), who began broadcasting R&B records over WJW in
Cleveland in the summer of 1951. Though the audience for the
records he played was predominantly black, his Judeo-Christian
benediction of the music served to draw an increasingly integrated
group of listeners. By 1953 his rock 'n' roll touring shows, which
featured the likes of Count Basie and Lester Young as well as of
Big Joe Turner, Wynonie Harris, Ruth Brown, and the Clovers,
were success and sensation, bringing him controversial celebrity
and fortune both. When he moved to New York to work at WINS
in the late summer of 1954—the cusp between rock 'n' roll's
golden and silver ages—he came as the most powerful disc jockey
in the land.

The man who took control of his career in New York was Morris
Levy.

"That was the secret of Moishe's success," I was told. "He controlled Freed." And, in those pay-for-play days, Freed, whose plays
were the biggest, got the biggest pay. "Every record company that
was in business selling R&B had a deal with Alan Freed. Atlantic,
King, Federal—all of them. And they all had to come up with the
money. That's the way it was." Freed made money. Morris made
money.

In a group, these are the things that are said, and in all of what is
said there is truth. These men know what they are talking about,
and there seems to be no special fondness for Levy among them.

There are a lot of stories from the Birdland days. It was Irving
Levy, Moishe's brother, who helped manage the joint.

"He was a sweetheart, Irving. I was there the night he was killed.
He had a hooker there, didn't want her there, and he chased her out.
Her husband caused a big commotion, stabbed Irving, killed him.
So then it was like open season. All the jukebox guys used to hang in
the Birdland mostly. And everybody's out for the husband."

"He loved broads," one says of Morris who would marry and
divorce several times.

But what of all the tales about Levy's being deeper into the Mob than the rest of them?

"Bullshit."

But alone, some speak differently. One takes me aside, his arm around me, whispering though we are in earshot of no one.

"Let me tell you," he says. His hushed words are delivered slowly and surely: "Morris simply could not have done what he did alone."

In 1959, it was announced that the House Subcommittee on Legislative Oversight was preparing to investigate commercial bribery in the music industry. Alan Freed, broken by the ensuing scandals of the lengthy payola hearings, died impoverished and disgraced in the year that later brought the sudden, exundant wave of rock 'n' roll's resurrection. As for Levy, he was charged in 1986 on counts of criminal conspiracy with several alleged mafiosi, was convicted of extortion conspiracy in 1988, and following the failure of an appeal, was scheduled to report to federal prison when, in the spring of 1990, aged 62, he died at the manor house of his estate, a 1,300-acre horse farm in Ghent, New York.

Of course, the payola scandals stopped nothing. Alan Freed was just the sacrificial fatted calf. Juggy Gayles, the legendary song plugger—the man who broke "White Christmas" for Irving Berlin, the man who got Kate Smith to take up Berlin's "God Bless America"—had known Freed since the disc jockey's early days in Cleveland. "What can I tell ya?" Juggy Gayles said a few years ago when I asked him about Freed and payola. Freed, he said, "was a genius, and he was a power to reckon with." But, at the same time, "Freed was a schmuck. He went around and shot his mouth off. They would've forgot about him if he had kept his mouth shut." As Gayles implied, rock 'n' roll and payola were inseparable. It went back to the big-band days. "Some of those Mickey Mouse bandleaders, we'd slip 'em 10 bucks to play a chorus because we needed a quick plug," said Juggy. But with the rise of rock 'n' roll, "payola was all over the place. . . . Booze, bribes, and broads: that was rock 'n' roll."

Inquisition, prosecution mattered not. At the masque of innocence, it was business as usual.

"There was nothing wrong with it," says one of the guys.

"What was that guy, the disc jockey from Boston who became
head of Warner Bros. Records?" asks Hy Weiss. "Joe Smith, that's
him. Well, what did he say about me? He said I made up the $50
handshake.

"One day the door opened and Internal Revenue walked in. I
said, 'Yes?' They said, 'Well, we understand you're doing business
with disc jockeys,' and so on. I said, 'What's wrong with that?
Everybody's doing business with disc jockeys.' He said, 'But you
gave somebody $5,000.' And I said, 'Who was that, pray tell?' He
said, 'You gave it to Alan Freed.' I said, 'I gave it to him?' He says,
'Yeah.' I said, 'Well, wait awhile, let me look at something.' I picked
out a check and showed it to him with a little note. He said, 'What's
that?' I said, 'It was a loooaan.' He laughed.

"That night we went out to the track, out to dinner, me and the
guy from the I.R.S. And I had to sit there and give him winners.

"I could tell you the end of the story," Weiss concludes, "but I
can't get a friend of mine in trouble."

That reminds someone of another investigating agent. "This
agent, he sounds all serious: 'I want to talk to you.' Then he holds
up this little hand-lettered sign: I'M WIRED."

Bookies, Broadway, the Brill Building, the Boys.

My buddy Geno Sculatti, a true connoisseur of the bizarreries
that lurk beneath the stones of popular culture's forgotten back
streets, went off in search of a guy named Tony Bruno, a singer who
in 1967 released an album called *The Beauty of Bruno*, "a post-rock
lounge record," as Geno has described it, full of wondrously "beefy,
button-popping vocals." *The Beauty of Bruno* is an artifact equal in
rarity and obscurity to *Little Joe Sure Can Sing!*, the album, released
a year later, that Joe Pesci recorded under the name of Little Joe
Ritchie.

Those were strange days, as Jim Morrison sang in the year of *The
Beauty of Bruno*. People remember "Strange Days," as well they

should. But what of Hank Ballard's re-appearance on the R&B charts in 1968—Hank Ballard, who had been at it since 1952, had shotgun-blasted the sensibilities of America in 1954 with "Work with Me, Annie" and "Sexy Ways," had originated "The Twist" in 1959, and was still only 32 when he came back with "How You Gonna Get Respect (When You Haven't Cut Your Process Yet)"? Well, as Jim Morrison also had it, and truly enough, people are strange.

My buddy Geno finally found Tony Bruno, who was living quietly in Florida. Bruno generously shared with him the story of how he had gotten into the music business, back in 1960:

"I was hangin' around the Brill Building, takin' action for this bookie from New Jersey. I was doing pretty well, so he set me up with an office, and we pretended it was a record label. I had my desk, a small turntable, and eight or nine phones."

The lettering on the office door read NOMAR RECORDS, the nonce word Nomar being a partial reverse spelling of the surname of Bruno's boss. It was inevitable, in that hive of aspiration and hustling which was the Brill Building, that someone should eventually knock on the door of Nomar Records looking for a deal. That inevitability came in the form of Maxine Brown, a young singer from South Carolina bearing an acetate demonstration recording of a song she'd written called "All in My Mind." To press and release the record would lend the bookmaking front a further illusory air of legitimacy.

But something went wrong. Maxine Brown's "All in My Mind," released by Nomar Records in December of 1960, entered the R&B charts during the following month and eventually became one of the major hits of the year, rising to No. 2 on the R&B charts, crossing over to the pop Top 20, and selling about 800,000 copies before it ran its course. Another Maxine Brown hit, almost as big, followed. By comparison, the bookmaking operation, eight phones and all, seemed little more than a chump-change racket. It was thus that Tony Bruno became a producer and songwriter, and, after years of prospering as such, gave unto the world *The Beauty of Bruno*.

Jubilee Records, founded in Washington, D.C., in 1946 by Herb Abramson, and taken over by Jerry Blaine in 1947, epitomized the scattershot approach of the mongrel labels: record, buy, or lease anything you could, get it out there, and see what shook. Jubilee put out records by the Delta Rhythm Boys, Charlie Mingus, Enzo Stuarti, the Orioles, and a slew of characters who specialized in risqué "party" records. The rarest of all rock 'n' roll records, the example of scattershot negligence par excellence, was released, nominally, by Jubilee in 1952: "Stormy Weather," by the Five Sharps, of which only one unbroken, 78-r.p.m. copy is said to exist—a disk now reportedly valued at more than $50,000.

Jerry Blaine also operated various Jubilee subsidiary labels: Josie records brought forth the Cadillacs and their hit "Speedoo"; Gross was reserved for albums by Doug Clark and the Hot Nuts. In the early 60s, Blaine started yet another subsidiary, called Chex.

It was in June of 1962 that young Freddy DeMann of Brooklyn began working for Blaine as a promotion man of the nondefenestrating kind. The exact date was June 5, Freddy's 23rd birthday.

DeMann, who 21 years later became Madonna's manager, remembers Blaine as a gruff-speaking man given to talk of lavish excess. He was at the Jubilee office when somebody came in looking to sell a recording to Blaine.

"Whaddaya want for it?" Blaine demanded.

A price of $500 was suggested with some hesitance.

"Five hundred?" growled Blaine. "Shit, man, I pay more than that for whores."

Blaine, however, gave DeMann nothing in the way of pay-for-play gelt when he sent him out in 1962 to promote "I Love You," by the Volumes, on the new Chex label. Without the cash, DeMann discovered, the record was trash.

Freddy met a fellow promotion man, a guy named Danny Driscoll who worked for Smash, a subsidiary of Mercury. Danny tried to shore him.

"He was a big fat guy," DeMann says. "Jovial. Funny. 'Call me Fat Ass,' he used to say. 'I'm not gonna call you Fat Ass,' I said. 'Come on, everybody calls me Fat Ass.' He was a colorful guy. Then one day they found him dead in a car. He was a fag, and the story I heard is that some sailor killed him or something like that.

But I don't know if that's the truth. Maybe the Boys got him. I have no clue."

That was one thing that Freddy learned quickly: it was a strange racket. The Boys cast a lot of shadows; there were a lot of maybes as to what went on. Like many of the promotion guys in the early 60s, he hung out at Al & Dick's, a joint on 54th Street near Broadway whose premises went back to the Volstead Act days. The entertainer Texas Guinan, the darling of the underworld, had run a club there, as well as many other Broadway *boîtes de nuit*, in cahoots with the Boys of that time. Texas Guinan, a role model and inspiration for Mae West, was remembered for her greeting to patrons: "Hello, suckers." But another remark attributed to her held its wisdom as the old days on Broadway gave way to the new: "Success has killed more men than bullets."

DeMann describes the clientele of Al & Dick's as "a Runyonesque group of people. They were all guys in suits with slick black hair. Pompadours, that kind of thing." The disc jockeys, the industry guys, the artists, the friends of friends. "We all looked alike."

"It was an exciting world to come into. And I was, believe me, brand-new. And, yes, I knew there were guys there that could 'get the job done.'"

In the end, without any cash to slip into the sleeves of "I Love You," Freddy, after a long, roundabout journey among unresponsive disc jockeys, found himself in Philadelphia. It was there, in the stu-dio-office of D.J. Jerry Blavat, that he laid down his lantern.

"So, anyway," Blavat tells me, "I'm doing the radio show, and the promotion men come to see me. I get a knock at the door, and I say to Kilocycle Pete"—a kid who worked at the station—"'Answer the door,' which he normally does.

"So it's this young guy. His name is Freddy DeMann. He says, 'I got a record I want you to listen to, and I've got a problem.' I said, 'What's the problem?' He says, 'Nobody will play this record. You're my last resort. I'm gonna lose my gig.' He says, 'There's no money on this record. I have no money for the record.' I said, 'Freddy, let me tell you something. Number one, I don't take money. If I like the record, I play it. My mother can come to me with a record and say, "Your uncle made this record." If I don't like the record, I'm not gonna play it. Because for my teenagers, for my audience, I have in my mind the sound I'm gonna present.' To make a long story short, he sits with me while I do the radio show. Nobody wants to play the record because they're all looking for this"—he rubs his thumb and two fingers in the universal baksheesh gesture—"and he doesn't have it. I play the record, bust the record wide open. From that moment on, Freddy DeMann and I became friends. His boss, Jerry Blaine, wanted to know, 'How did you get the Geator to play this record with no money?'" (That's Blavat, see, the Geator with the Heator, etymology approximately as follows: the nickname Geator derived from the nickname Gator so as to now rhyme with heater, as in let's-get-down-with-the-sound-and-turn-that-car-heater-up-on-this-cold-Philly-night.) "And Freddy explained to him, 'He liked the record, man, he liked the record.' And that's the way I was from the very beginning to now. You could be my best buddy, but if I don't like the record, I'm not gonna play it."

Blavat was 22 years old and making over a hundred grand a year.

"I mean, back in 1962, that's a lot of money for a little cockroach kid from South Philadelphia."

C'era una volta a Filadelfia . . .

Gerald Joseph Blavat was born, in Philly, on July 3, 1940. "See," he says, "when I was a kid growing up, there were four corners in the neighborhood. Pat's Luncheonette, the grocery store, the Tap Room, and a variety store. These were the four corners of South 17th and Mifflin Streets. The younger guys hung on one corner. Across the street were the older guys. Then, in the Tap Room, were the older wiseguys. And the variety-store corner, the people in the neighborhood would come in and buy blah, blah, blah, I don't know. And up the side street, the older guys would shoot craps.

"When you grew up in that neighborhood, you knew everybody. You knew everybody. They used to call me Shorts when I was a kid because I was the smallest little guy. But I always knew and respected older people. When I was 12, I was hanging out in the social club with guys, 17, 18 years old. By the time I was 16, I was donning a black Stetson, black Continental suit, going into clubs and bars. But I knew how to act, so I always acted older."

Like the Mob in America, Jerry was Jewish and Italian. His father, known as Gimpy Lou, or simply the Gimp, was with the Jewish crew. "He was in the numbers business. When I was a kid, they would ship me off to a day nursery at St. Monica's at six in the morning. We lived in a row house on a street where there were only six houses—everything else was garages—and our house would turn into a bookie joint with all the top Jewish guys working it. Moishe, Sammy, Mickey. When I came home from the day nursery at five, it would turn back into a regular house."

His mother came from the same town in the Cheiti Province of Abruzzi as did the wife of Angelo Bruno, the Sicilian-born mafioso to whom control of Philadelphia passed from Joe Ida in the late 50s. It was thus as a boy, through his father's involvement in the numbers racket, and even more through his mother's friendship with Angelo's wife, that Jerry came to know the ascendant boss before the advent of his imperium.

Blavat had been one of the kids who danced on the WFIL-TV show *American Bandstand* in the days before the show's original host, Bob Horn—banished in the wake of scandals involving drunk driving and allegations of sex with a minor—was replaced, in the summer of 1956, by Dick Clark, the cultural hygienist whose smile of cleanliness and rectitude was the smile of milk-and-cookies rock 'n' roll. Another of the dancers from the Horn show, Danny Rapp, had helped to form and was the lead singer in a local group called the Juvenairs. In 1957 the group became Danny and the Juniors. Their first record, "At the Hop," released toward the end of that year, was one of the biggest hits of 1958. When the group set out to tour, it was with Jerry Blavat as their road manager and shepherd.

"These kids were innocent," Jerry says. "I used to get them laid. That was the biggest thing they wanted to do. I was a kid, 18, on the road. I would take them to, say, Wheeling, West Virginia. One time

I went in, and I think it was 10 bucks apiece to get laid. They were only making 40 bucks a week. I handled all the money. So the one kid wanted to get fucked a second time. I said, 'You just got laid—you're not gonna be able to get it up.' Yeah, yeah, yeah. 'I'm in love with this fuckin' broad.' So I made a deal with the madam: 'He wants to go a second time.' She said, 'O.K., give me eight dollars.' He went back up to the room, and we're all waiting. The madam came and said, 'Look, he's gotta be outta there very shortly.' We're still waiting. The madam comes and she says, 'I'm getting him out of here.' She goes upstairs. I hear a commotion, yelling and screaming. He doesn't wanna leave until he gets a hard-on. She comes back down, she calls the cops. The cops come, and they almost pinch us because it was protected. He wants his money back, the eight bucks. I said, 'Fuck you and your fucking money—let's get out of here.'"

As immensely successful as it was, "At the Hop" was pretty much the end as well as the beginning of Danny and the Juniors. When Blavat came off the road with them for the last time, in 1960, they were fading fast; Danny Rapp would go on to commit suicide in the spring of 1983, aged 41. In 1960, however, Jerry was just getting started.

"There was this nightclub in South Philadelphia called the Venus. And, remember, this is when rock 'n' roll is not being featured in clubs. I mean, this was a lounge where wiseguys would go and drink and pick up broads and things like that. I mean, it was the Venus Lounge in South Philadelphia. So I had just made a score coming off the road. I think I had, like, 800 bucks, and I started to shoot craps at 17th and Mifflin with the older guys. And Don Pinto, who owned the club, was there. Guys were making bets. One guy says to Pinto, 'Yeah, he can help ya. What do you need?' He said, 'I'm gonna do a radio show out of my club.' This guy said, 'The kid can do it.' I said, 'Yeah, I'll do a radio show.' So Don said, 'I'll bet you on the next fuckin' throw you can't do it.' I said, 'Don't bet your money on the fuckin' throw, 'cause you're gonna lose. I can do a radio show from your club.' He rolls, he lost. He didn't get the fuckin' number. So he says, 'Bad day.' I say, 'I'm gonna make it up to you. You're gonna see, I'm gonna do a radio show.' I went up to WCAM in Camden. I said to the general manager there, 'I wanna buy an hour's worth of time. What would it cost me?' He said, 'A hundred dollars.' I said, 'O.K. How long?' He said, 'Thirteen-week contract.' I got him $1,300, and I had the contract. I went back to Don Pinto and his partners at the Venus. I said, 'Look, I'll do an hour's radio show. I want you to give me 120 bucks.' I then went out and I sold 15-minute blocks. Freihofer bread, 60 bucks. Crisconi Oldsmobile, 60 bucks. Dale Dance Studios, 60 bucks. Seven Up, 60 bucks. I made $240, and I had $120 from the club. Whoever comes through—Tallulah Bankhead, Rocky Graziano—I interview them at the club. Then one day a snowstorm hits the city, closes down the club. I owned the radio time. So I took my records up to Camden and started to play that music. The snow kept coming down, the kids were off from school"—he snaps his fingers: dual double-finger snaps, the loudest snapping known to man—"and that was that."

So came to be the Geator with the Heater, keeper of the flame and coolest of the cool.

Thirty-eight years is a long time, and Blavat and DeMann have seen a lot of things come and go, a lot of things go and come through those years, including themselves, a few times over.

Sitting with Jerry in New York, Freddy after a while seems to slough the skin of Los Angeles, where he has for so long lived and worked as a manager and label executive. It is as if a breeze from Brooklyn, a breeze of the past, reclaims him. They reminisce about the days and characters gone.

They were days of naïveté and exuberance: the sweet and celibate two-straws-and-a-milk-shake songs of Paul & Paula, the Singing Nun rising to the top of the pop charts. And, beneath it all, as Juggy Gayles had put it: booze, bribes, and broads.

Well, the Singing Nun is gone. She OD'd on pills in a suicide pact with another woman in the spring of 1985. But it's not the Singing Nun that these guys miss.

"Yeah, Abner was the best," muses Jerry.

"In New York, when I first broke in, there was a little ring of whores that everyone knew," says Freddy. That was the way it was.

Some took their bribery in the currency of flesh, and for others it was both money and broads. "I was always on the lookout, you know, who's gonna hook me up. When I went to Chicago, I got the names of three people to call for whores, and that was mandatory. Well, actually, he gave me one name and he gave me the name of Abner. I went to see Abner, just to say, 'Hi, I'm new in town.' And he said, 'O.K., here, you need some whores?' I said, 'Yeah.' 'Here's three, call them and use my name. And meet me every Friday night at the Avenue Motel. We have a bunch of guys coming around, and we all hang out, have drinks, and you look like a cool guy—you can come.' I was white and they were black. I would go every Friday to that Avenue Motel, and man, I'm telling you . . ." Freddy shakes his head; there are no words. "Abner drank Johnnie Walker Black straight up, and so I drank Johnnie Walker Black straight up. With a soda chaser."

They're talking about Ewart G. Abner Jr., who ran Vee-Jay Records, a company that had been founded in Gary, Indiana, in 1953, by Vivian Carter and her husband, James Bracken—Vee for V. Carter, Jay for J. Bracken—and had moved to Chicago in 1954. From the beginning—Vee-Jay's first release, by the Spaniels, a quintet formed at Roosevelt High School in Gary, established the group as one of the leading doo-wop acts of the Midwest—the company was one of the most powerful of the independents, strong in the full spectrum of R&B, from the Spaniels to the Dells, and from Jimmy Reed to John Lee Hooker. In 1963, under Ewart Abner—who, with the benison of Carter and Bracken, was the guiding force of the label—Vee-Jay became the Beatles' first American label. It was Blavat, the year before, who had convinced Abner that Vee-Jay could prosper with white artists as well as black, bringing him a quartet of Italian-American kids from New Jersey, the Four Seasons, who had a song called "Sherry," which became a No. 1 pop hit and a No. 1 R&B hit for Vee-Jay in 1962.

Abner was so cool that he wore velour jumpsuits when everyone else was wearing suits and ties.

He died two days after Christmas of 1997, aged 74. How I would love to have included the words of that voice, so recently but forever lost. I mean, damn, *velour* jumpsuits.

"I got him to pick up 'Sherry' at the 1962 convention, down in Miami, at the Fontainebleau. Association of Record Merchandisers," says Blavat. "I was with Morris Levy. I bump into Bob Crewe, who I knew forever. He wrote 'Silhouettes.' He says, 'I want you to hear something I just cut with these kids. It's a song called "Sherry."'" I hear it. I said, 'I think this fuckin' thing's a hit.' I play it for Morris; he says, 'That's the worst piece of shit I've ever heard.' I say, 'Crewe, don't get discouraged.' Now, Abner loves me for my ear, O.K.? Between 'He Will Break Your Heart,' by Jerry Butler, which I busted wide open for him, between this, that, the other thing—I mean, God gave me an ear. I take Crewe up to Abner's suite. Abner hears it. He says, 'You know, Geator, I think you got something here. But it's a white artist.' I said, 'Abner, who the fuck knows the difference on an acetate or a record if it's white or black? If a hit's a hit, it's got no fuckin' color, man.' They make a deal. I've got this kid with me who works for me in Philly. He's an orphan, maybe 15 or 16 years old. Crewe wants to celebrate. I say, 'This kid's never been laid—let's get him a hooker.' I go downstairs. Three hours later, I go back to the room. There's broads and characters all over the place, and there's this kid swapping spits with this fuckin' hooker that's been blowing everybody. He's naked, he's got a sheet around him: it's like a Roman orgy. He says, 'I'm in love.' I said, 'Forget about it.' The kid said, 'Why? She loves me.' I said, 'She's a hooker.' The kid turns white: 'No.' I have a drink in my hand. He spins around, goes to hug me from behind, I go down on the bed, the glass shatters, there's blood all over, the kid faints, they rush me to St. Joseph's. Forty-two stitches."

It was some convention. Freddy: "I remember that pussy-eating contest. What was his name? He was fairly short, chubby. It was Atlantic Records that he worked for. He and this other guy, this local promotion man out of Philadelphia."

Jerry: "The guy from Atlantic used to don a robe and come out like a fighter. I don't remember if it was how many they could do, or how long they could do it, or what."

"It was how long it would take for them to get the broads off."

"It was a spectacle. People were laying bets."

But with promotion men involved, suspicions of pay-for-play pseudo-orgasms were not to be dismissed out of hand.

"But I'm telling you," Jerry says, "it had to be for real." He adds: "I'm gonna tell you exactly when this convention was. My wife was pregnant with my second child. Stacey was born June the 27th. This convention was, like, June the 20th, because I didn't wanna go home, because I knew Patty was due any day, and I didn't wanna really . . . "

"Yeah, it's where everyone made the deals to get records played."

It was a time, all right. But as Heraclitus, greatest of pre-Socratic promotion men, long ago said: Nothing abides.

By 1980, when the gladiatorial cunnilinguists had many years since hung up their robes, the Geator with the Heator looked like he was down for the count: busted on weapons charges, and then arrested 10 months later for allegedly trying to run over a cop who was directing traffic at a road-construction site.

They All Sang on the Corner. So the title of a book about doo-wop, written more than a quarter of a century ago, by Philip Groia. It is a title that captures and expresses much. For, from the beginning, rock 'n' roll was of the corner: those four corners of Blavat's youth, and the countless corners of countless youths. Rock 'n' roll, in all its innocence, in all its wickedness, was, from the beginning, of the neighborhood.

And as the Church comprises many churches, so the neighborhood—I cannot capitalize that initial *n* no matter how strongly effect and meaning entice me to do so, for, here, to exalt the word would be to misrepresent the thing—comprises neighborhoods beyond number. This is not an idle analogy: the neighborhood is, or was, the embodiment of a spiritual ethos as supernal and puissant in reality as that of the Church in theory. As every neighborhood was a parish, and every parish was a neighborhood, so together they have died.

The true gauge of the freedom of any community is the measurement of the degree of equality with which the fruits of malfeasance are shared by the rulers and the ruled, the cop on the beat and the man or woman on the street. The essence of democracy, as of capitalism, is corruption. Only when the criminal in blue and the criminal in mufti, the peddler and the priest, and the alderman and the drunkard—only when they are neighbors of common root and conspiracy is any neighborhood safe for the old lady on the stoop on a hot summer night; only then is there true charity, only then is there a justice that is real, and only then is there life in the air. As the social clubs close, so the churches empty. This is fact, not metaphor.

These may sound to some like words beyond good and evil, but not to one who was neighborhood-born. Blavat was from the neighborhood. He was from the old school. But the walls of the old school came tumbling down.

Angelo Bruno, the Philadelphia boss who since Jerry's childhood had treated him with the love of a father, was murdered on March 21, 1980, reputedly in a killing arranged by his so-called *consigliere*, Antonio "Tony Bananas" Caponigro, who himself did not see the end of that year. Caponigro's naked body, tortured and mutilated, was found in a garbage bag in the South Bronx. Stuck up his dead asshole were $20 bills, not quite the deserts of avarice that the decedent had envisioned. Phil Testa, who had overseen this justice, took control, but his rule was not long. In March of 1981, pieces of him were blown into the street by a bomb planted on the porch of his South Philly home.

The murder of Angelo Bruno was when the walls of the neighborhood came tumbling down. It was not until after Bruno's death that Blavat, in February of 1981, was brought to trial for his alleged 1979 "aggravated assault" on the cop. The only thing that would have made this more bizarre would have been if he had not been acquitted. "I'll tell you about that cop they said I tried to run over," Jerry says. "First of all, he was an off-duty cop. He showed no sign of being a cop. He never identified himself as such. He showed no I.D." The cop disputed this at trial, but Jerry goes on: "The punch line is, the way this guy asks me to halt is he throws a flashlight at my head. You know the deal. You give some guy a badge, and . . ." Jerry's voice trails off mildly, as if there is no reason to reiterate universal truth. To this day he is not sure if the decision to prosecute him originated with federal agents, desperately seeking a rat to cast light, no matter how slight, on the baffling tumult that now embroiled the Philadelphia underworld, or with the state of New Jersey, which seemed intent on putting him out of business for motives upon which he can only speculate, involving state officials who cannot here be named.

Jerry had been doing good before his legal troubles waylaid his career. He had been spreading the old-time religion to converts, laying down that lean, mean music to those who had been following him for years. He was on radio. He was on television. He promoted shows. He had music stores, the Record Museums. He owned a club, Memories, in Margate, New Jersey. He was a partner in the best of the early oldies labels, Lost Nite, reissuing, with the help of Ewart Abner and Morris Levy, some of the finest recordings of the 50s. Most of his income came from hosting shows—no, "hosting" is not the right word. The Geator *performed.* I have heard of mercury poisoning. To experience the Geator in action was, and is, to witness what might be called adrenaline poisoning.

If you talk to every survivor of the days of pay-for-play innocence and of experience, among all the names bandied about, in malice or in joy or in both, Blavat's is one of the few that remain unsullied. He never took, they say. He was his own man, who had the wits and the ways to make it his way. Even when he got Crewe and Abner together, bringing about one of the biggest hits in the history of Vee-Jay, he refused the points that were offered him for "Sherry": a perfectly legitimate and legal offer that he chose simply not to accept.

"That's the difference between you and Dick Clark," says Freddy DeMann when this matter is broached.

"He took everything." Jerry smiles. "Even today he takes everything." Jerry shrugs. "God bless him."

He loved Crewe, he says. He loved Abner. He loved the record. He was making a fortune as it was. He never wanted to be beholden or have his freedom endangered, and that was that.

Jerry's not down anymore. He brought himself back up, starting over as he had started out after that crap game way back when: buying time, selling blocks on WCAM. Today he's broadcasting over five different radio stations heard in southern Jersey, Philadelphia, and Delaware, and doing shows on WQED, a Pittsburgh PBS channel. He's still got his club in Margate. That adrenaline is rushing as wild as ever. He hosts live shows and what he still calls "record hops," taking down up to $1,600 for a weeknight gig, $2,500 to $3,500 for a weekend night.

And if I had half of Freddy DeMann's money, I tell him, I'd burn mine. Yet even Freddy, sitting there shed of his L.A. skin, gives the impression that there were joys back there, in those days before truly big money, that have not returned.

"Phil Kronfeld's men's shop," he recalls wistfully. It was where la crème de la cool bought their threads. "I was making $50 a week or something like that, looking through that store window. I dreamed that someday I could afford to go in there and get a suit like the rest of those guys. That sharkskin suit and that silk tie, man. I had to have it. I had to do it."

Blavat has his own wistfulness. I don't even know if he and DeMann are hearing each other's words, or hearing merely the wistfulness.

"I'm having coffee one morning at my place with Blinky"—Jerry's talking about Blinky Palermo, the Philadelphia-based prince of the fight rackets under the lordship of Frankie Carbo—"and the phone rings. It's Sinatra. He calls me Matchstick; that's what he always called me. 'Where's the raviolis?' Blah, blah, blah. I said, 'My mother's making the raviolis. They'll be there by six, all right?' So Blinky's with me. He says, 'Who was that?' I said it was Sinatra. He says, 'That bum. I haven't seen him in—' I said, 'Well, I'm going over with the raviolis and the meatballs and the sausage. Come back at 5:30. We'll get the limo and we'll go and you'll say hello to Sinatra.' Sure enough, he comes back. We get in the limo with the raviolis, the meatballs, the sausage, and we go see Frankie." For a moment, it's not the past: "Frank loves my mother's raviolis. Because she's *abruzzese*. They're the best cooks."

"Hell," says DeMann, "later on, when I was a manager, you know how many guys approached me? I remember there was a guy came in with a suitcase full of cash when I represented the Jackson 5. He

wanted to be the promoter of a tour the Jacksons were going to do.
I said, 'Ah, come on, you're broke. I hear you're broke.' 'Here, here,
here'—he's pulling bundles out of the case."

"Was he a successful promoter?" I ask.

"He was. He did a lot of national tours, and then went to jail for
tax evasion or something, I don't know."

No, the two of them agree, payola never died. It just became a
drag.

"Payola today," says DeMann, "goes on in a much bigger way.
Now the stations absolutely hold you up. KISS in Boston, KISS in
L.A., they're doing a big summer show, or their Christmas show,
and it's 'Here's the act we want.' And you better supply them or they
won't play your record. They don't say it, but that's what they
mean." Freddy shakes his head, waves aside the current music business and its million-dollar corporate shakedowns, while Jerry turns
back to the days when the racket was exciting. "Who pulled the line,
who wasn't gonna pull the line. Who got paid. I'm telling ya, it was
incredible. The record business was like a Damon Runyon thing,
but with people who knew nothing about the record business."

And all the while, the kids dancing, aswirl, their own pulses
singing, never knowing, never hearing, the beat beneath the beat.

"Music was different," says DeMann. "The Mafia was different.
There was honor among thieves. Now there isn't any. There's nothing. There's nothing to hang your hat on these days."

Another day. I'm in New York with Wassel, Hy Weiss, and other
characters. Freddy is gone back to L.A., but these guys are saying
what he said in their own ways.

"Dead, all of it," somebody says.

"They took away the prize."

"Yeah," as Wassel says, intoning agreement with nothing, but
merely dismissal. "No more stand-up guys anymore." It is a once
common complaint, heard ever more rarely, testimony perhaps of
its increasing truth. "This city's dead," says someone else. "This guy,
this mayor, this *faccia di morte* here, he's . . ." The speaker shakes his
head, not for want of words, but in disgusted velleity.

Wassel hasn't been to jail in a while. I tell him of an arrest less than a year ago: the first time I was ever in a cell without a single obscenity scrawled on the walls. The walls were filled with only two phrases, in a hundred hands, a hundred intensities: KILL RUDY and DIE RUDY DIE. The notion seems to please all at the table, and inspires Wassel to speak again.

"Yeah"—same tone. "People say this guy's like Mussolini. They say he's like Hitler. I tell 'em no. Mussolini and Hitler had friends."

Even Hy Weiss grins. Then he leans forward, softly says. "You know why the government will never get the music business? It's because the people in the music business have never understood how it works."

Then Hy Weiss, a boyish gleam in his 77-year-old eyes, returns quite calmly to his eggs and his coffee and his silence.

Rock on, Hymie, rock on.

JONATHAN LETHEM

Not a Go-Betweens Piece

A Letter from Jonathan Lethem,
on His Favorite Band

New York City
October 23, 2000

Dear Stacy,

   When the Go-Betweens got back together and recorded a new album, I entertained fantasies of writing something about it. My first thought was to pitch it to *Rolling Stone*. I'd written an essay for them recently, and for reasons too elaborate to go into here, I've lately resurrected dormant fantasies of being a "rock writer." The truth is it'll never happen. I'm too paralyzed by reverence, both for the musicians and for writers like Greil Marcus and Lester Bangs, and conscious anyway that research and interviewing aren't really my strengths. Plus I suspect, or at least don't understand, my own motives. But my reasons for not pitching a Go-Betweens piece weren't only generic ones. They were strong and specific and they far outweighed the self-aggrandizing urge to announce myself in public as the Go-Betweens' biggest fan, or to meet the band. In a sort of Dylanesque "my weariness amazes me" way I found myself compelled by my own resistance to writing or thinking about the Go-Betweens reunion—to even buying the new record—compelled to such a degree that I began to want to write about *that*.

Before I start, I need to say that this form is strange. I hope it's not too soon for *Open Letters* to run a letter which acknowledges the existence of *Open Letters*. I've always had trouble with "sincere" first-person anyway, except in genuinely personal letters, ones with a single recipient in mind, and I don't remotely know how to pretend this isn't written for publication. It seems to me you've invented a very odd and exemplary new form, one which I find irresistible to read and consistently disingenuous: the fake private. It's very "web-like," I think, and if I were a better abstract thinker I'd tell you what I mean by that. Maybe it would even sustain a labored comparison to "Survivor." All I can say for sure is that when I wrote that bit above about "self-aggrandizing urge to announce myself in public the Go-Betweens' biggest fan," I'd stepped into a very odd writerly space, because though unlike a *Rolling Stone* piece this won't be read by teenagers stealing free reads from Borders' magazine racks, it will be read by most everyone I know in New York.

Anyway, here's why I can't write about the Go-Betweens reunion.

1. The Go-Betweens are my favorite band. I listened to them in two distinct periods in my life: in the mid-eighties, when they existed and when I was living in California, and in the mid-late-nineties, when their entire messy, elusive catalog was reissued on CD for the first time. Their songs are characterized by a complexity and self-awareness I want to call literary—in fact I'll do that. Their songs are beautiful and strange and emotional, but a lot of rock and roll is like that. The Go-Betweens are also smart and hesitant and not obvious. Not so much rock and roll is like that. There are a lot of historical facts surrounding the production of these songs: the punk context (they began in the late seventies, couldn't play their instruments at first, etc.) and the fact that they're from Australia but took up residence in England. I care and I don't care. I just don't want to shift my attention from the enduring, rewarding confusion of being the songs' devoted listener.

2. I have notions about the people in the band which are probably false, but they matter to me. Robert Forster and Grant McClennan are the Lennon/McCartney team at the heart of the band: they both write songs, they write some together, and they both sing. The third original member was a drummer named Lindy, and she's not on the reunion record. In my mind—and this is gleaned from reading bits of journalism about the band and from seeing them live, once, which I'll talk about in a minute—the friendship between these three people is beautiful and complicated. In a rich, fascinating evolution over the course of the six "original" Go-Betweens records these three people welcomed four new members (and learned to play their instruments), but that triangle always felt to me like the band's emotional and musical core.

3. Triangle, a key word. Here comes my falsely private confession: I've always imagined that Robert Forster and Grant McClennan were each Lindy's boyfriend in turn, and that the difficulties and ambiguities of this long arrangement and disarrangement are the impenetrable knot at the core of the music, the mystery that keeps me coming back. I know that the rock band love-triangle is a Fleetwood Mac cliché, but glimpsed (if I'm right that I glimpsed it) through the prism of the Go-Betweens sensibility, it felt profound to me. In the eighties, when the band existed, when I saw them play live, my own life was shaped by a long, devoted love triangle—one which persisted, though it was never static. I won't say anything more about this, except that if we three had been a band our six albums would have sounded as different from one another as the Go-Betweens' did. And we would have been as unmistakably the same band playing.

4. In Berkeley I lived on Chestnut Street, three blocks from a homely rock club called Berkeley Square. Every poor, scraping-along act touring California would get stuck there for a night, and it was rarely a full house. For years of afternoons I'd sit at home writing with the radio tuned to KALX, the college radio station, and when they gave away tickets to shows at the Berkeley Square I'd call up and answer a trivia question and get my name on the list, then walk over a few hours later and see the show. I'm good at

trivia. I saw the Proclaimers and the Violent Femmes and the
Throwing Muses there, along with other bands whose names I've
forgotten. I was once one of literally five people at Berkeley Square
for a My Bloody Valentine show on a Tuesday—we stood at the lip
of the stage and endured the harshest volume I've ever experienced.
When the announcement came that the Go-Betweens—an Aus-
tralian band, whose very existence seemed mythical—were coming
to the Berkeley Square I don't know whether I purchased or won
my ticket, only that I wouldn't have missed it, you know, for the
world. They played to about twenty-five or thirty people, a loosely-
packed herd of worshipers, but our worship couldn't console the
Go-Betweens, not this night. They were at the end of a tour that
must have been some kind of disaster, and twenty-five bookstore
clerks in Berkeley weren't going to turn it around. The band had
been arguing, I think, before the show even began, and Lindy, the
drummer, the original Go-Between, had been drinking. Really
drinking, so she was lurching and obvious and couldn't keep time.
By the fourth or fifth song Robert and Grant were both glaring at
her in turn, and expressly showing her their hands on the guitars to
try to dictate the tempo. The violinist, another woman, wouldn't
look at her. They were miserable. They made it through a song,
argued again, and then Lindy stormed off, between the two singers,
towards the bar. She weaved. At the bar she got something—
another drink? Water? Carrying it she lurched back to the stage,
and as she moved through the crowd she brushed me, a butt-
against-lap-swipe, the kind which happens late at night at crazy
parties, when intentions are blurry. I know this seems ridiculous,
but it happened. She was taunting one or both of the men onstage
by making physical contact with men in the audience, and in the
small, loosely-populated room it was apparent that it was having an
effect, though what sort I wouldn't presume to say. The horrible
intimacy, the unexpected access to the band's unhappiness, was
wrenching. It was also terribly sexy—I learned something that
night about how vivid a smashed woman can be.

5. Lindy, as I said, isn't on the new record. I bought it and took it
home today, and I listened to the first three songs in the car before I

started crying, for myself and who-knows-else, and took it off. "The Go-Betweens" are now Robert Forster and Grant McClennan and a bunch of names I don't recognize (they've also got the help of Sleater-Kinney, a good sign, probably, in a general sense). Now, forget love triangles for a minute, there's something I've always liked about Led Zeppelin's refusal to exist for even one minute after John Bonham's death. And I'd always felt the opposite about The Who—that they betrayed their audience by carrying on after Keith Moon. And that the saddest single fact about the Beatles' decline was that Paul McCartney played drums on some of the tracks on the White Album. Poor Ringo. I mean, songwriters come and go, but the drummer is the band. I'll certainly play this record, and I may come to like it, but I guess if I had to give you one reason why I'm not going to try to write about the Go-Betweens reunion, it's that I'm carrying a torch for Lindy. Her name isn't even in the *thank yous*. There's a story there, I know there is, and the thing is, having come as far as I have with the idea of the Go-Betweens standing in for so much I've felt and lost, I don't want to know it.

Best,
Jonathan

Singing Lead

The program notes to the February 7, 2000, performance of Aaron
Copland's "Lincoln Portrait" at Lincoln Center's Avery Fisher Hall
point out that the folk tune "Camptown Races" is quoted in the
score because it was one of Abraham Lincoln's favorite songs. Copland's piece, which sets Lincoln's writings to orchestral accompani-
ment (played here by the American Symphony Orchestra), was
narrated during the Avery Fisher performance by Al Gore, who, as
you may have heard, is running for president. This makes the
"Camptown" moment all the more prescient. For what song, other
than "We're in the Money," could a politician love more? It's a song
about a horse race, a gamble. And it never sounded more resonant
than in this, the primary season. Place your bets, fellow citizens, for
just as I might put my money on the bobtail nag, polls show that
you have a thing for the bay.

The hall bristled with the kind of energy that only Secret Service
agents provide. I couldn't take my eyes off the boxes, which is a natural post-1865 American habit when someone whose title includes
the word "president" attends a theater. Easily a third of the audience
was there to have some fun at Gore's expense. But there was something quaintly reassuring about the way the crowd clapped—some
even stood—out of respect for his office, which, lest we forget, is
only respect for the electorate and its judgment. Even in cool New
York, Americans are not above a little "He's here!" excitement over

the vice president, a man who once joked about himself that he is so boring his Secret Service name is Al Gore.

The "Lincoln Portrait" has a long instrumental introduction, which provided ample opportunity to watch Gore wait and wait and wait for his turn to speak. It was like watching the institution of the vice presidency in action. This must be what it's been like for him all these patient years, listening to someone else's noise until it's finally his cue.

Gore, who sat in profile next to conductor Leon Botstein, looked like the head on a coin. Which is to say he never looked more presidential. It's an easy trick to come off dignified while wearing a nice blue suit in front of tuxedo-clad violinists and orating the words of Lincoln. Then again, orating the words of Lincoln is itself a gamble. Who could begin to compare? The music on the stage wasn't coming from the woodwinds. It was coming from the page, from the grave, from the rhythm of "new birth of freedom" and the melody that "we cannot escape history."

Hearing words like that spoken by a presidential candidate was especially striking in the current climate of mind-numbing practicality among the campaigners for the job, who seem to think of the American people as a bunch of penny-pinching misers who are hoarding our precious votes for the candidate who might save us 40 bucks a year on the 1040EZ. I was delighted to take a brief, poetic break from the subject of tax breaks to sit there in Lincoln Center and ask, What is a president supposed to say? What should he sound like?

Should he sound like Lincoln? We think we think so, forgetting that Lincoln's voice was reportedly as squeaky as a 6-year-old girl's. Because of the eloquence of his words, documentary film producers hire narrators with stentorian timbres to deliver the Second Inaugural Address, all the while forgetting that Lincoln himself probably sounded more like David Sedaris than Gregory Peck—a thing Gore supporters might want to remember considering that the vice president was not born with his boss's oratorical gift. President Clinton was always a better artist than governor, and who knows what he might have stirred within me whispering Lincoln's call for us to "save our country." I would have been seduced by that voice—yet again.

But just as Clinton appealed to the rock 'n' roller in me, Gore's pencil neck tugs at my nerdy heart. I think the most endearing thing he has ever said can be found in a sentence in his book *Earth in the Balance: Ecology and the Human Spirit.* In it, he asks, "What happened to the climate in Yucatán around 950?" Something about the specifics of that query lit me up. For the first time, I could see casting my ballot for a man who would pose such a question. It was just so boldly arcane. The kind of mind that would wonder about temperature variations on a Caribbean peninsula a thousand years ago suggests that its owner has the stomach to look into any number of Americans' peculiar concerns. Paradoxically, this fervor for scientific facts—the thing that supposedly alienates him from voters because they see him as cold—requires no small amount of passion. You don't write a 400-page book about ecology unless you have the heart.

Maybe it was the Yucatán Gore who came to life at the end of "Lincoln Portrait." The piece ends grandly with the conclusion of the Gettysburg Address. Lincoln hoped "that these dead shall not have died in vain; that this nation, under God, shall have a new birth of freedom; and that government of the people, by the people, for the people, shall not perish from the Earth." At that last word "Earth," I did not think of Lincoln or Copland or you or me. I thought of Gore, because he owns that word more than any of us, and should trademark it, earn dividends and rewards. For what other candidate has thought more, read more, written more about the issue of whether we will have an Earth not to perish from?

After that he sang along with the New York City Gay Men's Chorus in the "Battle Hymn of the Republic" and during the stirring quiet parts the rest of us exercised our greatest concert-hall freedom: the freedom to cough.

DAVID RAKOFF

Barbra's Farewell:
A City *Verklempt*

It is High Holy Days weather in New York. And if you were to stand on the Upper West Side this evening, you might hear on the chilly breeze a great collective moan of sorrow. This is not the mass lamentation of a care-worn and inquiring people begging for forgiveness and inscription into the Book of Life for one more year. No, this is the full-throated wail, thousands strong, of those who have gathered at Madison Square Garden on 33rd Street—oh, do let's call it "Toity-Toid" just for tonight—to see the first of the two final concerts ever given by Barbra Streisand, our one true Jewish saint. These are indeed the Days of Awe.

She performed two nights last week in Los Angeles, as practice. I went to the first. And even though the message to her fans on the inside cover of the souvenir program says, "It's bittersweet to say farewell to live performing. But it feels right to say good-bye in the two cities I think of as home," and while she has certainly lived in L.A. for decades, we all knew the truth. It was to New York that she would always return—the place that gave birth to her, the place with which her ineluctable identification started, setting her on the road to stardom and, it must be said, self-parody.

I am not by any stretch of the imagination a Barbra queen, truth be told. She has never had that rare ability to make me feel simultaneously horrible about myself and good about the world that clinches my utmost devotion. On the Barbra spectrum—ranging from pure antipathy, like my friend Julie, who can only refer to her as "such a bitch!," to the girls with whom I went to high school, for whom Ms. Streisand was the Jewish Steven Biko—I'm somewhere south of the middle.

I am not unmindful of her very real talents. It's just easy to forget, given the annoying, obfuscating tsunami of her current Donna-Karan-confidante, Lincoln-bedroom, *Prince of Tides*-making persona. Ergo, my Streisand Talking Points: She is possessed of a remarkable voice; did have what was once an extraordinary comic sensibility—her performance in *What's Up Doc?* remains one of the great comic turns in American movies (and her rendition of "As Time Goes By" in same a contender for Platonic ideal of that song); and with her nose alone, she re-drew the parameters of physical beauty for millions of women—an achievement not to be underestimated.

There was lots of time to ruminate on such things during the 45 minutes we waited outside the Staples Center at Figueroa and 12th. Mostly, though, I spent my time being appalled at the ticket price. "Timeless" is not a benefit from what I can see, and at $375, my ticket was the second cheapest. For a paltry $150, one could secure a seat up in the stadium ether. At the other extreme, one could pony up $1,275, or truly go for broke and buy in at the super-elite, tippy-top level of $2,500—for which I would at least expect dinner. Actually, dinner and a speculum.

I make a list in my mind of just a few of the figures of equal cultural significance whom I have seen over the years for less money: Ella Fitzgerald, Sarah Vaughan, Count Basie, Vanessa Redgrave, Danny Kaye, Maggie Smith, Leonard Bernstein, Joni Mitchell, Simon & Garfunkel, Mikhail Baryshnikov, Rudolf Nureyev, Margot Fonteyn, Jessye Norman, Kiri Te Kanawa and Golda Meir.

We passed through the metal detectors. The tickets had an explicit "No Cameras/No Recorders" printed on them. It seemed a bit harsh to deny the thousands of fans who have foregone a month of prescriptions to afford to be here the opportunity of at least a picture of themselves. Even a grainy image of the distant pin dot that would be La Streisand herself couldn't possibly have posed a threat to any photo agencies here on this historic night. Frankly, I'm even skeptical that these are her last concerts, having some vague memory of a series of crypto-final engagements at Madison Square Garden about two years ago. It seems like she has come out of retirement to retire.

Judging by the lines at the souvenir kiosk, I was the only one feeling gouged and doubtful, as folks crowded dozens deep to purchase mementos of the precious memories they are sure to take away from the concert that had yet to begin. There were T-shirts abounding with that famous face, now of a certain age, serene and ingenuously nuzzling tea roses. Personally, I would have opted for the white cotton number with an archetypal His Master's Voice silhouette of Barbra seated in a director's cherry picker. Or the cinema auteuse at work: $30. Although the simple, scripted "B" in rhinestones on black for $40 was so very casually elegant, while the Barbra fleece pullover was functional and kicky at a cool $90.

"She's always been my Sinatra," said the man beside me. A friend of his, a blond Liz Smith type, said, "I first heard 'People' on the jukebox in a gay bar in Houston in 1964, and I said 'Who is that?' And it's been Barbra ever since." Barbra ever since, and Barbra ever after. Aside from myself and some dour-looking maintenance folk, everyone here—male, female, gay and straight—was a die-hard Barbra queen. I was seated among a nation indivisible under Barbra, anticipating the manifestation of her glorious presence.

That moment arrived at 8:30 sharp: The makeshift proscenium of enormous red velvet swags parted, revealing the huge Egyptian-themed set. The orchestra was seated on tiers made to look like the great sandstone blocks hewn by the Israelites, the backdrop an enormous pyramid against a starry sky. The overture started, a screen dropped down. Upon it, a dizzying assortment of dials and clock wheels, pendulums and a large watch face. (Timeless—get it?) A tap dancer in a billowing black velvet cape pushed the second hand counterclockwise, as time accordioned back to 1955. An actress playing a young Barbra (possibly, back then, still a young Barbara), accompanied by a hectoring Jewish stage mother straight out of Anti-Defamation League literature, entered a recording studio. Young B. was instructed to sing "You'll Never Know" as written. She bent the note with the keening suppleness that would make her a star, and pandemonium ensued as recording conductor and mother wondered what on earth they would do with this headstrong girl. The tap dancer returned, only this time a solemn harbinger: We knew this because his cloak was now lined in silver sequins—cross-cultural shorthand for Promising, Glamorous Future. Singing a trance-like "Who Knows?" from *West Side Story*, young Barbra was enfolded into the disco garment. We already knew what was going to happen and still we loved it, spontaneously getting to our feet as the caped one turned, knowing that on "May come cannonballing down from the sky," out would step Herself! And she did, in a sleeveless top and trousers with bronze sequins, a kind of *Owl and the Pussycat*–meets–Lufthansa stewardess evening look.

"Check the archives for her past concerts. I think this is the Vegas one," said the woman beside me, referring to Barbra's Millennium appearance last Dec. 31.

Recycled material or not, Barbra Streisand still has an amazing set of pipes—eerily so for 58 years old. She took us back in time to the Bon Soir, the little boîte where she got her start, singing a beautiful "Cry Me A River" and a heartbreakingly good "Sleeping Bee." A medley of songs from her *Funny Girl* period also didn't disappoint. Interestingly, the music was arranged so that she never actually said the phrase "I'm the greatest star" when singing that song. It's an omission almost sweet in its humility, given the throngs who have consigned their children to certain renal failure by having bought tickets. To them, she is the greatest star, a fact about which she does not seem complacent; she was not phoning this in. Begrudgingly, it must be admitted, she remains one of the great American singers. Whatever vocal elisions she makes in concession to her age—and they are far fewer than one might imagine—they are intelligent and as musically impressive as the pyrotechnics of her younger self. In two hours of concert, there was not one moment of embarrassment where I was looking at my shoes praying for it to pass.

Let me qualify that: In two hours, there was not one moment of musical embarrassment. But there was that inevitable, cringe-making ick factor endemic to latter-day Barbra. There is something profoundly uncool about Barbra Streisand. No father ever ripped a Streisand LP off a hi-fi declaring, "Not under my roof." She has never had counterculture cred; her aesthetic parentage is Broadway and Tin Pan Alley as opposed to Woodstock. This is not, in and of itself, an indictment. But now, watching her do the Fanny Brice thing 36 years later ("I'm a bagel in a plate of onion rolls!") was a lit-tle creaky and calcified.

The time when Barbra Streisand was unconventional (shockingly brief, given the fact that she was a full-blown star by age 22)—when she was that little spitfire who, with the face straight out of steerage, went on Jack Paar in 1961 and blew America's gasket of June Christy propriety with her staggering talent, unmediated New York *yiddishkeit* and hilarious shtick right off the dime—is long gone. Ms. Streisand's brand of ethnicity has become not just normative, but a caricature inauthentically trotted out seemingly everywhere but New York. I don't know a single Jew who says "*verklempt*," although I have heard Connie Chung use it. Ms. Streisand's been known to poke fun at her own eclipsing shadow with the *sang froid* of the cul-tural critic, fully aware of her metamorphosis into the poster child for a kind of middle-aged, middlebrow, suburban tackiness (making appearances with Linda Richman, Mike Myers' Streisand-obsessed character)—but, like the super-hero who can no longer take off his mask and live among normal people, she seems unable to rid herself of an intrinsic schlockiness. Schmoozing with the audience (about many of whom my mother might say, "It's a good thing they don't have to kill animals to get sequins"), she told us about a floral arrangement she just received backstage from a dear friend. "One hundred and fifty roses—I counted—and in the center of each one? Is a pearl." The audience fairly climaxed at this extra-classy Aaron Spelling image, and all I could think was, from what Summer's Eve box was this idea lifted?

Things were not always thus. Where once she was among the most gifted interpreters of Harold Arlen and Jule Styne, she has over the years allied herself with the poorly controlled hysteria and emotional ipecac that is the songwork of Marilyn and Alan Bergman. She actually demonstrated the devolution of her good taste, a *National Geographic* timeline in reverse, in what only I think of as a risky move: a montage of clips of her duets. It started with the sublime moment in 1963 when she and Judy Garland sang "Happy Days Are Here Again/C'mon Get Happy"—a meeting of god and titan exponentially more genuine and torch-passing than that Bill Clinton–J.F.K. photograph. Sadly, things degenerated almost immediately to footage of mistake after mistake: that Gibb brother (Barry?); Céline Dion; and culminating with her high school chum Neil Diamond, the most annoying man in the world. As this unholy alliance late of Erasmus Hall launched into "You Don't Bring Me Flowers" up on the screen, the audience went what can only be described as ape shit. (*"Well, it's good for you, babe, an' you're feelin' alright!"*) It was always a terrible song, and history has not been kind to it, either, although you wouldn't know it from the ecstatic awe over this coupling. We might as well have been watching footage of Buddha French-braiding Jesus' hair.

The cheese continued. The capper to the proceedings, I thought, would now be for James Brolin to emerge. He did make an appearance of sorts. A picture of Ms. Streisand's newish husband came up on the screen as she sang to it. I suppose if I had managed to nab a silver fox like James Brolin, I'd also probably rent out a stadium and sing about it. But the photos of him were so adoring, so poignant— the close-up tightening in ever nearer to the cerulean eyes and ax-head features in such loving tribute—that I found myself briefly wondering if he were dead.

Thoughts of mortality are not far off the mark. Retirement can be a tricky thing for artists as beloved as Barbra. Staying away from the spotlight must be an enormous challenge. The closest equivalent to these four last concerts are Sinatra's "final" appearance at age 55 in Los Angeles. He might have left it at that, exiting as he did on the last bars of "Angel Eyes," instead of coming back again and again to foist upon an unwitting public such sclerotic chestnuts as "L.A. Is My Lady." In addition to Sinatra, there are other cautionary tales she can look to: Liza, for one, who is barely Mabel Mercer now even on her best days. Even Garbo had the good sense to quit early, although anyone who has seen *Two-Faced Woman* knows she retired one film too late.

I don't see Barbra making the same mistake, if only for the fact that she doesn't even particularly like giving concerts, she lets it be known. She doesn't enjoy wearing high heels for 35 songs, she doesn't enjoy having to lose weight for an engagement, and there has always been talk of near-crippling stage fright for as long as she has performed. And, she tells us reassuringly, she will continue to make records and, heaven help us, movies. Given the anecdotal evidence over the years of her monstrously narcissistic self-possession, it's entirely conceivable that she would be sufficiently self-aware to know when to exit with dignity while her capacities are still intact.

And they are staggeringly, remarkably intact. By the time she reached her final song, "Happy Days Are Here Again," even I recognized the privilege of seeing her one first and last time. It was poignant. So poignant, in fact, that it demanded the encore we knew and hoped it would. She ended her concert as she began it, with a song from *West Side Story*, this time "Somewhere." The Man in the Cape appeared at the top of the Egyptian stairs, opening his garment; the Glittering Unknown winked at our Star as she ascended to meet her undetermined yet surely fabulous fate. Curtain. Crazed ovation.

And *noch* an encore, which was a series of jaw-dropping home runs: "The Music That Makes Me Dance," a wonderful torch song from the stage version of *Funny Girl* that was cut from the movie in favor of Fanny Brice's signature song, "My Man," which Barbra now sang. It was her Mrs. Norman Maine moment in the movie, an unadorned show-stopper about the vicissitudes of stardom. Indeed, the scene was filmed and sung live in front of an audience much like this one. It was doubly resonant this evening as she sent herself off.

So let us now give thanks, for thanks are truly due, to Miss Yetta Tessye Marmelstein, the ugly duckling who, by sheer force of talent, became beautiful by song's end. Bow your heads in the presence of that Voice, that shofar blast of perfect tone, as it makes its way up to the rafters of the Garden, and out into the night over the city that made her.

ROBBIE FULKS

If I Said You Had a Beautiful Gross Adjusted Income

Would You Hold It Against Me?

Chicago, Illinois
October 5, 2000

Dear muse-haunted friends,

Today, the day of our audit, we stop at a strip mall a few blocks from the IRS office in northwest suburban Chicago to get lunch. The particular European country being degraded here is Italy. Glassy-eyed office drones, potbellied bozos with pagers on their Dockers, anhedonic single moms, and desperate pink-collar climbers are grazing on semolina tubes clotted with quasi-cream and quasi-cheese and talking about people they know either from working with them or watching them on Survivor. My wife and I will have our sandwiches to go.

Once through the glass door marked "IRS, OFFICE HOURS 8:30 A.M. TO 4:30 P.M. MON.–FRI." in the multiplex office park down the street, we are in a tiny vestibule with a bulletin board on the wall in front of us and a locked door and intercom on the wall to our right. IRS CLEARED OF WRONGDOING, asserts the headline on a 1998 newspaper

clipping in the center of the board; CONGRESSIONAL INQUIRY FINDS
NO SUBSTANTIATING EVIDENCE OF INAPPROPRIATE TACTICS. We press
the button on the intercom a few times and no one comes, so I bang
heavily on the door. My wife likes this one, so I bang more and
harder. Then we spot another bulletin, advising visitors to ring 6441
on a phone hanging beside the board. My wife picks up the receiver
and dials 6441, but a screen above the touchtone pad simultaneously
registers "6461." She hangs up and dials the number again, with the
same result. We stand stupidly for 30 seconds. Then the magic door
opens and out steps a thin young black man dressed in that Pier One
translation of natural-fiber folk-art multicult chic. "I just had a feeling you would be here!" he exclaims.

I think: This is a fine development; for my instinctive reactions
are often those of the liberal reverse racist I used to be. I nod gravely
at my wife, to assure her: He's a brother. Everything will be all right.
Here is no busta-ass wigger bullshit-talkin' IRS chickenhead. This
man will not use the U.S. tax code to bully a pair of struggling
bohemians; he will not be so rock-ribbed or steel-hearted as to pursue some hairsplitting perversion of justice, unleavened by sympathetic understanding, in the course of setting aright whatever trivial
infractions he happens to uncover on our 1998 return; he will not
plow us over with penalties. These reflections, the effects of an
ingrained bad habit of attributing nobility to ethnic minorities, are
momentary. Within an hour I will feel like smashing this gentleman's head apart on his desk.

If I had come in here less blithely the day might have gone differently. But you see, we have been audited before, and despite the
horror the word is almost singular in provoking (almost, that is,
until the words "prostatectomy" and "SheDaisy" disappear from
use), I've not been worried this time around. "You know," I said to
my wife the night before as we tallied up the last subgroup of
receipts ("Promotional"), "I'm almost looking forward to this. It's
like a crucible, a big test, and we're as well-prepared as we could be.
In going back over the 1998 calendar so painstakingly I've gotten to
relive a lot of wonderful memories. And look how many errors
we've found that are in our favor—we might actually get some
money from them!"

"We're not going to call any attention to any errors, no matter who they seem to favor," said my wife, who does not quite share in my all-encompassing love of life.

"All right, but just remember, nothing can really happen to us. A couple hundred, a thousand bucks, but we've done nothing seriously wrong and we're not going to jail or anything." My wife has been on thin emotional ice during the preparations and so I try to help her look on the bright side, or skate on the thick patches, or whatever.

The auditor's name is Kelvin Peterson. His cubicle abounds with humanizing artifacts, predominantly watercolors of stoic Africans, including one man with sizzling raindrops in a band around the middle of his head and ghastly white seed-pods over both his eyes. There are also ribbons from two AIDS walks; a framed inspirational message of about 150 words, mainly "I," "try," "can," and "anything"; and—a puzzling touch—a single chain of little plastic Mardi Gras beads. Between two paintings hangs an unframed eight-by-ten sheet of beige paper bearing an octagonal silver seal with an eagle. "1993/This is to recognize/KELVIN PETERSON/for Five Years of service in the U.S. government." Five Years, capitalized. Beside that, an identical award from 1998 marking Ten Years. The overall effect of this office is, like its occupant, reassuring. Here is an auditor—"tax technician" according to the business card nestled in the pelvis of a reclining black iron stick figure—unafraid to wear a human face. Here is a man apart from the mediocrities down the street sipping marinara through straws, a man who recognizes that millennia before civilization, before language, and yes, before the U.S. tax code, our forebears transmuted their inchoate longings and sense of apart-ness from the beasts around them in crude etchings on cave walls. How fortunate that this adept of the fine arts has been charged with deconstructing my 1040, for my wife and I see ourselves as artists, after a fashion.

But first we have to explain exactly what we do and how we earn money, and this is a tricky matter requiring masterful exegetical technique. My wife does voiceovers for commercials, and she begins by explaining how it is that her robust ream of W2's comes from companies she has never been to or worked for. The companies are paymasters who compute her income based on how often commercials featuring her voice are played, at what time and in which markets. The payments are made to my wife's agent, who deposits the checks and pays my wife, who then pays back a commission. As a wrinkle, for reasons unknown to us, one of her payments in 1998 was reported on a 1099 rather than a W2. Kelvin Peterson is fixing his intelligence on this anomaly.

"So your business income for 1998 was actually $850; that is the amount that should be entered on your Schedule C."

"No, that's just a payment for one job which for some reason was reported on a 1099," says my wife. "If that were the only income entered on my Schedule C, I would be reporting a business loss of over $10,000, whereas I actually earned a net income of $44,000."

"You should tell these companies who send out your checks they should be issuing you 1099's instead of W2's. Then you can properly report them as self-employed business income."

"Hmm." We are both thinking of the tens of thousands of voiceover actors and actresses who file W2's from paymasters each year and wishing we had a snappy answer. It would be a shame to have to begin reporting giant losses that we didn't really incur. "There must be some other way . . . "

"Are any of these companies who issue you W2's your employer? Do they, for instance, tell you to be at work at 8 and leave at 5?"

This would seem to be a rhetorical question, since my wife has already detailed the irregular pattern of auditions and short jobs that constitute her workaday life. But she dutifully says, "No."

"Then," says Kelvin Peterson with a triumphant flourish, "they are not actually your employers and these W2's should never have been issued."

This certainly is a setback for us, but the audit is only beginning and there is plenty of time for improvement. The accounting methods of the ad industry have been exposed as fraudulent, and though this is surely thrilling in itself, we are preoccupied with the hazards ahead, such as my wife's mileage log, which she has lost.

"We moved last year and I just. Don't. Know. Where it went." Being an actress, she sometimes does that for effect. Kelvin Peterson's eyes are wide and full of fellowship, and I detect a malign after-effect of that congressional inquiry: human inter-relations training.

"That's really not good," he says.

"I know. And look, here's the thing. The 4,300 miles that are on there, that I drove from my house to Chicago in doing all my work that year—well, obviously I did it. I made the money from the commercials—in fact, I brought the contracts to show you—basically, I can demonstrate, I mean it's undeniable, that I did all this work. Which, logically, you agree I did it, since you're taxing the money I made from it. So if I did it, I had to have gotten there. Obviously, right?"

Kelvin Peterson is shaking his head with great sadness.

"Could I get some fraction of that 4,300?"

"No."

"I can't have any mileage at all?"

Kelvin Peterson pauses magisterially. "Let's see how generous I'm feeling by the end of this," he says.

Well, I for one didn't really expect to win that one. But this audit is not getting off to a good start. Our last audit was an hour and a half long and was conducted by a nice lady who tried to understand our occupations and proceed from there. At one point she singled out on my performance calendar a date where I had opened for Dave Alvin. "You went to Cleveland," she said. "Between personnel, motel, gas, and sundries you spent $900, and you made only $100. What were you trying to do?" I remember staring at her without quite knowing what to say. "Pass out business cards?" she suggested, trying to help me. "Make contacts?"

Good Lord, come to think of it, what on earth was I trying to do? My long, dogged pursuit of music business goals both childishly delusory (a major-label deal) and pathetically modest (a sustainable wage) suddenly seemed, in the light of What-are-you-trying-to-do, like a transparently absurd endeavor that I had kept afloat year after year only by suspending my entire capacity for sober self-examination. I might have dissolved in a pool of tears if my wife hadn't whisked a copy of my recent major-label release out of her pocketbook with a triumphant air, placed it before the audit lady, and announced: "This! This is what we have been spending all this money and time waiting for! This is it—the eventuality every struggling musician dreams of and prays for, this! The end of the rainbow! Our countless sacrifices vindicated by the endorsement of a giant corporation!" It was as though she had been polishing this Brechtian outburst for days. But her point was taken by the auditrix, and for the remainder of our session there were no inquiries into the hundreds of dollars daily disappearing into the voracious maw of my career during fiscal year 1996, the eventual sinking of hundreds of thousands of dollars into that very maw by a real record company having lent some legitimacy if not respectability to the boondoggle. (In an ironic footnote to this story, that company has now disappeared. I am still here.)

But this year's auditor is interested in succinct data to fill each field on the computerized form. "In this business you operate as a self-employed musician, where do you go to play music?"

"Um"—how to put it?—"bars."

"No, what I mean is, your engagements, do they take place primarily in and around Chicago?"

"No, they take place all over. Mainly in the United States."

"And who comes to hear you play?"

Again I am unsure what to say.

"For instance, do you play primarily for children?" The kinder, gentler, post-1998 tax examiner always keeps helpful mind-jogging instances at hand.

"No, primarily for adults. I put out records and theoretically people develop an interest in attending one of my shows after having heard a record."

"I see." He types the word "general" in the field and moves on to the next. "Who handles sales and production, would that be you?"

"You mean of the records? The records are produced, I guess you would say, by the record label. I sell some myself from the stage but most of the sales take place in stores where people go to buy records"—I am still trying to find a suitable diction for this weird discourse—"and are accounted for by the record label."

He types "lable" after the prompt "Sales" and "label" after the prompt "Production," and after comparing the effects, corrects the first. I am wondering how to get this on track. That no one outside of one's profession has a clear understanding of what one does, or how (or sometimes why) one does it; that one is condemned by one's occupational culture to exile from ordinary society; that one is, with one's casual attire, slouched posture, and stammering difficulty in answering a few generic questions, naturally ridiculous in the eyes of decent citizens; one must accept these symptoms of an ordered society with forbearance. But unfortunately, one also becomes inured to a special status that is usually easy to invoke when necessary. Look: I make records! I travel around entertaining people—not a lot of people, to be sure, but they are spread all over 48 states! I am written about in magazines! I'm even on the electric TV!

"Now, let's look at some of your Schedule C deductions. First, you reported $9,091 in travel expenses. What were those?"

I produce four thick manila folders full of tour receipts and income/expense breakdowns by month. "That's for hotels. Here are the receipts."

"These are hotels for . . . "

"For when we go to play our shows, which are attended by adults, and which occur mainly outside of Chicago. Afterward we sleep in hotels."

" 'We' is who? You and your band?"

"Yes."

Another sorrowful shake of the head. "The only allowable travel-related deductions are for yourself."

"I'm sorry?"

"You can't deduct others' expenses, unless they're your employees. The law is very clear on that point. Are these people your employees?"

The sickening sound is my all-encompassing love of life collapsing into a slough of despond. My wife steps in.

"These people are not our employees. Let me present a clear picture of our operation for you. We are not the Rolling Stones here. We are a small family business. We cannot afford to pay the people Robbie takes on the road Medicare or Social Security, nor do they expect us to. They are indispensable to my husband's career. He releases records featuring group performances, and so he needs to tour with a group."

"Then the group needs to pay their own way and claim their own expenses on their own returns."

"Musicians are not going to cover their own travel expenses! That's just not how! It! Is!"

"Well, I suggest you try looking for some different musicians. I'm sorry, but it's very clear." He reads a passage from a book which says what he just said, that travel deductions must be one's own or one's employees.

"Look," says my wife, trying a different and more fruitless tack, "this is what everyone does. And we ourselves have done this for years. Our travel expenses for Robbie's band passed our last audit, and passed two different, experienced tax preparers."

"I can't speak for what happened at your last audit, or what you have done in the past. Sometimes," he confides, "low-budget tax preparers are unreliable."

"This is absolutely insane," I suggest. "First of all, Geffen reimbursed me for all these expenses, and their reimbursements are reported here as income, so under your scenario I'm taxed on the reimbursement but can't claim the original expenses I paid out of pocket. Second, this tax law is plainly meant to cover pager-wearing schmucks who go to Cleveland for a seminar, not rock bands. It's not business-related travel, my whole business IS the travel. I have tens of thousands of dollars in expenses for my band, going back for years—not just hotels but air fares, cabs, drum heads, and a dozen other things." Maybe I shouldn't be saying all this.

"And none of that is allowed," smiles Kelvin Peterson. "You can't deduct other people's expenses. It's just absolutely clear. After all, how do I know that your band isn't claiming these same expenses on their returns?"

"What do you mean?" I pull from a folder a few pages of meticulously Scotch-taped hotel receipts. "I have the receipts! Here they are! Anyone else that claims these 2 rooms at the Red Roof on

August 9, 1998, in Trenton is clearly incorrect!" I am kicking at his desk impatiently and gesturing heatedly.

"Do not get angry at me, Mr. Fulks. I did not write the law. Talk to your congressman."

Neither of us can think of any other line of reasoning, and we can see little profit in continuing to object to something so clear.

"I'll ask my supervisor to confirm the law if you like." We nod mutely, and are left alone all of a sudden, Donna and I. There was, as Dorothy Parker put it, a long silence with things going on in it. After a minute I mumbled timidly, "Are these car dealer–type stunts or what? First the how-generous-I'm-feeling bit and now this. If he comes back saying 'Well, this is really your lucky day,' I'll asphyxiate him with my long form." (Tax jokes are usually a bit labored.)

But he returns without any developments to report, and informs us that it is time to move on to my mileage claim, which is 41,394.

"Were all these miles on one vehicle?"

"Yes."

"Did you use that vehicle for any non-work-related driving?"

"No."

"Did you keep a mileage log?"

"Yes."

"Let's take a look."

I recorded my mileage in my calendar book. At the end of every trip, on the page with the date on which I got home, I wrote down the miles driven with a box shape around the figure. Two-hour trip, number in a box; month-long trip, number in a box. There are perhaps 60 numbers in boxes. I read each one to Kelvin Peterson, slowly and deliberately, while turning 365 datebook pages slowly and deliberately. He runs an adding machine tape. The miles come up about 1,000 short.

"Well, that's odd," I say. "Maybe I missed one. Shall we double-check our work?"

He sighs, runs another tape, and I read through the book a second time, not much faster, and the number doesn't change. The return is adjusted accordingly. Kelvin Peterson's patience is being strained, and you can see some cracks, just barely. As for me, I'm not even here anymore. I am mildly interested in what magic sum will be declared at the end, but, despair having set like cement in my head, I would like to amuse myself for whatever time remains by playing daft and throwing spanners. When he turns to the meals deduction, which is based on the number of days out of town, I ask Donna whether she brought that sheet where I tallied my travel days. No, she didn't, and we go back to the datebook and count out 196 days, page by page, at the speed of mammal evolution. A couple times I lose the count—"47, no, wait, did I already say 47?"—but Kelvin Peterson sticks doggedly with me as he runs the tape. After this exercise he asks for the 1099's I filed for my band. "Um, did you bring those?" I ask Donna. Kelvin Peterson doesn't wait for the answer. He goes away again. I turn to Donna.

"What were we thinking? We should never have come here without bringing someone to speak for us, someone to speak to this man in his own tongue and find whatever fucking hidden clause it is that lets us earn a living the way we earn it and keeps the fucking IRS off our backs. We're over our heads and out of our element. And that sandwich is making me sick. Something was wrong with it."

"If he's right about your deductions, what are we going to do?" Donna says. "You can't go out on the road anymore if you can't claim most of the expenses."

"He's not right, and I can claim them, and what we're going to do is research case law, consult a half-dozen different tax lawyers and accountants, talk to other bandleaders who've been audited, and then appeal. We're going to spend half our productive time for the next month on this horseshit. We can't come back to this on our third audit." Almost everyone we know who has been audited once has been audited twice more.

"I think," Donna lowers her voice to the faintest whisper, "he's not going to ask you for documentation on your per diems." We haven't been able to locate any corroborating proof of the cash I paid my players in 1998 for meals on the road, and I've claimed (accurately) around $5,000. It was our top worry coming in, unable as we were to foresee the disallowed hotels or the agency paymaster brouhaha.

"I doubt it. I think he just hasn't gotten there." He walks back in, and it turns out he is indeed skimming past the per diems. He's just too eager to get this over with. "I" and "try" and "can" and "anything" have turned to "very" and "tired" and "go" and "home." This is not the sympathetic, soul-of-Job, post-congressional-hearings Kelvin Peterson of three-and-a-half hours back. This Kelvin Peterson stretches his arms languidly and sighs continually. Presently his phone rings. He tells the caller suggestively, "I'll call you back in three minutes."

"Are we through in three minutes?" my wife pipes up.

"I was using a turn of phrase," Kelvin glowers. But we are done in 15. The bill is $966. We ride home through rush hour traffic. As we pull in our driveway a girl from the neighborhood, a pretty 14-year-old with a somewhat confrontational style, is hanging around our lawn on her bike. People are hanging around our house a little more in the last week, since I did the Conan O'Brien show.

"I just wrote two songs," she tells me.

"I didn't know you were a songwriter. What are they called?"

"One's called 'Country Hillbilly' and one's called 'Down Town South.'"

"That's funny."

"I've got a lot of songs," she says. "Not all of them are finished."

"Stay out of the business," I advise her.

METAL MIKE SAUNDERS

Disney Dreams Up the Best Radio Station in 30 Years

The seminal moment of the teenpop era is of course in the *Clueless* movie, where Cher refers to college-rock R.E.M.–crap as "mope rock," or "dope rock," or "slope rock," whatever. When Hollywood says it in a script, it's alllllllll over. Anyone who runs into Alicia Silverstone remind her, and thank her. (The movie dates from when, 1995? Pre–Spice Girls, pre-Backstreet, pre-everything. They should recut the movie with a modern soundtrack dropped in—the Valley party would be better with "Genie in a Bottle" as "our song." LFO could be on the patio playing "Summer Girls," instead of that stupid ska band.)

Anyway, if you're collecting predictions on teenpop era span, I say through Year 2010 and beyond, EASY—that would be about 15 years, total. It's a gigantic land shift like the 1964 Beatles ("rock" era), or genre-wise like "heavy metal" (30 long years, right?—the last 20 mostly useless. . . . It's gonna take 20 years of new-era vocal groups just to neutralize that). Best spinoff would be if all the "serious musicians" and "singer-songwriters" gave up and went to work at Macy's. Can you imagine how preposterous a "singer-songwriter" would've seemed in 1963, 1964? (Actually, they were called folkies then.) From what I'm told they can't dance too good.

Funny that the truest pop underground of Year 2000 turns out to be grade schoolers (the trailing half of the 1996–1999 teenpop boom), but hardly surprising. This has been threatening to happen ever since Aqua snuck through 2.5 million copies of *Aquarium* in 1997–98 (ALL to preteens) in America—and throw in the Spice Girls' young kid–crowd for further confusion. So who knows how it will play out? Like, in 1982, who would've ever thought MTV would mean shit? It was all videos 24/7, and every 180 minutes you'd go, "OH FUCK, they're playing Sammy Hagar's 'Three Lock Box' AGAIN." But (along with Haysi Fantayzee's assassination of Ronald Reagan) it turned out to be one of the biggest music stories of the '80s.

I've finally figured it out, though—aliens landed several years ago, and Radio Disney is their beachhead! It's all very very clear: Hook the young minds, and then later start with the subliminal messages . . . "radio for kids!" is hardly one step away from "kill your parents" backwards three times per song. Or maybe *Jesus* came back, took a look around, and went, "Screw the grown-ups, I'm starting from scratch," and *he's* the PD for Radio Disney—nationally syndicated, now with actual airwave stations in about 80% of the U.S.'s largest markets including 1560 AM in New York, plus the Internet station at disney.go.com/radiodisney. They're not self-supporting, so they cross-advertise other Disney sectors heavily to get their money's worth. And Web-search business articles say their demographic is mostly ages two-to–11. (Wonder what songs those two-year-olds like? The *Pokémon* theme??)

Station IDs/promos in chirpy grade school voices ("Radio Disney . . . We're all EARS!") that drive high schoolers and other 12-to–20s out the door screaming, but charm the heck out of parents, aunts, and uncles (that's me!). It's like the old hippie cliché, where you take that "tab of acid," walk into the next room, and BOOM! Everything's now in Technicolor! Upbeat! Happy! Wacky! YOU NEED THIS STATION! PRODUCTIVITY WILL INCREASE BY XX%!

. . . Oh man, I give up. RadioD just ran Britney Spears's "Soda Pop" (I'm thinking, "I don't hate this QUITE that much," it actually sounded OK) straight into the Beatles' "I Want to Hold Your Hand," and neither song blinked. That Beatles song can sound re-allllll good when set up properly. (Fake reggae into exploding guitar—in 1964, Millie Small would have been the lead-in.) Thirty minutes later, Little Eva's "The Loco-Motion" is on the Disney deck (yesterday they played Kylie Minogue's), and not too long after, the Stones'—I mean Britney's—". . . Baby One More Time" into "Yakety Yak" from 1958.

I'm just jotting down the non-current–Top 30 tunes that spring out ('60s, '70s, and '80s), which keep getting more wack/astounding with each additional hour. Lots of novelty and dance songs spanning the last 40 years of hit radio . . . everything from "Yellow Submarine" to "Cars" by Gary Numan to a deranged version of "The Lion Sleeps Tonight," and over to "The Curly Shuffle" and "Do the Bartman" and Alvin & the Chipmunks disco ("Turn the Beat Around"). Lots of KC on weekends. And TONS of vintage Weird Al, this station/core audience's Numero Uno all-time act, sort of their parallel universe Beatles. (Hey, "I Want a New Duck" rocks!)

The most surreal segue I've heard on Disney so far is the Contours' "Do You Love Me" (certainly one of my Top 10 or 20 dance songs ever) right into "We Like to Party" by my beloved doofus Vengaboys: classic DJ synergy, where a great track makes an adjoining one sound better (and "We Like to Party" back on CHR-pop was truly annoying). Then there's the greatest pop sequence I've ever heard on commercial radio in my entire life: Toy-Box's "Tarzan and Jane" cavorting into the Backstreet Boys' fantab "I Want It That Way" sliding into the Archies' epochal "Sugar Sugar." "My Boyfriend's Back" and "I Got You (I Feel Good)" sandwiched around 'N Sync's new single (very catchy!). The *Jetsons* TV theme song, Little Richard's "Tutti Frutti," and the Isleys' "Shout," right next to Christina Aguilera, that damned Vengas bus, and the BSBoys. Joan Jett's glorious "Summertime Blues" hyperdrive Ramonesola, on a Monday afternoon! An insanely cute modern techno-ballad (movie track?) of Rosie and the Originals' "Angel Baby." The *Happy Days* theme, sounding as goofy as in 1976. Girl-pop-rock heaven: "Boys Will Be Boys" from the swell TLC–meets-new-wave 1998 *Beyond Pink* Barbie album. The great *Clueless* TV theme song (written by the Go-Gos' Charlotte Caffey), *full version* (can I buy this somewhere??), into Elvis's "Hound Dog." (Charlotte Caffey back-to-back with Scotty Moore? Don't think that's *ever* happened before on radio in this galaxy.)

An amazing playlist, I'm telling you, almost freeform! Plus their modern Top 30 is 100% hyper teenpop, simple as that—sometimes eight of the top 21 Disney chart slots are Backstreet or Britney. (On the Web page, you can play or download samples of most of the hits, if you have Real Player on your PC. And the most requested songs are compiled now, on two *Radio Disney Jams* CDs.) The square Top 40 scene is still polluted with creaky Celine/Mariah dinosaurs and snooze r&b and horrid faux-"rock" bands NOT heard on RadioDiz—Blink 182, Foo Fighters, etc., mercifully DON'T EXIST!! But they just played "Hand Jive" by what's his name (Johnny Otis?).... Why? They're trying to pass down the Diddley-beat? Or does that beat count as novelty? And they play "One Way or Another" regularly, too—the *Sabrina* version. Nuts.

Or 8 P.M. prime time, the Ramones' "Surfin' Bird"—guitars are obviously allowed if it's a "novelty song," Melissa Joan Hart included, so I figure Disney was just checking if the kids were paying attention. (I've heard them play the much superior Trashmen version several times.) "Crocodile Rock," "Na Na Hey Hey Kiss Him Goodbye," "Twist and Shout" by the Beatles, "We Will Rock You," 1910 Fruitgum Co.'s "Simon Says" (!), the eternally swank "Green Onions," SSledge's "We Are Family," all alternating in barely an hour's time with the week's current Top 30 fab hit teenpop sounds of BritneyChristinaBSBoysMandy'NSyncLFOVenga-boysRickyM-LouBegaEiffel65, all of whom completely hold their own in context. I heard the tail end (1965–66) of "screaming Top 40" radio in eighth or ninth grade, and it was cool—but not as cool as this! In '65 we just had the Beatles; oldies only on "oldies weekend," and they sounded silly back-to-back with Them or the Yardbirds or whoever.

The best thing about the teenpop era is that we're back to 1956 or '57 in the pre-Beatles(= pre-guitar bands) era, musically speaking.

Wiped the slate clean and started fucking over, back to when vocals meant something and had room to breathe. And those two million rock bands who've wasted everyone's time for the last 30 years are extinct as surely as Bobby Vee or Rydell were back in 1964, when that same initially swell "rock era" began courtesy of the Beatles. (You seriously think some 10-year-old's gonna listen to the Eagles or Fleetwood Mac? Not to mention U2 or R.E.M. or . . .) Until 1966 and artsy rock (*Revolver*), NO ONE but teenagers bought/followed rock and roll; it was a very small, self-contained, nutty little universe, with novelty records (or death tunes, sort of the same thing) every 30 minutes on the AM. Not unlike what the preteens seem to have going during this, their magic bubble of time.

All across the world—for a year now!—thousands of girls (ages 5 to 15?) have been screwing around in front of their moms' big mirrors, going, "I could do this!" Britney is their '65 Stones, i.e., the blueprint from which thousands copied ('65 Stones spawning roughly 66.7% of all 1966 garage bands). This current stuff's the best Top 40 girlpop since 1962–63, and MAYBE BETTER. 'Cause the beats are better, and there's even more diversity of "styles," white to black to Euro to domestic. ('60s girl groups being one of my favorite rock genres ever—they could really fuckin' sing—but they relied on a few too many lame, uninterested session drummers, once you got past Phil Spector's and David Gates's productions.) On the Disney AM, the "Drive Me Crazy" Stop remix is as relentless as "Satisfaction" in 1965 (meaning they play it *constantly*), altho I much prefer Britney's rhythm track.

And Backstreet get mega-all-hits rotation about equal to the Beatles of back then, so that's about a draw (Beatles—better songs; BSB—better beats). Harmony vocals are cool. Dancing is cool, always has been. I never had a problem with "I Want It That Way" being the greatest song of the century, but I'm getting into it after the fact. Which reminds me of my hostile initial reactions to at least two previous giant changings-of-the-guards in pop/rock: (1) the "heavy rock" of 1970, right before Sabbbath/realmetal happened . . . I HATED the stuff, as a '60s fan cranky about all the '60s bands going lame or worse. First couple times "Iron Man" came up early summer 1971 on latenite FM, me and my brother snickered, like, "how DUMB is this?" But by the fourth time we were air-banging our heads like Beavis and Butt-head. . . . It just *happened*, no conscious rethink involved. And (2) I REALLY hated the Ramones and '70s punk for one-entire-year-plus (from the first Ramones LP right up till the first Generation X album, 1978 U.S. version, which rocked hard enough to pull in us suburban metalheads). I mean, I wanted to KILL them; that's how much their brand-new take on rock offended my ears. I remember watching the Ramones' *Don Kirshner Rock Concert* 15-minute segment when it aired, and hating every single second.

So, it's hardly any surprise that I hated the BSB for a good while. . . . I was looking at them and not listening. But now that I'm hearing them constantly in the Radio Disney context, their best songs (without the irritating videos to distract) do indeed sound like a true refraction of the pre-Beatles white vocal groups. Who I think is a really great lead singer is the white guy who parts his hair in the middle—Nick, with the highest-pitched voice. He REALLY has the Belmonts vibe, sings like he MEANS it. Without a hint of retro on the surface, BSB are the first act since December 1963 to be a white male vocal group and be "cool." (Trust me, the minute the Beatles landed at the airport, Frankie Valli/4 Seasons were the epitome of anti-cool.) 35+ years is quite a stretch. In the Beatles' heyday, backing up 35 years would've taken you before swing music.

In 1962–63, the smart kids wouldn't touch the rock scene; they were off playing Coltrane or blues or ethnic folk and being beatniks. Likewise, Joni Mitchell (promoting some stupid cover song album) was in the paper last month grousing about "talentless puff figure" teenpop singers, and *Rolling Stone* and *Spin* these days run plenty of quotes from '80s rock fossils claiming, "MTV doesn't even play videos anymore!" Uh, sure—since *Total Request Live* = late '50s *American Bandstand* as a gonzo über-pop cultural touchstone, I guess *Bandstand* must NOT've played music. . . . It was just a mass cultural delusion. And the all-teen audience was a bunch of dozing sheep, just like the half-asleep bad-white-dancer kids in the *Bandstand* footage. (Twelve-year-old girls, ah, they're silly little kids, and they buy that silly music like, y'know, Elvis and the Beatles, and [their own kidlets] Madonna. I mean, where're the moog solos? The guitar jams? Some REAL music, y'know?) (Wonder what "real music" was in 1956—bebop??) BUT 38+YRS ONWARD, man, you get the total impression that the teenpop audience is culturally SHARP. Computer kids. The little elementary schoolers who call up the Radio Disney phone lines throw back one-liners as fast as any screaming 1965 AM jock. RDisney's weekly "mailbag" segment, where they play the new feature song of the week and dozens of listeners get to call in on-air (between subsequent songs) and voice their opinions, has more insightful comments than a roomful of rock critics high on Sterno. The record? Madonna's "American Pie." Sample comments? "I liked it 'cause it reminded me of Weird Al and he's my all-time favorite act!" "It's STUPID . . . it's sooooo messed up." "It's awesome! Better than the '50s original." Madonna just barely passed, favorable-over-unfavorable. Good thing they didn't play Pearl Jam.

I'm guessing this station would add .5 to anyone's GPA just as homework music. And the type of format Disney is pushing definitely makes it cool for boys to listen to their sisters' radio hits, too. But what % of actual genre sales are going to boys, and what acts would a 10-year-old boy *like*? Novelty songs? Sure can't imagine the real-life Stan and Kyle—who don't really like girls yet (so scratch Mandy and Brandy and Britney and . . .)—liking 'N Sync. But "Mambo No. 5" and "Blue," hell yeah. You'll recall that much of the youngest part of the mid-'60s pop audience gave us (my distant memory is flickering) punk/new wave—like, that great story about the Ramones trying to play "Indian Giver" upon forming, but it sounded like shit, so they just had to write their own attempted bubblegum songs instead. Well, I bet you my 401(k) the average really sharp eighth-grade boy would be trying to write a song like LFO right now—including to impress the girls! (You know it's a happening scene when the second-tier groups have great songs in them. Rich's lyrics on "Summer Girls" and "Girl on TV" are all-universe.) The kid'd be bright enough to figure out that the retard-rock-rap Woodstock-mosh stuff is duller than death. . . . It'd take about two seconds of watching dimwits à la Fred Durst to arrive at that con-clusion, obviously.

So whoever Disney's PD is, is a stone genius. Alan Freed, in 1954, only had current r&b cross-over breakthrough trends to work with and help mold. Disney's PD is taking 40 YEARS of the pop/dance/novelty side of rock music and mixing it into an artistic state-ment. And phone call-ins HAVE to be a certain % of their feed-back/input, once a pre-1996 song has been played once. (Can you imagine an eight-year-old going into a big all-formats mom-and-pop store and asking where he could find "Yummy Yummy Yummy"? They'd have a coronary.) Maybe Disney's PD was traumatized by hippie CSN&Y–lovin' parents, and the station is revenge? What goes around comes around, ya fuckin' pothead doobie-smoking mel-low fellow granolahead deadheads.

Underground? Check this: On Disney's Sunday February 6 Top 30 Countdown, those Swede wackokids the A*Teens' unspeakably great and happy-feet-inducing bubble-techno-pop Abba remake "Mamma Mia" was a breakout hit, up five to #22. Melancholic words? No problem, run it over with the happy truck. I checked the week's *Billboard* two blocks over from loading up the month's canned goods and bathroom groceries, and "Mamma Mia" wasn't even in the pop Top 100. The A*Teens' "Dancing Queen"—also not in *Bill-board* yet—EXPLODED on Disney, jumping from #27 to #10 in a week. Now it's inescapable: Wake up in the morning, it will find you. Come home from work, it has followed you. RD's playlist is a mile ahead of national CHR-pop on ALL the teenpop stuff (Han-son's new single every hour on the hour!), kinda like Murray the K breaking the Supremes' (total loser act till then) "Where Did Our Love Go" nationally out of his New York powerhouse show back in the days of classic Top 40. Keeping up with the pop underground could become a full-time job.

In fact, if Billie Joe of Green Day were truly the genius I've always claimed, he'd write a song about teenpop music, and make it funny, not sarcastic. "Getting High With Backstreet"—that'd make Green Day Dylan to the BSBs' Beatles. "One night I died/I got so high/And at the gates were Backstreet/They said you've got to dance/Like pigs a-squealin'/Sing like you mean it/With extra feelin'/I went to hell/And I don't care/I went to hell/And guess who's there/Singing I want it that way/I got it that way/Counting money for eternity/Printing contracts for you and me." Very last chorus refrain: "I got high with Backstreet/I got high with Backstreet/I got high with Backstreet/And I don't care."

ANTHONY DeCURTIS

Johnny Cash
Won't Back Down

On a sunlit afternoon, Johnny Cash sits in a large, comfortable chair in the Hendersonville, Tennessee, house he's shared with his wife, June Carter Cash, for more than thirty years. He's reflecting on his life. In 1997, he announced that he was struggling with a nervous-system disorder, and his public manifestations since then have been rare. But this afternoon, he is expansive, good-humored, and, above all, indomitable as he talks about the album he is recording, his plans, and his past.

"This room right here that you're in, this is the room I moved into when I decided to quit drugs in 1968," Cash says as he looks around the oval-shaped, dark-wooded den. "They didn't have treatment centers the way they do now, so this is the room that I climbed the walls in for thirty days.

"The doctor came to see me every day at 5 P.M.," he continues. "The first few days I was still rollin' stones. Amphetamine was my drug of choice, and I had pills hidden all over this room." He looks over to the many doors that line the wall opposite the row of windows overlooking Old Hickory Lake. He pauses, then laughs to himself. "I was serious about quitting—but not quite," he says, wryly. "About the third or fourth day, the doctor looked me in the eye and asked, 'How you doin'?' I said, 'Great!' And he said, 'Bullshit. I know you're not doing great. When are you going to get rid of them?' So I went and got them out of the closet and wherever else I had them hid, and we flushed them. Then I really started the program that he laid out for me. I came out of here feeling like a million dollars."

Being around Johnny Cash is a daunting experience. He is tall, and, though the illness he now lives with has broadened him around the middle and grayed that sleek mane of black hair, he remains a formidable physical presence. As he talks, he will occasionally put his hands over his eyes and rub them, as if he is in pain. Those eyes look as though they have seen everything, have absorbed all the lessons those experiences had to offer and now are hungry for more. His intelligence is keen, and his innate dignity informs every move he makes and every word he speaks. It is heartbreaking to watch him, a giant, struggle with his burden. The knowledge that Cash has walked both sides of the line separating sin and salvation only thickens the air of integrity that always surrounds him.

Right now, in the bright sunshine outside, a celebration is under way on the sprawling grounds of the Cash estate, just north of Nashville. Several hundred people—including such Nashville luminaries as George Jones, Tom T. Hall and Skeeter Davis—have gathered to celebrate the release of June Carter Cash's *Press On*, a moving collection of songs that honors her heritage as a daughter of the Carter Family, the founding family of country rhusic. But while the festivities go on, guests are quietly led back to the house for private audiences with Johnny. He's friendly to everyone, but he's pacing himself. He plans to perform a song with June in an hour or two, and he needs to conserve his energy.

In October 1997 Cash grew dizzy and nearly fell after bending down to retrieve a guitar pick during a performance in Flint, Michigan. He then told the audience that he had Parkinson's disease. Shortly afterward, he was diagnosed with Shy-Drager Syndrome, a progressive, Parkinson's-like illness for which there is currently no cure. The prognosis is terrifying: chronic degeneration over a period of years, then death. Cash canceled the remainder of that '97 tour. He has subsequently been hospitalized a number of times for pneumonia, and he has suffered other side effects of the disease and its rigorous treatment. Cash has fought his illness with characteristic will—so much so that there is now some question about whether the diagnosis of Shy-Drager is correct. While he suffers many bad days—and neither his doctors nor anyone in the Cash camp will publicly venture a more optimistic read on his health—Cash has fared far better than anyone had a right to believe he would.

It's hardly surprising, under such circumstances, that Cash's mind would turn to an earlier physical struggle—his tormented battle with drug addiction, a battle that, despite some notable backsliding, he eventually won. He does not like discussing his sickness. "It's all right," he assured the Michigan crowd after revealing his illness. "I refuse to give it some ground in my life." In the spring of 1999 he told *USA Today*, "I've made it a point to forget the name of the disease and not to give it any space in my life, because I just can't do it. I can't think that negatively. I can't believe I'm going to be incapacitated. I won't believe that." After that article appeared, Cash was so upset about its detailed discussion of his illness that he canceled some upcoming interviews.

Back in Hendersonville, Cash eventually leaves the house and, dressed in black tails and a black shirt, greets the family members, friends and guests who, to a person, are thrilled to see him. He takes the stage set up in the yard and affectionately introduces June. He looks flushed, and he moves with great deliberateness, spending his store of energy carefully, anticipating the exhaustion to come. Johnny joins June and her band—which includes their son John Carter Cash on acoustic guitar—to duet with June on "The Far Side Banks of Jordan," a tune that Cash first played for his wife twenty-five years before, telling her, "This is going to be our song." It's the sort of folk spiritual he used to sing with his family on their front porch in Dyess, Arkansas, decades ago, the kind of song that first sparked his love for music. He begins the song, accompanying himself on acoustic guitar. "I believe my steps are growing wearier each day," he sings. "Got another journey on my mind/The lures of this old world/Have ceased to make me want to stay/And my one regret is leaving you behind."

Johnny and June harmonize on the chorus: "I'll be waiting on the far side banks of Jordan/I'll be sitting, drawing pictures in the sand/And when I see you coming/I will rise up with a shout/And come running through the shallow water/Reaching for your hand."

Despite, or perhaps because of his illness, interest in Johnny Cash's music has reached a fever pitch. In May, Columbia/American/Legacy released an extraordinary three–CD box set of his work. Titled *Love God and Murder*, it is a thematically organized collection that explores the three grand subjects of Cash's forty-six-year career. Cash has also just released a stunning new album, *American III: Solitary Man*, his third collaboration with producer Rick Rubin. It is a brave, unflinching confrontation with his own mortality, the nearly inconceivable notion of leaving behind all the joys and sorrows that constitute a life. It's hard to imagine anyone else making an album remotely like it.

Like so many of the titanic heroes of rock & roll, Johnny Cash is a glorious mess of contradictions. The wild drugs and debauchery of Saturday night—and in Cash's case, pretty much every other night, too—have fought vigorously for his soul against the powerful Christian conviction of Sunday morning. Cash is the Man in Black, the noble outlaw, a fearsome figure whose Mount Rushmore face, piercing dark eyes and uproarious excesses helped make him one of the more combustible ingredients in the critical mass that exploded in Memphis in the mid-Fifties. In early songs like "I Walk the Line" and "Big River," he articulated a fierce vision of what country music—and its bastard child, rock & roll—could be. He hammered out a sound that is bare to the bone, without a single wasted note.

"I was a Johnny Cash freak," says Keith Richards, who first heard Cash's music as a teenager in England. "Luther Perkins, his guitar player, was amazing. Johnny's singing was, too. They taught me about the importance of silence in music—that you don't have to play all over the song. You just play what's necessary. If it's done wrong, it can be painfully monotonous. But when it's done right, it has this incredibly powerful focus and intensity, and that's what those early Cash songs were like.

"As far as early rock & roll goes," Richards continues, "if someone came up to me and for some reason they could only get a collection of one person's music, I'd say, 'Chuck Berry is important, but, man, you've got to get the Cash!'"

While he was making that groundbreaking music, Cash was also inventing what would soon become the myth of Johnny Cash. It is a larger-than-life persona that has had at least as much impact and influence as the music itself. "I was backstage at the Grand Ole Opry in Nashville when I met him in 1965," says Kris Kristofferson, whose career Cash helped to launch. "It was back in his dangerous days, and it was electric. He was skinny as a snake, and you just never knew what he was going to do. He looked like he might explode at any minute. He was a bad boy, he stood up for the underdog, he was exciting and unpredictable, and he had an energy onstage that was unlike anybody else.

"I shook hands with him," Kristofferson continues, "and that was probably what brought me back to Nashville to be a songwriter. He was everything I thought an artist ought to be."

Folk singer Eric Andersen remembers being introduced to Cash by Bob Dylan at the Newport Folk Festival in 1964. Dylan greatly admired Cash, and Cash, breaking ranks with Nashville orthodoxy, was an early, enthusiastic supporter of Dylan. "I was backstage, and Bob ran over and grabbed me," Andersen recalls. "'You've gotta meet Johnny Cash, man!' Cash was a hero to us, one of the original cats. So Bob brought me back to his tent, and I met John. He had just done his set, and he was really wired. He looked like a puppet whose strings were all tangled up—half cut, and half held together—and he was just jiggling around."

That darker, uncontrolled side of Cash has drawn generations of fans to him even as many of his contemporaries—and their progeny—have fallen out of favor. He is, after all, the man who, in "Folsom Prison Blues," sang, "I shot a man in Reno/Just to watch him die" in 1955, decades before gangsta rap was born. He demolished hotel rooms and stomped out the lights on the stage of the Grand Ole Opry while Keith Moon was still in short pants.

Those experiences also make Cash, who is now sixty-eight, sympathetic when younger musicians are attacked for causing violence by singing and rapping about it in their songs. "I don't think music and movies have anything to do with it," Cash says, when asked about the relationship between violence and popular culture. "I think it's in the person. I mean, I'm an entertainer. 'I shot a man in Reno just to watch him die' is a fantasy. I didn't shoot anybody in Reno—and I didn't kill Delia," he adds with a chuckle, alluding to a grisly folk song he adapted on his 1994 *American Recordings* album.

"But it's fun to sing about those things," he continues. "Murder ballads go way back in country music. Even the Carter Family, they got some really bloody records. There's 'The Banks of the Ohio' with all that 'stuck a knife in her breast and watched her as she went down under the water, and the bubbles came up out of her mouth, and the water turned red.' And Jimmie Rodgers—'I'm gonna buy me a shotgun/Just as long as I'm tall/And I'm gonna shoot poor Thelma/Just to see her jump and fall.' That's right up there with 'shot a man in Reno.'

"But these songs are just for singing, and singers always knew that. I'm not suggesting that anybody consider learning how to shoot a gun. I'm not suggesting that they even own one. Although I do. I used to collect antique Colt pistols. But they weren't for shooting. They were like ancient coins—I collect those, too. But the coins aren't for spending, and the guns aren't for shooting."

Inevitably, the discussion about violence leads to the deeply held religious beliefs that are the other pull in Cash's divided soul. They are the salve to the urges most aptly described in the title of a Nick Lowe song he covered a few years back: "The Beast in Me." "There's something missing there," Cash says. "There's a spiritual hunger in people for goodness and righteousness. There's an emptiness in people that they're trying to fill. And I don't know why they go about it the way they do."

Bono recalls visiting Cash in Hendersonville during a drive across the U.S. He and U2 bassist Adam Clayton sat down for a meal with Johnny and June. "We bowed our heads and John spoke this beautiful, poetic grace," Bono says, "and we were all humbled and moved. Then he looked up afterwards and said, 'Sure miss the drugs, though.'"

Cash is content to let his convictions, however conflicted, speak for themselves. "I believe what I say, but that don't necessarily make me right," he says, laughing. "There's nothing hypocritical about it. There is a spiritual side to me that goes real deep, but I confess right upfront that I'm the biggest sinner of them all." He even views his battle with drug addiction in spiritual terms. "I used drugs to escape," he says quietly, "and they worked pretty well when I was younger. But they devastated me physically and emotionally—and spiritually. That last one hurt so much: to put myself in such a low state that I couldn't communicate with God. There's no lonelier place to be. I was separated from God, and I wasn't even trying to call on him. I knew that there was no line of communication. But he came back. And I came back."

That sense of spiritual wisdom garnered through grueling experience has given Cash the moral strength, as an artist and a person, to always stand his ground. Throughout his life Cash has pandered to no specific audience or constituency. In the Sixties and early Seventies, he performed for American troops and protested the Vietnam War. He defended Native American rights long before it became fashionable. He has both played in prisons and supported organizations that assist the families of slain police officers. And he stands by his friends.

"I opened for John in Philadelphia a few years ago, and I dedicated a song to Mumia Abu-Jamal," Kristofferson recalls. Abu-Jamal is an African-American journalist who is currently on death row for allegedly murdering a police officer—in Philadelphia. His case has become a flash point for activists, who believe Abu-Jamal was railroaded and who want him to get a new trial. It's a flash point as well for law-enforcement organizations, who view him as a cold-blooded killer. "The police at the show went ballistic," Kristofferson continues. "After I came off, they said that I had to go out and make an apology. I felt pretty bad, because it was John's show. But John heard about it and said to me, 'Listen, you don't need to apologize for nothin'. I want you to come out at the end of the show and do "Why Me" with me.' So I went out and sang with him. John just refuses to compromise."

Johnny Cash became a superstar in his mid-twenties, enjoying an impressive run of hits between 1956 and 1958 on Sun Records, the Memphis label run by Sam Phillips, the man who originally signed Elvis Presley. Like Presley, Cash soon left Sun to sign with a major label, in his case, Columbia. On Columbia, his success continued, beginning with "All Over Again" and the classic "Don't Take Your Guns to Town" in 1958. "Ring of Fire" (1963) was his next major hit, and it's a song with a gripping story behind it.

Cash first laid eyes on June Carter when, on a high school class trip, he saw her perform with the Carter Family at the Grand Ole Opry. He liked what he saw then, and when he met her in person backstage at the Opry six years later, he told her, "You and I are going to get married someday." June laughed and said she couldn't wait. The only problem was she already was married. In his autobiography Cash deadpans: "She was either still married to Carl Smith or about to be married to Rip Nix, I forget which. . . . "

Of course, Cash was married himself, so nothing much happened until 1962, when June joined Cash's roadshow. "We got married in a fever/Hotter than a pepper sprout," the two would sing in "Jackson," the song that became their signature, and from the start the attraction between them was strong and undeniable. Composed by June and country star Merle Kilgore, "Ring of Fire" is the story of those first, overwhelming feelings of danger, lust, and love. June, after all, was a daughter of country royalty, and Cash, his addictions raging, had already more than earned his wild-man rep. "Love is a burning thing," the song begins, "And it makes a fiery ring/Bound by wild desire/I fell into a ring of fire."

"I never talked much about how I fell in love with John," June recalls about writing the song. "And I certainly didn't tell him how I felt. It was not a convenient time for me to fall in love with him—and it wasn't a convenient time for him to fall in love with me. One morning, about four o'clock, I was driving my car just about as fast as I could. I thought, 'Why am I out on the highway this time of night?' I was miserable, and it all came to me: 'I'm falling in love with somebody I have no right to fall in love with.'

"I was frightened of his way of life," she continues. "I'd watched Hank Williams die. I was part of his life—I'm Hank Jr.'s god-mother—and I'd grieved. So I thought, 'I can't fall in love with this man, but it's just like a ring of fire.' I wanted so to play the song for John, but I knew he would see right through me. So I gave it to my sister Anita, and she recorded it—her version was like a folk song, like bells ringing in the mountains. When John heard it, he said, 'I want to do that song.'"

Cash, needless to say, knew exactly what the song was about from the start. "I remember she had some lyrics," Cash says. "She had a line where she called herself 'the fire-ring woman,' and then she changed that. I said, 'You got it right when you called yourself a "fire-ring woman," because that's exactly where I am.' We hadn't really pledged our love—we hadn't said, 'I love you.' We were both afraid to say it, because we knew what was going to happen: that eventually we were both going to be divorced, and we were going to go through hell. Which we did.

"But the 'ring of fire' was not the hell," he continues. "That was kind of a sweet fire. The ring of fire that I found myself in with June was the fire of redemption. It cleansed. It made me believe every-thing was all right, because it felt so good. When we fell in love, she took it upon herself to be responsible for me staying alive. I didn't think I was killing myself, but you're on the suicide track when you're doing what I was doing. Amphetamines and alcohol will make you crazy, boy!

"She'd take my drugs and throw them away, and we'd have a big fight over it. I'd get some more, and she'd do it again. I'd make her promise not to, but she would do it anyway." He laughs. "She'd lie to me. She'd hide my money. She'd do anything. She fought me with everything she had."

By the time June and Johnny got married in 1968, his career had reached another peak. The live album he released that year, *At Fol-*

som Prison, sold extremely well. Then, in 1969, he enjoyed the biggest hit of his career, albeit with a novelty song, Shel Silverstein's "A Boy Named Sue." He began hosting his own network television series, *The Johnny Cash Show*, and used it as a forum for a bold array of musical talent, from Bob Dylan (who appeared on the opening show) to Louis Armstrong, Pete Seeger, Linda Ronstadt and Carl Perkins.

As the Seventies progressed, however, Cash's star waned. Early in the decade, the singer-songwriter movement in rock and the outlaw movement in country provided him with aesthetic vindication and a raft of spiritual heirs. But he shared nothing with later phenomena like disco and the urban-cowboy craze, and the connections between his music and punk rock would only become apparent later. The glitz-obsessed Eighties and the onslaught of MTV did little to help matters. Cash made some strong albums in this period—and some bad ones—but he seemed to have lost his artistic compass.

He remained a powerful draw on the road, however, and in 1985 he joined the Highwaymen, an occasional alliance with Willie Nelson, Waylon Jennings and Kris Kristofferson that would continue until the onset of his illness. In the meantime, Rosanne Cash, a daughter from his first marriage, and June's daughter Carlene both launched their own musical careers. As often is the case with children of the greats, rebellion and resentment battled love and support on all sides. Carlene's insistence, for example, that she wanted to put "the cunt back in country" was obviously designed both to shred the Carter Family mantle and to crack the iron reserve of her mother's husband. It worked on both counts.

For her part, Rosanne remembers her struggle to escape her father's looming shadow. "I was very rebellious," she says. "I couldn't stand the constant references to him. I wanted to do it on my own. That's not unlike any person in their early twenties, but it just so happened that my dad was very public so I had to rebel a little harder—and I rose to that test [*laughs*]." That her father was experiencing his own career woes only exacerbated the situation. "When I was having hit records, my dad and I felt competitive with each other," Rosanne says. "He admitted it later. I mean, he would

ask me about my contract and how many points I was getting
[*laughs*]. We went through that phase. But when he felt that I was
pulling away from him, he gave me a lot of space. I think it probably
hurt him some."

Cash regained a focus in his work after meeting producer Rick
Rubin in the early Nineties. Rubin had made his reputation with
albums by LL Cool J, Public Enemy, and the Beastie Boys, but he
was determined to sign Cash to his label, American Recordings.
Cash had no idea who Rubin was or what conceivable interest the
producer could have in him. "From the very beginning, I couldn't
see what he saw in me," Cash says, bluntly. But Rubin felt he understood exactly who Johnny Cash is. "He's a timeless presence," Rubin
says. "From the beginning of rock & roll there's always been this
dark figure who never really fit. He's still the quintessential outsider.
In the hip-hop world you see all these bad-boy artists who are jug-
gling being on MTV and running from the law. John was the origi-
nator of that."

The three albums Cash and Rubin have made together, *American
Recordings* (1994), *Unchained* (1996), and, now, *Solitary Man*, have
helped Cash discover a voice suitable both to a man of his age, dis-
position and accomplishments and to contemporary times. *American
Recordings* received a Grammy for Best Contemporary Folk Album,
while *Unchained* won for Best Country Album.

"From the first day, working with Rick has been easy, laid-back,
relaxed and trustworthy," Cash says. "We trusted each other to be
honest. I said, 'I'm gonna sing you a song and if you don't like it,
you tell me. And if you got a song that you like and I don't, you've
got to listen to me. I can't sing it if I don't like it.' But he's come up
with some really fine songs, and he never pushed anything on me.
We get along beautifully."

Solitary Man typically reflects the wide range of music that has
shaped Johnny Cash's soul. "There's a Bert Williams song written in
about 1905 called 'Nobody,'" Cash recounts. "You ever hear
'Nobody'? [*starts to sing*] I ain't never done nothin' to nobody/I ain't
ever got nothin' from nobody no time/And until I get something
from somebody sometime/I don't intend to do nothin' for nobody

no time." He laughs, clears his throat and begins again: "When wintertime comes with its snow and sleet/And me with hunger and cold feet/Who says, 'Here's two bits, go and eat'?/Nobody."

He laughs again. "It's a great old song," he says. "Then there's a new song I'm recording next session called 'The Mercy Seat'—it's a Nick Cave song. And I'm writing three or four songs myself at the same time. It's the first time I've ever had them bombard my brain like that. I hadn't written for more than a year since I got sick, but when I started recording, the ideas started coming. I'll finish them as we work."

For his part, Rubin also found some songs for Cash, including Neil Diamond's "Solitary Man," which became the title track, and Tom Petty's "I Won't Back Down," the album's opening song. Cash was unable to put in long days in the studio, but, according to Rubin, his illness didn't really affect their work together. "He's been fine; we just have to take breaks," he explains. "Whenever he feels comfortable, we record. It's been very pleasant."

The process of working on the album energized Cash. Even the setting proved restorative. "We're recording in a log cabin in the woods, right straight across the road from my house," Cash says. "I built it in '78, and it's just one room. It's got a kitchen, a bathroom off the back, and state-of-the-art equipment. We're surrounded by goats, deer, peacocks, and crows. We have to stop taping sometimes because the goats get on the porch and tromp around."

Rubin was similarly inspired by the locale. "It feels appropriate, him singing these songs in that environment," he says of the studio. "Lyrically, this album is intense, but musically it's relaxed.

"One thing is a little bit different," Rubin adds a moment later, thinking back to the question of Cash's health and its impact on their work. "John is a little more self-conscious about his vocals. There's no need for him to be—they're spectacular. But when he listens to them, he often feels, 'I can do better than that.' Meanwhile, everyone in the room is like, 'That was amazing.' I think because he doesn't feel well physically all the time, he's projecting that onto the work. But I don't hear it. I hear these strong, beautiful songs.

"He loves music—it is his life," Rubin says. "After one session, he said to me, 'You know, I think this is going to be my best album ever.' He's made what, 200 albums? It's exciting to be around someone who's done that much work and still wants to make his best album."

Grace is a word that suggests both spiritual blessings and dignity of action, and both those definitions fully apply to *Solitary Man*. He turns in a splendid version of U2's "One." His voice does falter a bit on "I Won't Back Down," but while the song seemed in search of a meaning when Tom Petty sang it (and Petty turns up on this version as well), in Cash's hands it takes on a staggering gravity. That refusal to go gently gets picked up in Will Oldham's scarifying "I See a Darkness," on which Cash sings, "You know I have a drive to live/I won't let go/But can you see/Its opposition comes rising up sometimes. . . . And that I see a darkness?"

Cash plans to start working on a new album right away. As Rick Rubin said, music is Cash's life. "I didn't like that 'public figure' business," Cash says. "I didn't like that 'American statesman' stuff. I didn't like that 'great spiritual leader' stuff. I am a very private person about those things. So many times, when there would be something I'd have to do that I didn't have my heart in, I'd say, 'All I ever wanted to do was play my guitar and sing a simple song.' And that's still all I want to do."

These days, Johnny Cash doesn't have to do anything he doesn't want to do. In a merciless way, illness can clarify your life. "Yeah, well, most of 'em are dead," he says with a grim insouciance when asked if he ever sees any of the people with whom he helped create rock & roll. "Carl Perkins and his brothers are all dead. Bill Black. Elvis. Roy Orbison, who was not only my best friend, but my next-door neighbor for twenty years.

"Of the ones who are still left, I talk to Marshall Grant, who played bass for me for so long. He and I are friends. [Producer] Jack Clement and I are still really close. We don't really do a lot of 'good ol' days' sessions, but if something comes up, we'll argue about who's right about it. But I don't see many of them, no, I don't see many people at all since I got sick."

The Carter Family's staunch Appalachian will to survive courses in June's blood, along with a Southern woman's determination to cheerfully make the best out of whatever travails fate may bring. She is now seventy-one, and her devotion to her husband is absolute. "Even now, since John's been sick, we've just had so much fun," she says. "When he first got ill, I said, 'We're going to quit work for a year, and then we'll see how we feel.' And we'll quit another year if we want to. Who says we have to work? We've got a lot of front porches—we'll go sit on them."

"There's unconditional love there," says Cash about his marriage. "You hear that phrase a lot, but it's real with me and her. She loves me in spite of everything, in spite of myself. She has saved my life more than once. She's always been there with her love, and it has certainly made me forget the pain for a long time, many times. When it gets dark, and everybody's gone home and the lights are turned off, it's just me and her."

Johnny and June spend as much time as they can with their family, and they travel among their homes in Tennessee, Virginia, and Jamaica. Despite being a longtime road horse, Cash will not be able to tour in support of *Solitary Man*. "It depresses him," says Rosanne. "He's not used to sitting around. He's a very powerful person and to not feel well, that's really hard for him. He spent over forty years on the road, and suddenly he's not out there. When that energy comes to a screeching halt, there's a lot to deal with just inside yourself."

Whatever he needs to deal with, either inside or outside himself, Johnny Cash will make do and not complain. He doesn't know any other way. "I wouldn't trade my future for anyone's I know," he writes in the liner notes to *Solitary Man*. "I believe that everything I've done and lived through is what has brought me to this part of my life right now," he says, as he looks around his den and remembers the many roads, rough and smooth, he's traveled down. "I like to say I have no regrets. And I really don't."

WILLIAM GAY

Sitting on Top
of the World

The week before MerleFest I went by to check on Grady, and he was putting a fuel pump on his RV. It was a huge RV so ancient it looked like something the Joads might have fled the Dust Bowl in, and something was always going wrong with it. Grady had skinned knuckles and a half-drunk beer and a home-rolled Prince Albert cigarette stuck to his lower lip that waggled when he talked.

He was not in the best of moods.

"I don't think I'm going to this one," he said. "It's got to where all this traveling around costs too much money. I believe I've about seen everything anyway."

I looked at the RV. It was emblazoned with hand-painted legends memorializing bluegrass festivals past. The Bean Blossom Festival, the Foggy Mountain Festival, MerleFest '96, '97, '98. Maybe he *had* seen everything. He told me about Dylan at the 1964 Newport Folk Festival, cracking a bullwhip and preening as the newly crowned King of Folk. Another time at Newport, his RV had been parked next to the one belonging to Mother Maybelle Carter. They had sat in lawn chairs and watched twilight come on, and she had shown him how to play the autoharp, placing his fingers just so to form the chords.

Grady told me a lot of things, but he had the goods to back it all up. The walls of the house he rented were papered with a surrealistic collage of photographs of the high and the mighty, the late and the great: Bill Monroe, the Stanley Brothers, Flatt and Scruggs, Don Reno and Red Smiley. Grady was in a lot of the pictures. Bill Monroe was embracing him like a long-lost brother in one, and there were pictures of Grady's own band, the Greenbriar Boys, skinny guys in Hank Williams suits standing before old-timey WSM microphones as if they were frozen back in the black and white '40s.

"If you go, go up and talk to Doc Watson," Grady said.

"I may. I always wanted to know where he got that arrangement for 'Sitting on Top of the World.'"

"He got it off that old record by the Mississippi Sheiks."

"I heard that record. That's not the arrangement."

"Well, hell. Just go up and ask him. Walk right up to him, he'll tell you. He's not stuck up like a lot of them are. He's a hell of a nice guy."

"Well, he's blind. Maybe that makes him a little more approachable."

Grady didn't want to hear it. "A blind man can be a prick the same as anybody else," he said. "He's just a hell of a nice guy."

Early in the morning of October 23, 1985, Arthel "Doc" Watson received the worst news a father can get: His son was dead. Eddy Merle Watson had been plowing on a steep hillside when the tractor he was driving overturned and rolled on him.

It was a blow that Doc almost did not recover from. It was a blow that resonated on a number of levels: Aside from the incalculable loss of a child, Doc had lost a friend and a fellow musician. For a time it seemed he might even lose the music as well, because Merle and Doc and the music were inextricably bound together.

In 1964, when he was fourteen, Merle had learned to play guitar while his father was away. He had learned to play it so well that when Doc went back on the road, Merle went with him. That fall they played the Berkeley Folk Festival, and he was all over the place on Doc's next album, *Southbound*. They toured and recorded together for the next twenty-one years, right up to that morning in 1985.

Merle became a proficient blues guitarist, and some of the albums subtly reflect his love for the genre. But he could pick flattop guitar with the best of them, and he could frail the banjo in the style of country performers like Uncle Dave Macon. When he died he was a few days away from winning *Frets* magazine's Bluegrass Picker of the Year award.

In what may be one of the few purely altruistic gestures in the music business, a handful of folks decided to do something. A friend of Doc's, Bill Young, together with "B" Townes and Ala Sue Wyke, approached Doc with a proposition. Townes is Dean of Resource Development at Wilkes Community College, in Wilkesboro, North Carolina, and the three of them convinced Doc to play a benefit concert on the campus. The funds raised would be used to create a memorial garden in Merle's honor.

Doc agreed, and a few of Merle's friends, including the banjoist Tim O'Brien, volunteered their time and ended up playing from the beds of two flatbed trucks.

That was the first MerleFest, in 1988. By contrast, the festival in 1999, while still held on the college campus, was a vast sprawl of tents and stages and concessions accommodating more than a hundred performers and over sixty-two thousand people in the audience.

There was not a flatbed truck in sight.

The first night of the festival was cold and rainy, but the performances went on inside tents, where hundreds of folding chairs were arranged in rows. When you came out of the tents, the wind would be blowing and the rain would sting your face, but nobody seemed to mind. Earlier there had been a little grumbling when the performer list had been released: Hootie and the Blowfish? Steve Earle? These were not the direct descendants of Bill Monroe. Earle had been touring with the bluegrass great Del McCoury, but there was a loose-cannon quality about him, and he was a lot more edgy and confrontational than, say, Ralph Stanley.

But never mind. This audience could take it in stride. They had come to have a good time, and by God they were going to have a good time.

There is some kind of common bond between participant and observer; common heritage maybe, the unspoken reverence for certain values: Family, home, and the tattered remains of the American Dream. Disparate elements of the audience mingled as easily as Freemasons meeting far from home and exchanging the password. Except here no password was needed. The fact that you were here seemed password enough.

The second day was sunny and as perfect as days in April get, and the shuttles were busy early ferrying folks down to the main gate. The parking lot is a mile or so from the festival, and buses carry festival-goers down a winding road to the entrance. Watching this potential audience disembark, you are struck by the fact that there seems to be no type, no average, and that every spectrum of America is repre-sented: middle-aged hippies and their new–SUV–driving yuppie offspring; farmers and farmers' wives; factory workers; the well-off in expensive outdoor gear from L.L. Bean; and longhaired young men in beards and fool's motley who seem determined to be ready should the '60s clock around again.

And just as you are about to decide that there is no common ele-ment among the spectators, you notice the percentage of people carrying instruments. Guitars and banjos in hardshells. Cased fid-dles tucked under the arm and God knows how many harmonicas pocketed like concealed weapons.

You don't see this at a rock concert or at the Grand Ole Opry, folks coming equipped to make their own music should the need arise. But bluegrass is widely perceived as handmade music, as opposed to, say, the output of song factories on Nashville's Music Row. The people who love bluegrass love it enough to learn to play it, and they are intensely loyal—to the music, to the performers, and to one another. That love of music is the common factor, the source of the brotherhood that seems to radiate off the audience like good vibrations.

Music is always in the air here. Wandering past tents and the open-air stages, you hear it segue from bluegrass to old-time rustic to a tent where a Cajun saws his fiddle at breakneck speed, and young girls jerk and sway with their partners on sawdust-strewn floors. There are vendors everywhere. MerleFest is a growth industry. Attendance has grown every year that the festival has been in existence, but not as fast as the number of vendors and service providers: You can buy the usual tapes and CDs of your favorites, t-shirts and sweatshirts and blankets and plaster busts of musicians and folk art and homemade jewelry; Italian food and Mexican food and down-home American food; anything you want to drink, unless you want it to contain alcohol—alcohol is forbidden on the festival grounds.

During the course of the four-day festival, you learn that a lot of these people know one another. They know one another well enough to remember the names of their respective children and what everybody does for a living. They will meet again before the year is out, whether they live in Alabama or Pennsylvania. They begin in the spring, at MerleFest, and through the careful allocation of vacation days or the advent of three-day weekends, their paths will cross at bluegrass festivals in the South, or in Midwestern states like Michigan or Indiana, where bluegrass is almost a religion. They will see the shows and late in the day will get together and grill out and catch up on old times. Likely they will drink a beer or two and make a little music themselves.

Like family. In a sense they are a family, loose and nomadic but keeping in touch, and at the very bottom of things family is what they believe bluegrass music is all about.

Family and Doc Watson.

Doc Watson, blinded by an eye infection during infancy, first learned to play the harmonica. From there he went to a banjo with a drum made from the skin of a house cat. But when he'd listen to records, the guitar was what he liked, and he began fooling around with one his brother had borrowed. His father heard Doc and told him that if he could learn a song by the end of the day, then he would buy Doc one of his own. When his father came in from work that night, Doc played "When Roses Bloom in Dixieland," and the next day Doc owned his first guitar.

Watson was playing on the radio at age nineteen, and in the years between learning that first song and becoming an icon, he played roadhouses and church socials and square dances. He played all

kinds of music—country, rockabilly, swing, Appalachian ballads
about young women wronged by their lovers.

It is amazing to listen to the Folkways records Doc made with
Clarence "Tom" Ashley in the early days of the '60s. His style
seems fully formed—the complex picking, the impeccable inter-
action between bass and treble strings, the breathless, death-defying
runs he interjects into spaces of time so small there seems scarcely
room to accommodate them. You keep listening for him to miss
a note, deaden a string, but he does not. There have been countless long and drunken arguments over how many guitars, one or
two, were playing on a particular track. It was one guitar, Doc's
guitar.

In every great performer's life there are watershed concerts,
events that forever alter the rest of the career from what has gone
before. For Doc one of these came in 1963, when he was brought to
the Newport Folk Festival by the folklorist Ralph Rinzler. Doc was
forty-one years old. He sang about blackberry blossoms, shady
groves, houses of the rising sun, and the sad fatalism of sitting on
top of the world. When he began, he was an unknown guitarist with
a pleasant baritone, on a long and winding road from Deep Gap,
North Carolina. When he was helped from the chair and led from
the stage, he was on his way to a contract with Vanguard Records,
and he had reinvented forever the way folk musicians approached
the guitar.

As has been said, there are more than a hundred performers here,
and there are no slouches. These are the heavy hitters and brand-
name pickers of bluegrass, everyone from hardshell traditionalists to
the avant-garde, folks who through virtuoso playing and infusions
from jazz are moving bluegrass into new and uncharted territory.

But no one questions what this thing is all about.

The Texas singer-songwriter Guy Clark usually performs his
song "Dublin Blues" during his sets, a song that has the quatrain:

> I have seen the *David*
> I've seen the *Mona Lisa* too

I have heard Doc Watson
Play "Columbus Stockade Blues"

At the mention of Watson's name there is an outbreak of applause, thunderous and spontaneous. It happens the same way before different audiences each time Clark performs the song.

When Doc is led up the wooden steps to the stage, he approaches from the rear, and the first thing you see is his silver hair. At the first sight of it, the audience erupts. Doc is guided across the stage to where folding chairs have been positioned before the microphones. He is assisted into a chair, and he feels for the guitar in the open case beside his seat. He takes the guitar and sits cradling it, his face turned toward the crowd he can feel but not see, waiting until the applause dies down.

A stocky young man with a black beard has seated himself in the chair beside Doc's. He has taken up a guitar as well. He touches Watson's arm, and Watson leans toward the microphone.

"This is my grandson Richard," he says, "and he's going to help me out a little here. This is Merle's boy."

The crowd erupts again. The torch has passed.

Doc's guitar kicks off a set of country blues, old Jimmie Rodgers songs, and the song Clark referenced. The third generation holds his own with ease, as if perhaps guitar playing was simply a matter of genetics.

Between songs Doc jokes easily with the audience, tells a couple of stories. The audience eats it up. They're eager to laugh at his stories, and maybe they've heard them before—their laughter anticipates the punchlines. They love him. He could sell them a used car with a blown transmission, a refrigerator that keeps things warm instead of cold. His voice is comforting and reassuring. He could be a neighbor sitting on the edge of your porch, or rocking right slow in the willow rocker.

Except for the playing. The picking is impeccable; it's what you expect Doc to do: the hands sure and quick, the notes clean and distinct, and the absolute right note to go where he picks it. Those cannot be seventy-six-year-old hands, the audience is thinking.

Maybe they are not of a mortal at all, maybe they are the hands of a king, a god.

And with the guitar clasped to him and his fingers moving over the strings, he is a god, the king of what he does. They are the hands of a man sitting on top of the world.

But every set has to end, and when this one does, and Doc begins to rise, his hand reaching for the hand that without seeing he knows is reaching for his own, and the hands touch, the illusion shatters: The audience sees that he is not a god at all but a mortal with frailties like the rest of us, and this somehow is more endearing yet.

The applause erupts again.

"Chet Atkins is the best guitar player in the world," Doc said.

"I figured you'd say Merle Travis."

"Well, Merle was a great influence on me. I named [my son] Merle after him, and we finally met when we did that *Will the Circle Be Unbroken* record. But Chet's the best. He can play anything."

"That's what people say about you," I said.

"I'm slowing down a little. I'm getting older, and I can feel my hands stiffening up. I don't tour as much as I used to. I can feel myself slowing down, some of the runs are slower."

Close-up, Watson's face is pleasant, ruddy, the silver hair a little thin but waved neatly back, every strand in place. He does not wear dark glasses, as most blind performers do, and in fact, it is easy to forget that he is blind: The lids are lowered, the eyes just slits, and he looks almost as if he's just squinting into strong sunlight.

"Where'd you come up with the picking on 'Sitting on Top of the World'?"

Watson laughed. "I made that up," he said, "that's my arrangement. I heard it off that old Mississippi Sheiks record. You might not have heard of them. But I changed it. I just played it the way I wanted it."

"What do you think about the way MerleFest has grown? It's pretty big business now."

"Well, it's good for the music. It's good for Merle, to keep people thinking about him. And people have to make a living, have to sell records. It's good to know so many people love this kind of music enough to come way down here to hear it."

"Do you think it's changing? Music, I mean?"

"Music is always changing," Doc said. "But it's all music, just people getting together and playing. One thing I noticed though, somebody told me there were some complaints about one of the performers using some pretty rough language over the mic during his show. I don't care for that. This has always been a family thing, women and kids, and that young fellow needs to remember where he is."

It was almost dark, and gospel music was rising from the tents when I walked down the road toward the parking lot. It was Sunday, the last day of the festival, and gospel was mostly what today had been about. There had been Lucinda Williams, of course, but mostly it had been gospel, like Sundays on old-time radio when the Sabbath was a day of respite from the secular.

Off to the right were the campgrounds. You could see the RVs, but they were hazy and ambiguous through the failing light, and music was rising from there, too—the plinking of a banjo, a fiddle sawing its way through some old reel.

What you could see best were the campfires scattered across the bottomland, and for an illusory moment, time slipped, and it could have been a hobo camp or a campground for Okies on their way to the Golden State. There was a gully beyond the camp area. It was shrouded with trees, and fog lay between the trees like smoke, and it was easy to imagine Tom Joad slipping through them like a wraith, fleeing the vigilante men on his way upstate to organize the orange pickers. Or Woody Guthrie himself might ease up out of the fog, his fascist-killing guitar strung about his neck, a sly grin on his face that said all the world was a joke and only he was in on it. He'd warm his hands over the fire, for the night had turned chill, and he'd drink a cup of chicory coffee before heading down one of those long, lonesome roads Woody was always heading down.

Then I was closer, and I saw that the fires were charcoal and gas grills, where ground beef sizzled in tinfoil, and hot dogs dripped sputtering grease, and I saw that these people were much too affluent to be Okies and that the guitars they played were Fenders and Gibsons and Martins. They were guitars that Woody would never have been able to afford.

After a while Grady wandered up. I knew he'd made it, since I'd seen him a couple of times in crowds and had seen him playing guitar in a tent with other players, guys with homemade basses and washboards and Jew's harps and whatever fell to hand. I hadn't talked to him yet, though.

"You learn what you wanted to know?"

"Doc heard it off that old Mississippi Sheiks record," I said.

"I told you that."

"He invented the arrangement, though. It's his song now."

"But he did talk to you. Was I right about him, or not?"

"I guess you were right," I said.

I thought about it. It seemed to me that Doc embodied the kind of values that are going out of style and don't mean as much as they used to: self-respect and a respect for others, the stoic forbearance that Walker Evans photographed and James Agee wrote poems about. Something inside that was as immutable and unchanging as stone, that after a lifetime in show business still endured, still believed in the sanctity of womanhood, family, property lines, the church in the wildwood, the ultimate redeemability of humankind itself.

Life sometimes seems choreographed from the stage of a talk show, where barbaric guests haul forth dirty linen and a barbaric audience applauds, where presidents disassemble themselves before a voyeuristic media, where folks sell their souls to the highest bidder and then welsh on the deal. It was nice that Doc was still just being Doc, just being a hell of a nice guy.

But Doc's getting old, and those values are getting old, too. Maybe they're dying out. Maybe in the end there will just be the music. For there will always be the music. It is what Doc loves above all things—from show tunes like "Summertime" to music leaked up through time from old, worn 78s by Mississippi string bands, from the hollow, ghostly banjo of Dock Boggs to the contemporary folk of writers like Tom Paxton and Bob Dylan.

All kinds of music that will endure and help us endure. The music will never let you down.

Seeing Music:
Django Reinhardt

The brilliant Gypsy guitarist Django Reinhardt was born Jean-Baptiste Reinhardt, near Liverchies, Belgium, on January 23, 1910, and died, of a stroke, in Fontainebleau, on May 16, 1953, after a pleasant day of fishing on the Seine. Between 1934, when he and the violinist and pianist Stéphane Grappelli formed the Quintet of the Hot Club of France, and the late forties, when the electric guitar and bebop began closing in on him, he made hundreds of recordings, appeared all over Britain and Europe, and became one of the most famous jazz musicians in the world. Charles Delaunay, who created the first jazz discography and shepherded Django through much of his sometimes chaotic professional life, said of Reinhardt, during a visit to America in the seventies, "There were two personalities in him. One was primitive. He never went to school and he couldn't stand a normal bed. He had to live in a Gypsy caravan near a river, where he could fish and catch trout between the stones with his bare hands, and where he could put laces between the trees and catch rabbits. But Django also had a nobility, even though he could be very mean to the musicians who worked for him."

Male Gypsies exist in a timeless macho continuum in which obligations and appointments are largely meaningless. In 1946, Django, dreaming of sitting with Hollywood stars by their pools, finally got to America for a three-month tour. He travelled with the

Duke Ellington Band in its private railroad car, and it played in
Chicago, Cleveland, Detroit, and Pittsburgh before finishing up
with two nights at Carnegie Hall. But, on the evening of the second
concert, Django ran into the French boxer Marcel Cerdan, who had
a scheduled bout at Madison Square Garden, and, slipping into
Gypsy time, went to a bar with Cerdan to drink and talk about life
and France. When he suddenly remembered where he was supposed to be, he jumped into a cab and, because he spoke almost no
English, ended up somewhere on the East Side. He got to Carnegie
Hall at eleven o'clock and probably played the same four numbers,
backed by the band, that he had played in Chicago—a blues, a variation of "Tiger Rag," one of his own dreaming pieces, and "Honey-
suckle Rose." (The Chicago concert was recorded.) The applause
was reportedly thunderous. Ellington, in his autobiography, *Music Is
My Mistress*, says of Reinhardt, "Among those I think of as citizens
of Paris was Django Reinhardt, a very dear friend of mine, and one
whom I regard as among the few great inimitables of our music. I
had him on a concert tour with me in 1946, so that I could enjoy
him the more."

Delaunay, who was the son of the unique and celebrated Parisian
geometric colorists Sonia and Robert Delaunay, supervised most of
Reinhardt's recordings. This, he said, is what music meant to Reinhardt: "Life for Django was all music. He was full of constant
enthusiasm when he played—shouting in the record studio when
someone played something he liked, shouting when he played himself. . . . When he was accompanying in the bass register he sounded
like brass, and in the treble like saxophones. He had a constant
vision of music—a circle of music—in his head. I think he could see
his music." Reinhardt's style had such presence and power and
imagination that, in the manner of masters like Charlie Parker and
Sidney Catlett and the Armstrong of the early thirties, he surpassed
his very instrument. He created an almost disembodied, alternately
delicate and roaring whorl of music. Charlie Christian, who flourished between 1939 and 1941, when Django was near the top of his

powers, became the first consummate electric guitarist and, following Lester Young's lead on tenor saxophone, fashioned long, horn-
like lines that had their own flawless logic and beauty. (Jim Hall, the
paramount guitarist, still idolizes Christian, and Hall, in turn, is
idolized by such contemporary guitarists as Pat Metheny. Reinhardt's utter originality largely confounds imitation.) But Reinhardt
turned the songs he played inside out, decorating them with his
winging vibrato, his pouring runs and glisses, his weaving and duck-
ing single-note lines, and his sudden chordal tremolos and offbeat
explosions. All these sounds were controlled by an adventurous
rhythmic sense. Like Billie Holiday and Red Allen and Jimmy
Rowles, he could leap ahead of the beat, or fall behind it, or ride it
mercilessly. And this rhythmic sense was constantly colored by his
dynamics, which moved back and forth between flutters and whis-
pers, talking tones, and cascades and roars. Two peculiarities shaped
Reinhardt's playing: he had enormous hands, and the two smallest
fingers on his left hand—his fret-board hand—were permanently
bent at the second knuckle. (They had been burned in a fire in his
caravan, and he was so badly injured that his wounds never healed
properly.) The huge hand made the crippled fingers work nonethe-
less: thus the mysterious chords and melodic lines that no one had
heard before.

Reinhardt might start a medium-tempo ballad with three or four
bars of slightly altered melody, played in single notes behind the
beat, each phrase graced by his vibrato (almost a tremble), pause for
a beat, and go into a brief mock double-time, rest again, drop in an
abrupt, massive chord, and release a hissing upward run. Then he'd
cut his volume in half and turn into the bridge with a delicate, fern-
like single-note variation of the melody, letting his notes linger and
bend and float on his vibrato. Just before the end of the bridge, he
would loose another offbeat chord, let it shimmer for three or four
beats, work through a humplike arpeggio, lower his volume again,
and return to a single-note variation of the original melody and come
to rest. Almost all his solos in the thirties and early forties have an
exotic romanticism, a hothouse quality; the notes roll and echo with

Eastern European and Spanish overtones. Armstrong and Ellington had taught him to swing and be cool, but he filtered them through his Gypsy mind.

The original Quintet of the Hot Club of France grew indirectly out of various string groups led by the violinist Joe Venuti and the guitarist Eddie Lang in the late twenties and early thirties. But its instrumentation of violin, solo guitar, two rhythm guitars, and bass was unique. From the beginning, it was a swinging, lithesome group, at ease with big-voiced up-tempo numbers, twirling ballads, and direct haunting blues. It certainly presaged Benny Goodman's small groups, Artie Shaw's Gramercy Fives, and even the Modern Jazz Quartet (consider John Lewis's beautiful anthem "Django"). Grappelli and Reinhardt experimented ceaselessly with the quintet on its recordings. They used one or two violins, they subtracted a rhythm guitar, there were violin-and-guitar duets, guitar-and-bass duets, and solo-guitar numbers. Grappelli occasionally played piano (he loved Art Tatum), and later in the quintet's life, if Grappelli was unavailable, one and sometimes two clarinets were added. The original quintet (with some personnel changes) lasted from December 2, 1934, when it gave its first public performance in Paris, until September 3, 1939, when Britain and France declared war on Germany. The group had been touring Britain with great success, and Grappelli decided to stay in England, where he lived off and on for the rest of his life. Reinhardt and the remainder of the quintet took one of the last boats back to France, and they somehow survived, and even flourished, despite the Nazi interdiction on Gypsies. (Django kept on the move, working in the South of France and in North Africa, disappearing occasionally into the Gypsy netherworld, and once trying to cross the border into Switzerland.) Grappelli and Reinhardt were reunited in England in 1946 (the first number they played together was the "Marseillaise"), and they made their last recordings in Rome in 1949.

More than half of the hundred and nineteen numbers in a new Mosaic reissue (*The Complete Django Reinhardt and Quintet of the Hot Club of France Swing/HMV Sessions 1936–1948*) are by the quintet or its variations and are full of such beauties as the spaces between Django's notes on "Solitude," and his rustling tremolos behind sweet Grappelli (who finally found his strength and fervor in the sixties, when he began playing worldwide to great acclaim); his delicate, barely audible opening chorus on "When Day Is Done"; the astounding train piece "Mystery Pacific," which has roaring staccato chords, played at a blinding tempo by three low-register guitars; his four exquisite choruses on "I'll See You in My Dreams," accompanied only by a bass, and the wild, elbowy up-tempo "You Rascal You," again done with just a bass; and the almost atonal notes in "Little White Lies," with the clarinettist Hubert Rostaing's lifting "organ" chords behind Reinhardt. American music was outlawed by the Nazis, so "Exactly Like You" became "Pour Vous," "Little White Lies" became "Petits Mensonges," and "Dark Eyes" became "Les Yeux Noirs."

In 1935, when the quintet was barely a year old, Django, already sought after, began sitting in on occasional recordings with visiting American musicians, among them Coleman Hawkins, Benny Carter, Bill Coleman, Dicky Wells, Rex Stewart, Barney Bigard, Eddie South, and Larry Adler. These recordings are not part of the Mosaic issue, but fifty-seven of them are on a DRG album, *Django with His American Friends.* He is given solo space on roughly half the numbers, starting with the loose, joyous sides made by Coleman, Shad Collins, and Bill Dillard on trumpets, Wells on trombone, Dick Fullbright on bass, and Bill Beason on drums. Django takes a floating blues chorus on "Bugle Call Rag," while the trumpets riff softly in the distance, and he delivers one of his great shouts near the end of "Between the Devil and the Deep Blue Sea." He has a full chorus on the classic slow blues "Hangin' Around Boudon," with Wells and Coleman behind him, and he fashions one of his pre-bebop solos on "Japanese Sandman." Bill Coleman reappears with a French-American group, and Django solos on the slow "Big Boy Blues," backed only by the drummer, who plays a stark press roll with his sticks. Then the Hot Club Quintet accompanies the celebrated American harmonica player Larry Adler, who, despite his massive ego, was not much of a jazz musician. He pushed his melodies into odd shapes, and he had a harsh sound. But Django counteracts him on "Body and Soul," on "Lover Come Back to Me," on a strange, fast "Melancholy Baby," and on "I Got Rhythm," often working in his ringing low and middle registers.

In 1939, Rex Stewart, Barney Bigard, and the bassist Billy Taylor arrived in Paris with the Duke Ellington band and set down five numbers with Reinhardt that remain timeless small-band performances. Stewart, dark and brooding, loved queer squeezed notes that he produced by pressing his valves halfway down, and Bigard, cheerful and circular, was the last of the rococo New Orleans clarinettists. Django's solos are easy and gentle; he sounds as if he had grown up with Stewart and Bigard. Listen, in particular, to the slow blues "Solid Old Man." Django solos twice, Bigard accompanying him—so the story goes—with whisk brooms on a suitcase. His opening solo has several silences and he uses only five or six notes, but his second solo is full of little announcements and complex hilly phrases. Stewart stays mainly in his low register, releasing a tremolo and a couple of tight half-valvings, and Bigard soars a little and finally lands down in his chalumeau register. Each of the four other numbers the quartet made has its special beauty.

Reinhardt and Grappelli have turned up elsewhere in the past several months. In the movie "Sweet and Lowdown," Woody Allen's American guitar-playing hero regards Django with fear and awe. And Grappelli bursts out of the recorded background music of the dance comedy "Contact," at the Vivian Beaumont, with "My Heart Stood Still" and "Sweet Lorraine." Grappelli, of course, knew Django as well as anyone on earth, and here is what he told me in 1974: "Ah! The troubles he gave me! I think now I would rather play with lesser musicians and have a peaceable time than with Djangoo and all his monkey business. One time, Djangoo and I were invited to the Élysée Palace by a high personality"—probably Charles de Gaulle. "We were invited for dinnair, and after dessert we were expected to perform. Djangoo did not appear. After dinnair, the high personality was very polite, but I can tell he is waiting, so I say I think I know where Djangoo is when I don't know at all. The high personality calls a limousine and I go to Djangoo's flat, in

Montmartre. His guitar is in the corner, and I ask his wife where he is. She says maybe at the *académie* playing billiards. He was a very good player of billiards, very *adroit*. He spent his infancy doing that and being in the streets. His living room was the street. *Alors*, I go to the *académie* and when he sees me he turns red, yellow, white. In spite of his almost *double* stature of me, he was a little afraid. In the world of the Gypsy, age counts, although I am only two years older than him. Also I could read, I was instructed. He have two days' *barbe* on his face and his slippers on, so I push him into the limousine and we go back to his flat to clean him up a little and get his guitar. Djangoo was like a chameleon; *à toute seconde*, he could change keys. He was embarrassed about everything, but his *naturel* self came back, and when we arrived at the Élysée and the guard at the gate saluted the limousine, he stick up his chin and say, 'Ah! They recognize me.'"

And here is a different Django. Phoebe Jacobs, who has spent much of her life smoothing the way for the likes of Duke Ellington and Benny Goodman and Louis Armstrong, met Django two years before his death, when she was travelling in the South of France with Lucille Armstrong, Louis's wife, and Moustache, the huge Parisian club owner. "Django seemed nervous and overanxious next to Moustache, even though it was probably because of who Lucille was," she said recently. "He patted Lucille's arm and behaved almost like he was smitten with her. And when he played for her, the tenderness that came out in his music was like a man stroking a woman's breast."

FRANCIS DAVIS

Our Lady of Sorrows: Billie Holiday

Few people alive today, even among her most ardent fans, have heard Billie Holiday other than on recordings or seen her other than in photographs and random film clips. Holiday was eighteen years old and a worldly former prostitute when she recorded "Your Mother's Son-in-Law" with Benny Goodman in 1933; she died from the cumulative effects of heroin and alcohol in 1959, a ravaged forty-four. Yet with the obvious exception of Frank Sinatra, who was born in the same year as Holiday but outlived her by almost four decades, no other recording artist from the first half of the twentieth century seems more real to us—more like our contemporary.

Jazz aficionados have always enjoyed nothing more than debating the relative merits of different performers. But when conversation turns to Billie Holiday, the only way to start a fight is to state a preference for early, middle, or late—her jaunty recordings of the 1930s, her diva-like ballads of the 1940s, or her work from the 1950s, when she had almost nothing left but compensated for her husk of a voice with the intimacy of her phrasing (closer to speech than song). That Holiday was the greatest woman jazz singer ever is accepted as incontestable fact, no matter how fond you or the person you're talking to might be of Mildred Bailey, Ella Fitzgerald, or Sarah Vaughan.

But Holiday has never appealed exclusively to jazz listeners, nor has her appeal ever depended solely on her vocal artistry. As was true in 1939, when she first sang the anti-lynching song "Strange Fruit," to an audience consisting mostly of bohemian artists and left-wing intellectuals at Café Society (a Greenwich Village nightclub whose owner, Barney Josephson, and regular patrons were as committed to racial integration as they were to the finest in jazz and cabaret), many people today are unable to listen to Holiday without projecting into whatever lyric she happens to be singing their sense of her as a martyr to an uncaring world and to her own bad judgment.

Holiday, born Eleanora Fagan, was black, the child of an unwed mother. Rumored to be bisexual, she was drawn to abusive men; on her recordings of the song "My Man" the lines "He beats me too / What can I do?" are disturbing less for the sentiment than for the near-ecstasy with which she delivers them. Raised as a Catholic, Holiday, according to at least one biography, may have seen her inability to conceive when she was married as divine retribution for having aborted a teenage pregnancy by sitting in a bathtub full of hot water and mustard. She was a substance abuser whose name recognition made her an easy target for publicity-hunting police departments; during her final hospitalization she was arrested for illegal possession of heroin, fingerprinted, and photographed for mug shots on her deathbed. As a convicted user, she was prohibited by law from performing in New York City nightclubs for the last twelve years of her life.

Singing should have been her salvation, and perhaps it was. But there is a widespread belief that she was discriminated against even as an artist, especially toward the beginning of her career, when, according to a dubious bit of folklore, white performers fed off Tin Pan Alley's choice cuts and black performers were forced to make do with the musical equivalent of intestines and jowls. Although famous, Holiday never achieved the mass popularity of some white big-band singers, possibly because the liberties she took with melody and rhythm required of listeners a sharper ear than most of them had. Or was it, as she may have thought, simply because she was black?

Holiday was, I think, a victim of both injustice and her own vices—a week's worth of *Oprah*, with the requisite confessional streak. She may have sung that what she did was nobody's business (on a fiercely independent number she borrowed from her girl-hood idol Bessie Smith), but she made it everybody's business with the publication of her "frank," if not always factual, autobiography, *Lady Sings the Blues* (1956), actually written by the journalist William Dufty. A prior knowledge of Holiday's hard knocks darkens some listeners' perception of even her earliest recordings, which were ebullient more often than not. The singer nicknamed "Lady Day" or just "Lady" has become an all-purpose Our Lady of Sorrows—embraced by many of her black listeners (and by many women and gay men) not just as a favorite performer but as a kind of patron saint. She touches such fans where they hurt, soothing their rage even while delivering a reminder of past humiliations and the potential for more. Especially since the 1972 Diana Ross movie, loosely based on Holiday's loose-to-begin-with autobiography (and perversely enjoyable as a color-conscious variation on an old Lana Turner or Susan Hayward tearjerker), part of Holiday's allure has come from her intuitive swing and the interpretive depth she acquired with maturity—qualities matched by no other woman singer, and among male singers only by Louis Armstrong (in headlong swing) and Frank Sinatra (in depth of interpretation).

Even leaving aside the morass of race and sex, Holiday is a giant subject for a biographer. A friend of mine, a fellow music critic, gave up on the idea of writing a book about her when he realized that each photograph of her seemed to show an equally beautiful but otherwise entirely different woman—a phenomenon not fully explained, he thought, by her mounting drug habit and evident fluctuations in weight. There are at least four full-length biographies of Holiday; the one that achieves the best balance of empathy and detachment is Donald Clarke's *Wishing on the Moon* (1994), but still the reader comes away from it convinced that Holiday and her moods were finally unknowable.

In *Strange Fruit* (2000), a slim volume expanded from a 1998 article in *Vanity Fair*, David Margolick approaches Holiday sideways, examining her relationship to a single song. The lyrics of *Strange Fruit* are from a poem written by Abel Meeropol, a Jewish schoolteacher from New York, who, following the execution of Julius and Ethel Rosenberg in 1953, adopted and raised as his own the Rosenbergs' two sons.

> *Southern trees bear a strange fruit,*
> *Blood on the leaves and blood at the root,*
> *Black body swinging in the Southern breeze,*
> *Strange fruit hanging from the poplar trees.*

In her autobiography Holiday recounted how she and the pianist Sonny White, working closely with Meeropol (who wrote under the pseudonym Lewis Allan), came up with a melody for "Strange Fruit." Reference books, however, list Lewis Allan as the sole composer, and Margolick offers evidence to substantiate that Meeropol wrote the melody as well as the words. Margolick presents one person after another telling of having been chilled to the bone on first hearing Meeropol's disturbing imagery and Holiday's restrained, almost serene delivery, whether in performance or on recordings (the assembled witnesses include Tori Amos, Cassandra Wilson, and a member of the lesbian a cappella group Amasong, all of whom have recorded versions of "Strange Fruit"). Along with its readability, the book's virtue is in shoehorning so much useful anecdotal information—about Holiday, Meeropol, Café Society, and the mixture of rapture and disdain with which "Strange Fruit" was originally greeted—into a brief text.

Margolick shows how Holiday became identified with "Strange Fruit," and because he is a scrupulous reporter, he also questions to what extent and on what terms she identified with it. (He wisely dismisses persistent speculation that the poorly educated singer was only dimly aware of what the song's lyrics were about.) In Holiday's own book she told of once refusing to honor a request for "Strange Fruit" from a "bitch" who called it "that sexy song [about] the naked

bodies swinging in the trees." Margolick repeats the story, but earlier offers this surprising observation from a black woman named
Evelyn Cunningham, a former reporter for the *Pittsburgh Courier*:
"The song did not disturb me because I never had the feeling that
this was something [Holiday] was very, very serious about. . . . Many
times in nightclubs when I heard her sing the song it was not a sadness I sensed as much as there was something else; it's got to do with
sexuality." Cunningham saw couples moving closer and holding
hands as they listened. Holiday usually performed "Strange Fruit"
as her last song, rightly convinced that nothing could follow it. But
the late Jimmy Rowles, once Holiday's accompanist, told of a night
in a Los Angeles club when she opened with it, after a beating from
her husband and a shouting match with a customer at the bar.

According to Rowles, Holiday stormed offstage after that one
number. If the story suggests that "Strange Fruit" ultimately became a way for her to release her anger, it also suggests that her
anger could be unfocused, her racial indignation mixed up with
resentment at her mistreatment by the men in her life, her perse-
cution by the law, and the public's preference for blander female
singers. Though I hear nothing sexual in her recordings of
"Strange Fruit" (including the original, 1939 recording, which
was reissued earlier this year on the CD *The Commodore Master
Takes*), I think I understand how Holiday herself and those couples
Cunningham noticed might have. Once Holiday added "Strange
Fruit" to her repertoire, Margolick tells us, "some of its sadness
seemed to cling to her." And some of the carefree sexuality she
projected on her earliest recordings may have rubbed off even on
"Strange Fruit."

Though "Strange Fruit" was unofficially banned from radio, and
the label to which Holiday was then under contract refused to let
her record it for them (she wound up recording it for Commodore,
an upstart jazz specialty label operating out of a New York record
store), the song had unexpected commercial benefits: in addition to
establishing her credentials as a "race woman" (her own term for a
woman committed to the cause of racial equality), it transformed
her in the public's perception from jazz singer to cabaret artist. As

Margolick points out, however, "Strange Fruit" is unlike anything else she ever recorded. The only numbers even close to it, in terms of having lyrics that could be heard as pertinent to Holiday's being a black woman (neither of them remotely a "protest" song), are "God Bless the Child," about knowing what it's like to be poor and hungry, and "Don't Explain," about forgiving a cheating husband or lover to whom the singer is in sexual thrall. Holiday is officially credited with having written both songs in collaboration with Arthur Herzog Jr., though many believe that Herzog wrote them alone, using Holiday's anecdotes as a starting point and cutting her in on the credit as a reward for her recording them.

Except for coming up with a few impromptu blues lyrics at recording sessions, Holiday was certainly no songwriter. Yet we listen to her sing "Strange Fruit" and "God Bless the Child" and "Don't Explain" and imagine that the lyrics represent her innermost thoughts. And we think we hear her keeping an ironic distance from the fluffier numbers that first earned her a following, in the late 1930s—improving them by virtually rewriting their melodies on the spot, and also implicitly offering a critique of the dreamy sentiments expressed by their lyrics, which were presumably of no relevance to someone with her knowledge of the seamier side of life.

It's easy to see how the idea got started that Holiday and other black recording artists were denied access to the best material of the late 1930s and early 1940s. From 1933 to 1942 Holiday, on her own or as a featured vocalist with all-star groups led by Teddy Wilson, recorded 153 numbers for Columbia, Brunswick, Vocalion, and Okeh (this material is chronologically assembled on the nine volumes of Columbia's series *The Quintessential Billie Holiday*). Although she had the honor of being the first nonoperatic singer to release a version of "Summertime" and was given a shot at "You Go to My Head," "Easy Living," and "These Foolish Things" when they were brand-new, nobody would remember many of the other songs she recorded as a young singer—including "Me, Myself, and I," "Foolin' Myself," and "What a Little Moonlight Can Do"—if not for her alchemy. But did Holiday think of these songs as shabby goods? Did Wilson and her black sidemen? Did the record-buying public, including Holiday's black fans?

The evidence overwhelmingly suggests not. According to Teddy Wilson, before each of their recording sessions he and Holiday would go through the new songs submitted to their record company by music publishers, and she would pick out the ones she liked best. Often "they were pretty good songs," Wilson once said, by which he may have meant that many of them became hits.

In the 1930s Holiday was what would today be called a cover artist—recording her own versions of current songs originated by other performers. The term seems not to have come into widespread use in the recording industry until the mid-1950s, when Pat Boone and other white teen idols began "covering" rhythm-and-blues hits by Fats Domino and Little Richard, in direct competition with them for a place on the charts and with a distinct advantage in being white. But the practice is as old as the record business itself. Black performers have covered whites and also one another. The aim of Holiday's first recording sessions with Wilson, in 1935, was to stock jukeboxes in black neighborhoods with cover versions of songs her label thought might soon become hits by white singers. In one sense almost everybody making pop records in those years was a cover artist: a song would be introduced by Fred Astaire or Alice Faye in a major motion picture, and other singers would see who could get a version into the stores first. Two or more performances of the same song, recorded within days of each other, might become best sellers simultaneously, sometimes appealing to slightly different markets. Most consumers didn't particularly care whose version was the original—only which version they liked best.

In 1937 Holiday recorded "A Sailboat in the Moonlight," one of her most thrilling performances, with the tenor saxophonist Lester Young. This is often cited as the most obvious instance of her transforming the dross available to her into gold. But as Holiday entered the recording studio, Guy Lombardo's version of the song was already on its way to the charts, eventually to become No. 1; it wasn't necessarily a good song, but it was a hot property.

Among the famous composers and lyricists whose work Holiday recorded during the 1930s and early 1940s—when, myth has it, she was limited to songs beneath the contempt of white performers—were Cole Porter, Irving Berlin, Jerome Kern, George and Ira Gershwin, Harry Warren and Al Dubin, and Jimmy McHugh and Dorothy Fields. The list of performers Holiday covered, or with whom she shared a hit song, includes many of the popular white singers of those decades, some of whom were featured with society orchestras and swing bands: Bob Eberle, Skinnay Ennis, Charles Chester, Bea Wain, Helen Ward, Helen Forrest, Edythe Wright, Jack Leonard (Frank Sinatra's predecessor with Tommy Dorsey), and Harriet Hilliard (Ozzie Nelson's wife and Ricky Nelson's mother). The performer she covered most frequently— no fewer than nine times, beginning with "I Wished on the Moon," in 1936—was Bing Crosby, who had his pick of new songs, even though he didn't always choose well (does anyone remember "One, Two, Button Your Shoe," which he introduced in the 1936 movie *Pennies From Heaven*, and which Holiday covered that same year?). The runner-up was Fred Astaire, from whom she borrowed seven of the songs he introduced in *The Gay Divorcee*, *Swing Time*, *Shall We Dance?*, and *A Damsel in Distress*. So much for the notion that the best popular songs of the late 1930s and early 1940s were, symbolically, cordoned off behind a sign that read for whites only.

Not every song Holiday sang in that era had a pedigree; some of them, including "Eeny, Meeny, Miney, Mo," an early effort by Johnny Mercer, really were mutts. But it's wise to remember that many songs that strike us as nonsensical today were intended by their composers as "rhythm" songs; Holiday had fun with them, and so did her listeners. Did she find anything relevant to her own experience in the lyrics that movie stars like Astaire and Crosby sang to court their virginal leading ladies? Anyone reflexively answering no should be informed that the former Eleanora Fagan read romance magazines, longed for the day when she could record with strings, and adopted the name "Billie" from the silent-movie star Billie Dove.

Many 1930s leftists, disdainful of movies and popular music unless they delivered a forthright message along with entertainment, would have been appalled at such middle-class inclinations. In the view of many white intellectuals of the thirties, Holiday was a standard-bearer for the downtrodden who had more in common with the Scottsboro Boys or the kitchen help at Café Society than with white performers like Crosby and Mildred Bailey. I fear that this is the view of Holiday that has prevailed, even among some black intellectuals.

Holiday herself added to the confusion in *Lady Sings the Blues*, misleading readers (and possibly herself) about the early influences on her. She said she admired Bessie Smith for her big voice and Louis Armstrong for his feeling—no argument there. But she omitted Ethel Waters, the great black star of vaudeville and Broadway, whose influence Holiday may have been reluctant to admit because of a long-standing animosity between them (Waters was territorial about her songs, and the younger Holiday had made the mistake of singing one of them right in front of her). Holiday and Lester Young are often called musical soulmates, because his tenor saxophone and her voice were similar in timbre. Soulmates they were, but Holiday's phrasing and relationship to the beat were more like Armstrong's than Young's.

From time to time early in her recording career, Holiday would revive an older song closely associated with another performer. She did her own versions of numbers first made popular by Waters ("Sugar," "Trav'lin' All Alone," and "Am I Blue?"), Armstrong ("All of Me"), and Bessie Smith ("St. Louis Blues"). But as if giving her audience a clue to her larger ambitions, she more often revisited songs first sung by and still closely associated with the most flamboyant white torch singers of the 1920s and early 1930s—Ruth Etting ("Mean to Me," "More Than You Know,"and "I'll Never Be the Same"), Marion Harris ("The Man I Love"), Helen Morgan ("Why Was I Born?"), Libby Holman ("Body and Soul" and "Moanin' Low"), and Fanny Brice ("My Man"). At that point Holiday was arguably better suited to upbeat love songs with a hint of self-mockery—among them Jimmy McHugh and Dorothy Fields's

"I Must Have That Man," whose clever lyrics ("I need that person much worse'n just bad! / I'm half alive and it's drivin' me mad") let her indulge her rhythmic playfulness and a boundless *joie de vivre* that we tend not to associate with her, though maybe we should. It was a few years later, almost eerily coinciding with her first recording of "Strange Fruit," that Holiday acquired the maturity a singer needs to make her listeners feel as though they're the ones carrying a torch. (*The Commodore Master Takes* includes a haunting version of Jerome Kern and Otto Harbach's "Yesterdays," also from 1939, which seems to have been a turning point.)

What part heroin or brutal men or racial oppression played in Holiday's gaining greater depth we should be hesitant to speculate about. Not everybody who suffers becomes a great artist. Heroin bespeaks a death wish, but to the user it must also seem, if only at first, a life force—a source of defiant pleasure, like risky sexual encounters or an adolescent's first cigarette or drink. This self-abandonment is the animating quality I hear in Billie Holiday's early recordings, when she was defying social convention and her threatened marginalization as a black woman—and in her later recordings, when she was defying not only all of that but also the damage she had inflicted on herself. In fighting to become her own woman she also became her own victim, and nobody else's.

GREIL MARCUS

Raising the Stakes in Punk Rock: Sleater-Kinney

Two Sundays ago, some 10,000 people gathered in Dolores Park in the Mission District here for Soupstock 2000, a day of music celebrating the 20th anniversary of Food Not Bombs. With chapters around the country and overseas, the anarchist collective was founded to fight militarism; more recently, in San Francisco, the group has organized tenants to oppose gentrification and often clashed with police over unauthorized, on-the-street food distribution to homeless people. But this was a sunny day. The riotously tattooed crowd was very young, no one was hungry ("Have you had any of the food?" asked an announcer from the stage; "It's free; everything here today is free"), and Sleater-Kinney, a three-woman punk band founded in Olympia, Washington, in 1994, was out of place.

The guitarists Carrie Brownstein and Corin Tucker and the drummer Janet Weiss—all three sing—put out their records on Kill Rock Stars, a small independent label that functions very well as the center of its own universe: its slogan used to be "Olympia, Birthplace of Rock," which was a way of saying that rock 'n' roll can be born again and again, anywhere and at any time. "There's nothing that we do that can be separated from where we're from," Ms. Weiss said four days after Soupstock: she lives in Portland, Oregon, as does

316

Ms. Tucker; Ms. Brownstein lives in Olympia. "It's rainy. And it's gray. It allows you to be more internal than a place with an outdoor, extroverted climate. It allows for and fosters our ability to break out. To get away. To make a difference. And it fosters our ability to go home and regroup and rebuild."

The band had flown in from Denver near the end of a five-week, 29-date tour. They were flying, you could imagine, on the momentum generated in their recently released fifth album, *All Hands on the Bad One*. It's get-out-of-the-way music: "Is It a Lie?," a song that steps back from itself, viewing the disaster it recounts as if it were a reverie, starts in the middle of a dead run.

Most punk bands get less fierce, less demanding, as they learn to play better; they substitute technique for bravado, because they're so pleased to discover they can master a technique. Though from *Sleater-Kinney* (1995), *Call the Doctor* (1995), *Dig Me Out* (1997) and *The Hot Rock* (1999) to *All Hands on the Bad One*, Sleater-Kinney's sound has gone from crankily primitive to frighteningly grand, the band has grown not out of ferocity but into it: "Instead of a locked room," as the critic Howard Hampton says of "All Hands on the Bad One," it is "a storming of 'The Shining's' castle-keep's endless corridors, haunted rooms and menstruating elevators," until everything is in jeopardy and no destiny is fixed.

This was the argument many made from the stage in Dolores Park, but not the feeling. Everything was in jeopardy—the right to live in a city being transformed by unlimited amounts of new dot.com money, with long-time tenants evicted and people working ordinary jobs forced to flee rents they could never imagine paying ("You're no longer wanted here," a speaker told the crowd, and for a moment the sunny day chilled)—but everything was enclosed in that locked room. The speakers seemed tired of their own words, their outrage rote. Their worry that the people gathered before them were present only to hear bands they'd already heard of was inescapable. When "Diamond" Dave Whitaker, Bob Dylan's mentor in Minneapolis's Dinkytown in 1960, introduced the combo Folk This as a link to a long tradition of song and protest—"Back to

'Cisco, Woody and Lead Belly too," Mr. Whitaker said, quoting Dylan's 1962 "Song to Woody"—you could hear him try to unlock the door. Offering a smug version of "There'll Be Pie in the Sky When You Die," a broadside by Joe Hill, the I.W.W. songwriter who was executed by a Utah firing squad in 1915, the group went right back to nothing-new-under-the-sun. They followed with a horrible workers' anthem ("March, march, you toilers"), translated from the Polish.

What wasn't hectoring was sentimental, and Sleater-Kinney were out of place because they were neither. "We're more interested in raising the stakes," Ms. Brownstein, 25, said here on June 8, just before the last show of Sleater-Kinney's tour, at the Fillmore. That's just what the band did at Dolores Park—that, and change the language.

Setting up, they were three demure-looking women. There was no hint of the world-claiming hugeness of the voice that comes out of Ms. Tucker, 27—probably the biggest voice in pop music since Arlene Smith of the Bronx's Chantels, and that was in the 1950's— or of the magnetic, absolutely determined presence of Ms. Weiss, 34, or Ms. Brownstein's leaps all over the stage. But by the time the band reached "Call the Doctor," four songs into its set, everything had changed.

Some of the words to "Call the Doctor" could have been read out by one of the day's speakers ("They want to socialize you" is the first line). But a lyric sheet is not a song. "It's the ability of the sounds and the melodies and the rhythms to sometimes counteract, to create tension, sometimes to work as a complete whole," Ms. Weiss said. "Sometimes the sound of the song can create the meaning of the words—create a duality for the words." That is what happened. It was as if the shibboleth that opened the song was there only for its language to be destroyed by the Superman leaps of the band's sound—a sound Ms. Weiss always kept open even when Ms. Tucker's wail seemed so big it would blow the performance up.

"The sound of Bob Dylan's voice had more to do with changing the world than anything he sang about," Robert Ray, a musician and professor of English at the University of Florida, has written; the same is true of the sound Sleater-Kinney makes. One could imagine that first line was there only to remind a listener of how far one had come by the shocking end of the piece, with Ms. Brownstein screaming into her microphone, making a noise that went in human and came out inhuman, and Ms. Tucker commanding "Call the doctor! Call the doctor!" as if more than one life was at stake. "I was frustrated," Ms. Brownstein later said of the moment. "But sometimes when there's a sense of desperation when we play, I can muster up that kind of inner . . . monster."

Ms. Tucker's whole performance can seem like Ms. Brownstein's moments. "I'm your monster, I'm not like you," Ms. Tucker chants a few lines into "Call the Doctor" (following later with "I'm no monster, I'm just like you"—but then, you think, with her voice ringing in your head, which? who am I?). It can be thrilling, confusing, scary, but it's no effect: it's a voice that was discovered, and passed on.

The story goes back to the teenage radical feminist milieu that called itself riot grrrl, an explosion of bands, fanzines and cross-country committees of correspondence, a milieu with an especially strong presence in Olympia. "I was 18," Ms. Tucker said on the last night of the band's tour. "I went to a show that Bratmobile and Bikini Kill played"—respectively, the three-woman punk band that would open the Fillmore show, and the startlingly extreme three-woman, one-man riot grrrl band led by the singer Kathleen Hanna. "It was February 14, 1991. And Kathleen Hanna was . . . terrifying. People were just freaking out. She was saying things"—with the slogan "Revolution Girl Style Now" singing songs about rape, incest and resistance, sometimes with words like "Slut" scrawled on her stomach—"that were really direct and really emotional at the same time. She was so powerful. People were crying. And some people were like, 'They're the worst band ever.'

"It was the first time I'd seen feminism translated into an emotional language," Ms. Tucker went on. "That I saw those kinds of thoughts and ideas put into your own personal life, that's not in a textbook or an academic discussion. For young women to be doing that, basically teenagers on stage, to be taking that kind of stance, that kind of power, was blowing people's minds. And it totally blew my mind. I was like," Ms. Tucker said with happy determination, "O.K., that's it. That's it for me—I'm going in a band, right now. You had the feeling they had started the band the week before: you can do it too"—that is, you too can stand up and speak in the town square, even if you have to create the town square yourself.

As a kind of public secret society, riot grrrl became an almost instant meal for the media, and the movement turned inward. "The outside world reacted so intensely we had to band together," Ms. Tucker said. "We suddenly had *Newsweek* reporters hiring women to come to our shows, and not tell us they were journalists, and say that they were fans, and this was so important to them, buying our really personal fanzines. And the press that happened about riot grrrl was extremely sexist, and really targeted. Taking these young women and trying to make them look absolutely inarticulate. That it was just a fashion thing, that people were doing it just to get attention. There were valid issues that were being presented in the music, or in the words that we were saying: rape and sexual abuse, issues that young women face, that we face."

As Ms. Brownstein added, it was a small revolution in many hearts that was soon enough "completely collapsed into the Spice Girls: T-shirts with 'Girls Rule' or 'Girl Power'—even if the Spice Girls would never know where that came from." But this was also the voice that is passed on by Sleater-Kinney. Ms. Tucker has a particular gift that turns that voice into a thing in itself: a force of will disguised as a force of nature.

Over seven years, Sleater-Kinney have found an intense following all over the country. Though their music is almost never played on commercial radio, and for good reason—like Sex Pistols music, it is so strong, so quick and far-reaching, it makes nearly everything that today might surround it on the radio feel cowardly—their albums now sell about 100,000 copies: a figure, Ms. Brownstein said as Ms. Weiss and Ms. Tucker nodded in agreement, that "seems like so much. It's still amazing for us to think that many people have our record, who sit there and listen to it."

The three make a living as musicians, and manage themselves financially. "I don't think people realize," Ms. Tucker said, "how important it is for a band to know about how records are sold, how things are made, what percentage of profits you're going to get, how touring happens, how to make money on tour." All three agreed that collaborating with a small, independent label strengthened, not weakened, their ability to treat a musical career as at once a form of free speech and real work.

"I give you the best band in the world," an announcer said from the wings as Sleater-Kinney walked onto the stage at the Fillmore. The impossible encomium didn't seem pretentious, didn't seem like anything anyone had to live up to—not the band, not the crowd, which in contrast to the two-thirds female audience in Los Angeles two nights before was at least two-thirds male; in contrast to the crowd at Dolores Park, where people who looked over 30 were a rarity, here there were a lot of people who looked over 50. The feeling was all anticipation: Aren't we lucky to be here?

For an encore, the band chose "White Rabbit," with Ms. Tucker walking in the footsteps worn into the Fillmore stage floor in 1966 when Grace Slick sang it with the Jefferson Airplane. It sounded unnatural—for punk bands, pre-punk rock numbers often feel like they're being performed in a second language, because they are—as Creedence Clearwater Revival's 1969 "Fortunate Son" had not when Sleater-Kinney played it at Dolores Park. Whatever its chords or its melody, Creedence's old, still-fresh curse on privilege had the hurry and worry that is Sleater-Kinney's first language.

"Sometimes," Ms. Brownstein said in between the two shows, "when we're listening to music in the van, from the 60s and 70s, we always are so surprised that some of these songs that are so political and so meaningful ever were on the radio, and hits. You miss that feeling of such cultural power, such belief, that music could have an effect on so many people. Because right now, I feel like people have lost faith in music, in popular music, having the kind of efficacy it did before."

"In the 60s," Stanley Booth writes in the new edition of his *The True Adventures of the Rolling Stones*, "we believed in a myth—that music had the power to change people's lives. Today we believe in a myth—that music is just entertainment."

"I like that first myth so much better," Ms. Weiss said. "Bob Dylan—for someone saying those words to break into the mainstream, I think it's amazing. I think he handled it really well. He developed, and changed, and took chances. It's like he was the original punk rocker. And still is."

Bob Dylan was not exactly missing when Sleater-Kinney went into their last number at both the Fillmore and Soupstock 2000—that last number in both cases being the storming "Dig Me Out." He was present as an imagined comrade, just as, keeping his own counsel, he had been present in spirit at Soupstock's progenitor, the Woodstock festival of 31 years before. "Dig Me Out" was a desperate celebration at the Fillmore—the end of a traverse of the nation, a cry of having made it through with nothing lost, with other musicians from the tour, male and female, madly go-going across the stage in full "Shindig" absurdity. In the crowd, you had to wonder how long it would be before you saw anything so funny, or heard anything so unafraid. But at Dolores Park, the feeling was different. There were still shows to play after this one, and the song was not an occasion for revelry; it seemed like a last chance.

Sleater-Kinney came out of the self-created community of riot grrrl. When you ask what a community is for, one answer is to create events like the one at Dolores Park. In a conversation years ago about what "politics" would mean in the political philosopher Hannah Arendt's ideal city, where what she called "the social question"— hunger, want, poverty—had been solved or banished, one person answered seriously, "People would decide what plays to put on." They'd decide if they wanted to take a chance on a play as extreme as that performed inside "Dig Me Out." Dig me out, dig me out—as the words were chanted in Dolores Park, chanted as if they were the whole of the language Sleater-Kinney was speaking, you could in the instant feel buried by the social question, by the money that was changing the city and that you would never have, buried by whatever you feared was set against you in the world at large.

Then "Dig me out" was no longer a line in a song by a punk band but something in the air, a warning, or a promise, or an event taking place as you listened. "They will do it again, the threads of youthful dissidence in Paris and Texas and Prague and Berkeley and Chicago and London," Jan Hodenfield ended his *Rolling Stone* report on Woodstock in 1969, "criss-crossing ever more closely until the map of the world we live in is viable for and visible to all of those that are part of it and all of those buried under it." "The Drama You've Been Craving," Sleater-Kinney titles one of their songs; that is the drama they are craving, and the drama they are making.

OTHER NOTABLE
ESSAYS OF 2000

Andy Battaglia, Michelle Goldberg, Andrew Goodwin, and Joe
  Heim, "Radiohead's Kid A" (*Salon.com*, October 25, 2000)
Larry Bohter, "Rock en Espanol is Approaching its Final Border"
  (*New York Times*, August 6, 2000)
Zev Borow, "Radiohead: The Difference Engine" (*Spin*, November
  2000)
David Bowman, "Emmylou Harris" (*Salon.com*, September 11,
  2000)
Ethan Brown, "The X Factor," (*Vibe*, October 2000)
Mike Bruno, "Sue 'Em All," (*Ironminds*, April 28, 2000)
Robert Cantwell, "The Ghost in the CD," (*Village Voice*, August 8,
  2000)
Robert Christgau, "The Noise Boys Ride Again: Impolite Dis-
  course," (*Village Voice*, July 4, 2000)
Jason Cohen and Michael Krugman, "Kid A to Zzzzz—A Radio-
  head Reaction-ary," (*Rollingstone.com*, October 24, 2000)
Peter Cooper, "Snake Lady," (*No Depression*, March/April 2000)
Chuck D, "Death of a Nation—Where Ignorance is Rewarded for
  a New Race Creation: The Niggro," (*Rapstation.com*, September
  26, 2000)
Eddie Dean, "Hair Today," (*Washington City Paper*, May 26–June 1,
  2000)
Matt Dellinger, "Beef Stew," (*New Yorker*, November 27, 2000)

Erik Flannigan, "Outside the Wall," (*No Depression*, May/June 2000)

Geoffrey Himes, "A Joyful Noise—Sacred Steel Guitar: It's Not Just For Churches Anymore," (*Chicago Tribune*, September 17, 2000)

Ted Gioia, "A Megastar Long Buried Under a Layer of Blackface," (*New York Times*, October 22, 2000)

Jesse Green, "Forever Johnny," (*New Yorker*, July 3, 2000)

Don Heckman, "Not Exactly All that Jazz," (*L.A. Times*, August 7, 2000)

Stephen Hedricks, "The Singer," (*DoubleTake*, Winter 2000)

Geoffrey Himes, "From the Hills: How Mid-Century Migrants from the Mountains Brought Bluegrass—and More—to Baltimore," (*Baltimore City Paper*, January 12, 2000)

Joseph Hooper, "The Ballad of Little Jimmy Scott," (*New York Times*, August 27, 2000)

Camden Joy, "The Greatest Record Album that Ever Was," (*Puncture*, Summer 2000)

David Kamp, "Live at the Whiskey," (*Vanity Fair*, November 2000)

Alan Kozinn, "Looking for the Real John Lennon," (*New York Times*, December 7, 2000)

Courtney Love, "Courtney Love Does the Math," (*Salon.com*, June 14, 2000)

Mitch Myers, "The Sound and the Fury: Lou Reed's Metal Machine Music," (*Magnet*, April/May 2000)

Eva Neuberg, "The Marshall Mathers LP," (*New York Press*, July 7–13, 2000)

Joe Nick Patoski, "Doug Sham: We Remember," (*Texas Monthly*, January 2000)

Ann Powers, "No Last Hurrah Yet for Political Rock," (*New York Times*, December 31, 2000)

Mike Ruffino, "Tour Diary: The Unband, On & Off the Road," (*New York Press*, August 16–22, 2000)

Kyle Ryan, "The Crash," (*Punk Planet*, September/October, 2000)

Strawberry Saroyan, "Oops, She's Doing it Again," (*Salon.com*, May 22, 2000)

Peter S. Schlotes, "In the Company of Flow," (*Minnesota City Pages*, November 29, 2000)

John Schulian, "One Album to His Name, but it's the Stuff of Legend," (*New York Times*, August 27, 2000)

Dinita Smith, "When Women Called the Tunes; Rediscovering the
  Players Who Kept Things Swinging After the Men Went to
  War," (*New York Times*, August 10, 2000)
R.J. Smith, "Punk Rock on Trial," (*Spin*, February 2000)
Kate Sullivan, "Corporate Rock Still Sucks," (*Minnesota City Pages*,
  September 27, 2000)
Daniel Wolff, "Directions to the Promised Land," (*DoubleTake*,
  Spring 2000)
Chris Ziegler, "Death in Texas," (*Punk Planet*, March/April 2000)

LIST OF
CONTRIBUTORS

Lorraine Ali is the music critic at *Newsweek Magazine*, where she has written about everything from Texas rapper South Park Mexican to the fabulous Dolly Parton. She has also contributed to the *New York Times*, *GQ* and *Rolling Stone*. She is currently working on a book about growing up Arab American.

Whitney Balliett has been covering jazz for the *New Yorker* since 1957. His most recent book is *Collected Works: A Journal of Jazz, 1954–2000*.

Eric Boehlert is a senior writer at *Salon.com*.

Bill Buford has been fiction and literary editor of *The New Yorker* since 1995. He has served as editor of *Granta* and publisher of Granta Books, for which he edited three anthologies. He is also the author of *Among the Thugs*. Born in Baton Rouge, Louisiana, he now resides in Manhattan after eighteen years in Britain.

Carly Carioli commits rock criticism and other petty crimes in the pages of *Boston Phoenix*. He lives in Wakefield, Massachusetts, with his wife and daughter. Their top favorite songs to sing in the car are "The Gorilla" by the Ideals; "The Vowels of Love" by the Poets; "Shake a Tail Feather" by the Five DuTones; and "E.I." by Nelly.

Steven Daly is a contributing editor at *Vanity Fair*. In a previous life he played drums for Scottish indie band Orange Juice.

Francis Davis is the author of *In the Moment, Outcats, The History of the Blues, Bebop and Nothingness, Like Young*, and a forthcoming biography of John Coltrane. A contributing editor of the *Atlantic Monthly*, he also writes about music for the *New Yorker* and the *New York Times*.

Anthony DeCurtis is a contributing editor at *Rolling Stone* and host of "The A List" on GetMusic.com. He is the author of *Rocking My Life Away: Writing About Music and Other Matters*, and editor of *Present Tense: Rock & Roll and Culture*. He won a Grammy for his liner notes for the Eric Clapton retrospective, *Crossroads*.

Born in Jersey City, New Jersey, the year the Beatles arrived in America, **Jim DeRogatis** began voicing his opinions about rock 'n' roll shortly thereafter. He is currently the pop music critic at the *Chicago Sun-Times* and a contributor to *Spin, Guitar World, Modern Drummer*, and *Penthouse* magazines. He is also the author of two books, *Kaleidoscope Eyes: Psychedelic Rock from the '60s to the '90s* and *Let It Blurt: The Life and Times of Lester Bangs, America's Greatest Rock Critic*.

Mike Doughty wrote a pseudonymous column called "Dirty Sanchez" for the *New York Press* from 1998 to 2000. He was also the singer, songwriter, and founder of Soul Coughing, which recorded three records for Slash/Warner Bros. in the 90s. Now he's just some jerk with an acoustic guitar; his folky CD, *Skittish*, is available at www.superspecialquestions.com.

Steve Erickson is the author of *The Sea Came In at Midnight, Days Between Stations, Rubicon Beach, Tours of the Black Clock, Leap Year, Arc d'X, Amnesiascope*, and *American Nomad*. He has been acclaimed as one of the most individual and important contemporary novelists by Thomas Pynchon, Greil Marcus, William Gibson, and many others.

Robbie Fulks is a singer-songwriter living in Chicago. His most recent record is *Couples in Trouble*. "If I Said You Had a Beautiful Gross Adjusted Income . . ." originally appeared on *Robbiefulks.com*.

Gilbert Garcia writes for *Phoenix New Times*. He is a graduate of Harvard University and the University of Texas Graduate School of Journalism. He is also a musician who has released two CDs with the Memphis band Mea Culpa.

William Gay's two novels are *The Long Home* and *Provinces of Night*, and his short fiction has appeared in various magazines, as well as in *New Stories from the South* and *O. Henry Prize Stories 2001*. He writes about music for *The Oxford American*.

Author-filmmaker-producer **Robert Gordon** wrote *It Came From Memphis* and produced the book's two companion music CDs. His biography of Muddy Waters will be published by Little, Brown in 2002; he is directing the companion documentary. He has written for most music magazines, including *Rolling Stone*, *Spin*, and *Mojo*.

David Kamp is a contributing editor at *Vanity Fair* and *GQ*. He writes infrequently about music.

Monica Kendrick developed unhealthy passions for music and writing as the only child of boho outsiders in a small Appalachian town. In 1995 she stumbled into a typesetting gig with the *Chicago Reader*, where she's now a staff writer. Recently she has also contributed to the *Wire, Resonance, Maxine, Bridge*, the *Journal of Country Music, Spin*, and *Salon.com*.

Nathan R. (Sonny) Kleinfield has written for the *New York Times* since September 1977, most recently for the metropolitan section. He is the author of several books, among them *A Month at the Brickyard, The Hidden Minority, The Biggest Company on Earth, The Traders, A Machine Called Indomitable, Staying at the Top*, and *The Hotel*. He has also contributed to a number of popular magazines including the *Atlantic, Harper's, New Times*, and *Esquire*.

Jonathan Lethem is the author of *Motherless Brooklyn* and other novels.

Bob Mack was a staff reporter at *Spy*, a contributor to *Spin* and *Village Voice*, even a producer of MTV's *Top 20 Countdown* prior to becoming a founding editor of *Grand Royal*, where he authored, among other pieces, the cover story that resurrected Lee Scratch Perry's cult/career, the original essay on the Mullet, and a memorable shouting match with Ted Nugent inspired by his hero, Paul Morley. Mack now lives in Los Angeles and writes primarily for *GQ*.

Rian Malan is a journalist, a contributing writer to *Rolling Stone*, and the award-winning author of *My Traitor's Heart: A South African Exile Returns to Face His Country, His Tribe, and His Conscience*. He live in Johannesburg, South Africa.

Charles C. Mann is a contributing editor to the *Atlantic Monthly*, the author of four books, an occasional hired gun on television and movie scripts, and a member in plausible standing of pho.

Greil Marcus is the author of *Double Trouble* and *The Old, Weird America*. He is a regular columnist for *Interview* and *Salon.com*. In 2000 he taught the American Studies seminar "Prophesy and the American Voice" at the University of California at Berkeley and Princeton University.

Richard Meltzer has been in on the rockwrite racket since day one (or is it minus-one?) and has authored both its seminal manifesto, *The Aesthetics of Rock*, and most cornucopial song & dance, *A Whore Just Like the Rest: The Music Writings of Richard Meltzer*, not to mention its earliest and most thoroughgoing deconstruction, *Gulcher*.

David Rakoff is the author of *Fraud*, published by Doubleday. He is a regular contributor to the *New York Times Magazine*, *Outside*, and Public Radio International's *This American Life*, and has written for *GQ*, *New York Observer*, *Salon.com*, *Lingua Franca*, and *Harper's Bazaar*, among other publications. He lives in New York.

Lori Robertson is *American Journalism Review*'s assistant managing editor.

Metal Mike Saunders graduated from Hall High (Little Rock), 1969. Graduated from University of Texas/Austin, 1973. Twenty-four years to date in the accounting profession. Plays/played in a punk rock band (1977–2001), cussed a lot doing it. Can and will do Eurobeat dance steps to the A*Teens, Toy-Box, and all other spiritual descendents of Betty, Veronica, 'n' Jughead.

Nick Tosches is the author of *The Devil and Sonny Liston, The Nick Tosches Reader, Country, Unsung Heroes of Rock 'N' Roll, Hellfire, Power on Earth, Cut Numbers, Dino,* and *Trinities.* He lives in New York City.

Sarah Vowell is the author of the books *Take the Cannoli* and *Radio On.* She is a contributing editor for PRI's *This American Life.*

CREDITS

July 14, 2000. Copyright © 2000 Chicago Reader, Inc. Reprinted with permission. All rights reserved.

"Neil Young on a Good Day" by Steve Erickson. Copyright © 2000. Originally appeared in the *New York Times Magazine*, July 3, 2000. Reprinted by permission of Melanie Jackson Agency, LLC.

"West Bank Hard Core" by Lorraine Ali. First published in *Raygun*, Summer 2000. Copyright © 2000 by Lorraine Ali.

"Northern Light" by Robert Gordon. First published in *Oxford American*, July/August 2000. Copyright © 2000 by Robert Gordon.

"Invisible Man: Eminem" by Eric Boehlert. This article first appeared in *Salon.com*, June 7, 2000, at http://www.Salon.com. Reprinted with permission.

"The Tao of Esteban" by Gilbert Garcia. This article first appeared in *Phoenix New Times*, September 21, 2000. Copyright © 2000 Gilbert Garcia.

"The Heavenly Jukebox, Part 3: They're Paying Our Song" by Charles C. Mann. First published in *Atlantic Monthly*, September 2000. Copyright © 2000 by Charles C. Mann.

"Napster Nation" by Carly Carioli. First published in the *Boston Phoenix*, August 3–10, 2000. Copyright © 2000 the *Boston Phoenix*.

"Golden Oldies" by Lori Robertson. First published in *American Journalism Review*, July/August 2000. Reprinted by permission of *American Journalism Review*.

"Delta Nights: A Singer's Love Affair with Loss" by Bill Buford. Copyright © 2000 by Bill Buford. Originally published in the *New Yorker*, June 6, 2000. Reprinted with the permission of The Wylie Agency, Inc.

"Hipsters and Hoodlums" by Nick Tosches. First published in *Vanity Fair*, December 2000. Reprinted by permission of the author and the author's agents, Scovil Chichak Galen Literary Agency, Inc.

"Not a Go-Betweens Piece: A Letter from Jonathan Lethem, on his favorite band" by Jonathan Lethem. Copyright © 2000 by Jonathan